PELICAN BOOKS

FREEDOM, THE INDIVIDUAL AND THE LAW

Professor Harry Street was born in 1919. He was educated at Farnworth Grammar School and Manchester University, where he gained his LL.B in 1938. He qualified as a solicitor in 1940, but during the war served as a Flight Lieutenant in the R.A.F. Since 1946 he has been a university teacher. He was Professor of Law at Nottingham University from 1952 to 1956. Since then he has occupied the same position in his own university at Manchester. In 1957–8 he was Visiting Professor at Harvard Law School, U.S.A. He has published several books on legal subjects, and contributed articles to numerous English, Canadian, and American journals. He is married, and has three children.

H. STREET

FREEDOM, THE INDIVIDUAL AND THE LAW

PENGUIN BOOKS

Penguin Books Ltd, Harmondsworth, Middlesex, England
Penguin Books Inc., 7110 Ambassador Road, Baltimore, Maryland 21207, U.S.A.
Penguin Books Australia Ltd, Ringwood, Victoria, Australia

—

First published 1963
Reprinted 1964
Second edition 1967
Third edition 1972
Reprinted 1973

—

—

Made and printed in Great Britain
by Hazell Watson & Viney Ltd
Aylesbury, Bucks
Set in Intertype Baskerville

CONTENTS

PREFACE TO THIRD EDITION

THE purpose of this book is to provide a survey of the present content of civil liberties in England. No book has previously attempted such an account of the legal and administrative basis of the various executive interferences with the citizen's liberty. It is hoped that, besides satisfying the demands of the general reader for a guide to his freedoms, the student of constitutional law or government, whether in university, technical college, or sixth form, will find it useful.

The task of keeping this book up to date in successive editions is a mammoth one; hardly a day passes without a new development in the sphere of civil liberties. 'Law and order' and 'the Permissive Society' are not the whole story. There have on the whole been many changes for the better. Much of what I have criticized in the past still remains unaltered, though others have recently joined in the criticism. The denial of any right to a passport, the laws of official secrets, the uncertain scope of police powers, the complexity of the law about demonstrations, invasion of our privacy are prominent examples.

Parliament has done much that has been advocated in previous editions. The Immigration Appeals Act 1969 greatly improved the procedures for treatment of immigrants, theatre censorship has been abolished, Race Relations Act Mark II is a greatly superior version, the 'protect the consumer' campaign has found tangible reward in the Trade Descriptions Act. The Immigration Act 1971 is to be commended for clarifying this complex area of law but the increase in administrative discretion and the conferment of additional powers on the police are seen by many as retrogressive. The Industrial Relations Act will take the place of immigration legislation as the branch of law the complexities of which defeat the attempts of the quality newspapers' leader writers and legal correspondents to understand and expound it.

The police have given the courts plenty of opportunities to develop the law about the rights of the citizen against the police. The meaning of 'deprave and corrupt' is as elusive as ever. Sir John Black convinced a magistrate that he should destroy *Last Exit to Brooklyn* (private prosecutors cannot avoid jury trial like that any more), but the publishers of the book survived separate proceedings in the Court of Appeal on indictment even though the judge refused to have any women on the jury; Edinburgh finds Beardsley's etchings obscene and London thinks even worse of *Oz*, but *Oh! Calcutta!* escapes the Director of Public Prosecutions' lash. To stop Harold Wilson reading the lesson in a Brighton church by criticizing his Vietnam policy is, holds the Lord Chief Justice, to be guilty of *indecent* behaviour, but our new Lord Chancellor could write inaccurate comments in *Punch* on a case without being guilty of contempt because his criticism was honest. The courts thought the alleged 'trial' of Savundra by David Frost intolerable and deplorable; his reply, unusual for him, was that he had no opportunity of being heard. The *Sunday Times* was found guilty of contempt of court, but has won other contests in defence of liberty, the *Observer* was criticized for contempt of Parliament, the *Spectator* fell foul of the Royal Court, the police did not like *The Times* reporting on the doings of some of its senior officers, but forebore to prosecute; the editor of the *Sunday Telegraph* was acquitted at the Old Bailey, to the lasting benefit of those who oppose the Official Secrets Acts. A British citizen from Guyana will survive in the law books for establishing that his union could not treat him unfairly without incurring substantial damages. Melford Stevenson J. will remember the Garden House Hotel trial. When last was an English judge criticized so much without contempt proceedings following?

There is no longer a Roman Catholic Index, the banned books in the British Museum are to be more accessible, the British Board of Film Censors has altered its classifications. The running battle between the Press Council and the *People* and the *News of the World* continues : Christine Keeler memoirs condemned, varied fates for the biographies of the train robbers and their spouses, but O.K. for the *Daily Telegraph* to publish the names of heart donors against their will, and for a photograph of the Queen in bed to be reproduced in the *Daily Express*. *Mrs Wilson*'s *Diary* was too offensive for the I.T.A.'s taste, her husband and Chapman Pincher no doubt both think that they were victorious over 'D' Notices. The politicians altered the rules about political broadcasting in part by meeting the criticisms I made of the aide-mémoire – but they declined to change the laws of parliamentary contempt so as to give citizens the standard ingredients of a fair trial, and their rules about election broadcasting have been redesigned so as still to meet their convenience regardless of the preferences of the licence-fee-paying electorate. The pressures on the B.B.C. to obey the politician's are mounting and must be resisted.

I have tried to describe in detail, and assess the importance of, all these changes and many more; thousands in all. Through the kindness of many of the departments and public and private organizations with whose activities this book deals I learn more about them all the time. I gratefully acknowledge their help, and I hope that none of them will think it churlish of me if the changes I have made in this edition do not always even now make my views correspond to theirs.

Finally, I thank the large number of readers of previous editions who widened my knowledge of the subject by writing to me about their experiences.

H.S.

INTRODUCTION

ENGLISHMEN pride themselves on the freedoms which they
enjoy. In no one place, however, can they find an account
of those freedoms. This book is an attempt to fill that gap.
Each of the fundamental liberties will be looked at in turn
with a view to ascertaining what the law (whether laid down
by Parliament or the courts) and practice have to say about
their content. By the time the reader has finished he will
know (to mention a few matters) just what are the relations
between himself and the police, what freedom he has to
organize meetings, how much censorship there is in Britain,
how far the law recognizes his freedom to work, and what
restrictions have been imposed on freedom in the interests
of national security. One large topic which may be thought
relevant has been excluded : the growth of delegated legislation and administrative justice, the exercise of powers over
the citizen by Ministers and administrative tribunals, town
planning and compulsory acquisition of property. That is
the one topic which has received adequate coverage in books
intended for laymen. In a sense that subject is plainly sever-
able from other aspects of civil liberties, and to include it in
this book with proportionately the same detail as for the remainder of the contents would have been greatly to expand
the book without perhaps greatly adding to the fund of
knowledge readily available at present.

We shall see that any evaluation of the limits on our liberties must always balance the competing interests at stake.
Nowhere is this better illustrated than in the discussion in
1963 of the treatment of the reporters Foster and Mul-
holland, who went to prison rather than disclose the sources
of their information. The Press used all its power to protest
at their imprisonment : it made telling points in contrasting
the privilege of solicitors with the rightlessness of journalists;

it represented the affair as an interference with the freedom of the Press and as another triumph for bureaucracy against the individual. Against all this, other factors must be weighed. Traditionally, freedom of the Press means freedom to *publish* – this case effected no interference with that – not licence for the Press to *acquire* news as it thinks fit, immune from the restraints of the law as it does so. The Lord Chief Justice is not preaching totalitarian doctrine merely because he recognizes that in some circumstances closely and directly affecting national security the need for a court to know the source of a journalist's information in order to test possible leaks in our security outweighs the freedom of a journalist not to reveal the sources of his news. This is how English law goes about its job of defining limits on our freedoms. The citizen may do as he likes unless he clashes with some specific restriction on his freedom. The law does not say : 'You can do that'; it says 'You cannot do this', which means that you can do everything else except that which it says you cannot do. Whenever such a prohibition is made, the reason will be that some other interest is rated more important than that freedom on which it impinges. The reader will make up his own mind as he progresses whether the line has always been drawn at the right point, but first let him acquaint himself with the present law, which is hard enough to ascertain in many instances. Many decisions will inevitably be seen as compromises; some, it will be contended, have paid excessive regard to the claims of the state.

What is distinctive in form about the English arrangements is that the citizen will not find his freedoms set out in any written constitution. This is in contrast not only with the historic American and French Constitutions but also with twentieth-century trends. As members of the Commonwealth secure their independence they tend to have written constitutions : India, for example. On the international scene, also, the pressure is for statements of principle such as the Declaration of Human Rights. Membership of the European community might spark off further developments.

In the United States there are hundreds of books dealing

with civil liberties. So far as is known, this is the first book which attempts to survey comprehensively the state of civil liberties in Britain. One reason for this striking difference is that it is easier to expound a written constitution than to grub in the law reports, Hansard, and newspaper files, to inquire in Whitehall and of the various 'fringe' bodies like the British Board of Film Censors and the Independent Television Authority, whose activities raise issues concerning our liberties. It is in the belief that our liberties will be the more firmly established the better their extent and limitations are appreciated, that the following survey is attempted.

CHAPTER I

PERSONAL FREEDOM AND
POLICE POWERS

In England, the policeman's main task is to detect and catch people suspected of crime so that the courts may try them for the acts which they are alleged to have done. What powers, in carrying out that task, do the police enjoy and how are they exercised? Does the Englishman's cherished idea that he does not live in a police state match up to reality? Are police powers hedged around with adequate protection for the citizen? This opening chapter considers personal liberty, our most vaunted freedom, against the realities of police behaviour, and follows the police from their powers of arrest to the restrictions imposed on the searching and entering of premises, to police questioning, then to bail and *habeas corpus*, and finally to an extended discussion of the controversial powers of telephone tapping and intercepting mail.

The reader will be constantly reminded that somehow two public interests must be balanced : the need to ensure that criminals are caught on the one hand, and on the other the right of the citizen to go about his business without unnecessary interference.

ARREST

English law recognizes (and rightly so) that a policeman needs greater powers than the rest of us. It is a sensible provision that a policeman who believes a certain person to have committed a crime can make a sworn statement before a justice of the peace or other judicial officer, whereupon the justice may at his discretion issue the policeman with a warrant which authorizes him to arrest the person named. A policeman who arrests that person on the authority of the warrant is fully protected by the law even though it turns out that the man arrested was innocent. Warrants are not issued to the ordinary citizen.

Unfortunately those in the know have long been aware that the police abuse the warrant system by taking doubtful cases to a magistrate whom they know to be lax or accommodating in the signing of warrants. Only when an influential person like Lady Diana Duff Cooper became a victim in 1968 was it found necessary to do anything about it. The only information on which the police procured a warrant to search her home for drugs was an anonymous phone call. The Home Office has since issued a directive to police and magistrates about anonymous complaints, but in other respects the system's defects remain.

There is not always time to seek out a magistrate before making an arrest. Here again we see the difference between the powers of a policeman and the rest of us. Shops with open counters have many of their goods stolen and frequently employ store detectives (who are merely employees of the shop, not policemen, and therefore have the same powers as other private citizens) to protect them against shoplifting. The shop detective who believes that somebody in the shop has stolen goods may arrest him, provided that he takes him to the police station or before a justice within a reasonable time in order to be charged with the offence. But he makes the arrest at his peril; if either the goods have not been stolen or they have been stolen but a reasonable man would not in the circumstances have suspected the man arrested of being the thief, the shop employee and his employer will both be liable for false imprisonment to the person arrested. For instance,[1] W. H. Smith & Son Ltd thought that one Walters was in the habit of stealing books from their bookstall at King's Cross railway station; their employee challenged Walters while in possession of one of their books and took him to the police station. Walters was charged with stealing and found not guilty by a jury who accepted his plea that he did not intend to steal. Walters was able to recover damages from W. H. Smith & Son Ltd for the false arrest although the court found that they had reasonable grounds for believing Walters guilty, because the book had not in fact been stolen by Walters or anyone else. This may seem harsh on the company, but an alternative course of action had been open to them. They could have reported the facts to a policeman and left him to charge Walters, whereupon they would not have been answerable for false imprisonment, and the policeman would have been protected as long as he acted on reasonable suspicion, even though no crime had actually been committed by anyone.

The Criminal Law Act 1967 creates a category of arrestable offences : these are offences for which the sentence is fixed by law or for which a statute authorizes imprisonment for five years, and attempts to commit those offences. Offences like theft come within that provision. It is only for those offences that the common law gives a citizen the power to arrest on reasonable suspicion that the person arrested is the one who has committed the offence, and gives a policeman the power to arrest on reasonable suspicion that the offence has been committed by the person arrested. A citizen as well as a policeman can arrest for breach of the peace committed in his presence. For all other offences, including summary offences tried only before magistrates, private citizens cannot arrest, and policemen may do so only in the exceptional cases where an Act of Parliament authorizes it. For many of the 1,000 and more different crimes a warrant is required for an arrest. The astute policeman might justify any arrest by asserting a reasonable suspicion of stealing, but he will have to think of this one quickly, as the following case shows.

Leachinsky was a dealer in rags or waste who bought supplies from time to time from Michaelson in Leicester.[2] In August 1942, he bought three bales of waste, and in picking them up he asked Michaelson if he had any remnants from which he might make a dress for his wife. Michaelson said he had, and Leachinsky bought a considerable number of remnants and had them packed in a single bale. The four bales were shipped to Leachinsky's warehouse in Liverpool and they were all described as waste. At the time of the purchase of the remnants war-rationing restrictions on the purchase and sale of cloth were in effect.

When the goods arrived in Liverpool the police, being suspicious, examined the goods and discovered that one of the bales contained cloth and not waste. When Leachinsky started to unload the bales, he himself set aside the bale of cloth. Christie and Morris, police officers, then questioned Leachinsky about a bale of cloth and the latter professed to know nothing about such cloth. The officers, not satisfied with the explanation, arrested Leachinsky under the provisions of the Liverpool Corporation Act 1921. This Act provided that if a person's name and address were unknown, he could be arrested and brought before the court to give an explanation of his possession of goods believed to have been stolen by someone, although not necessarily by the person arrested – the charge usually referred to as 'unlawful possession'. The two police officers knew Leachinsky's name and address and later, in evidence, Christie admitted that he knew that he had no power to arrest under the Liverpool Corporation Act and that he had made the arrest in this way simply because it was 'more convenient'.

Leachinsky was charged in the police court with 'unlawful possession' and after spending a night in gaol was brought before a magistrate on 1 September, when a remand of one week in custody was granted. During this period the police saw Michaelson in Leicester and the latter denied that he had sold the goods to Leachinsky and claimed that they had been taken from him without his authority. When Leachinsky was brought before the magistrate on 8 September, a further remand was granted of one week, under bail, and at the hearing on 15 September the police withdrew the charge of unlawful possession and Leachinsky was discharged. Before he could leave the court he was re-arrested for theft of the remnants. At his subsequent trial, he was acquitted, and Michaelson was proved to have been lying. Leachinsky sued Michaelson for libel and recovered £250. Leachinsky then brought an action for false imprisonment against Christie and Morris: anyone, whether policeman or citizen, who arrests another when he has no authority at law to do so commits this wrong of false imprisonment and is liable to pay heavy damages to the person whom he unlawfully arrests.

At the trial before Mr Justice Stable the defendants obtained judgment, the trial judge taking the view that the two police officers had reasonable grounds for suspecting Leachinsky of theft, and although the arrest on the 'unlawful possession' charge was improper, they could justify the arrest by their state of mind at the time of the arrest. As he put it, 'Why did they arrest him? If they arrested him because they believed he had committed a felony and there were reasonable grounds for so believing, they do not lose the protection of the law.' The Court of Appeal reversed this judgment, and the House of Lords affirmed the award of damages for false imprisonment made in the Court of Appeal. The House of Lords held that even though the policemen had valid grounds for arresting Leachinsky on reasonable suspicion of stealing, they chose to arrest him for an offence under the Liverpool Corporation Act, which did not in the circumstances authorize the arrest. Viscount Simon said:

(1) If a policeman arrests without warrant upon reasonable suspicion of felony, or of other crime of a sort which does not require a warrant, he must in ordinary circumstances inform the person arrested of the true ground of arrest. He is not entitled to keep the reason to himself or to give a reason which is not the true reason. In other words a citizen is entitled to know on what charge or on suspicion of what crime he is seized. (2) If the citizen is not so informed but is nevertheless seized, the policeman, apart from certain exceptions, is liable for false imprisonment. (3) The requirement that the person arrested should be informed of the reason why he is seized naturally does not exist if the circumstances are such that he must know the general nature of the alleged offence for which he is detained. (4) The requirement that he should be so informed does not mean that technical or precise language need be used. The matter is a matter of substance, and turns on the elementary proposition that in this country a person is, prima facie, entitled to his freedom and is only required to submit to restraints on his freedom if he knows in substance the

19

reason why it is claimed that this restraint should be imposed. (5) The person arrested cannot complain that he has not been supplied with the above information as and when he should be, if he himself produces the situation which makes it practically impossible to inform him, e.g., by immediate counter-attack or by running away. There may well be other exceptions to the general rule in addition to those I have indicated, and the above propositions are not intended to constitute a formal or complete code, but to indicate the general principles of our law on a very important matter. These principles equally apply to a private person who arrests on suspicion.

What happens when the person arrested is ultimately acquitted of the charge for which he was arrested? He can ask the court to make him a grant towards the legal costs he has incurred in defending himself. Only in comparatively rare instances, when the court feels that the charge should never have been brought, is the court likely to make any grant towards his costs. When a person acquitted can establish that the prosecution was instituted out of spite or for some purpose other than bringing him to justice, and that there was no reasonable and probable cause for believing him guilty, he may after his acquittal sue his prosecutor in damages for malicious prosecution. In practice it is so difficult to prove all these essentials of this wrong that those acquitted very rarely succeed in obtaining damages for this.

TAKING A SUSPECT TO THE POLICE STATION

The detective story and the daily press regularly tell us that the police detain citizens for questioning. When the B.B.C. put on a programme about police practices a former Scotland Yard superintendent vouched in the *Radio Times* that the programme would be accurate in every detail,[3] and at the end of the programme an assistant chief constable of a large city stressed that the actions of the police were authentic. In the programme a man was told by a policeman that the policeman would have to detain him pending inquiries, although no charge was then preferred against him. Occasionally, it emerges in the course of a trial that the accused was detained against his will before being charged and without having been arrested. There is much more similar evidence that it is the practice of the police to take a suspected person to the police station in order to question him with a view to ascertaining whether he is to be charged with some offence. Yet courts from the House of Lords downwards have frequently had to make it clear that the police have no power to require a person to go to the police station in order to answer questions. This direction to the jury by Mr Justice Devlin (as he then was) is typical :

> You may sometimes read in novels and detective stories, perhaps written by people not familiar with police procedure, that persons are sometimes taken into custody for questioning. There is no such power in this country. A man cannot be detained unless he is arrested.

In a 1966 case the Lord Chief Justice ruled that a man who refused to tell a policeman his destination and his name and address was not guilty of the offence of obstructing a policeman in the execution of his duty, because the citizen had no legal duty to answer the policeman's questions.[4] In 1970 it was held that when a policeman touched the citizen on the shoulder in the course of inquiry into an offence, and the policeman knew that the citizen did not want to speak to him, the citizen was guilty of assaulting the policeman in the execution of his duty when he struck him.[5] This decision is of doubtful merit and must not be allowed to give the police the right to detain for questioning an unwilling citizen.

If, then, a policeman is to compel a citizen to accompany him to the police station, he must arrest him and, as we have seen, inform him of the reason for the arrest. If he takes him to the station, or detains him there, against his will, this is the wrong of false imprisonment for which the victim can recover damages from the policeman. Still less, of course, can a policeman lawfully insist that a witness visit the station in order to make a statement or to answer questions, or indeed that he make a statement anywhere. The citizen can be served with a subpoena ordering him to attend as a witness when the case comes into court for hearing, but that is all. And it is the court, not the police or the prosecution, who alone can issue a subpoena.

What then happens in practice? It may be supposed that the police experience little difficulty in securing the attendance at the police station of those whose presence they require. No doubt the first reaction of the Englishman, if not of the Irishman, is to do as a policeman asks. One distinguished judge has attributed this readiness, rightly or wrongly, to 'the Englishman's tolerance of, and indeed affection for, the unwritten rule; his natural instinct is to act according to what he believes to be the general understanding among his fellows as to how he should behave rather than to look for a rule permitting or prohibiting what he proposes to do and to study its terms'. The witness will recognize his public duty to aid detection of crime by giving the police all possible assistance. The innocent suspect will welcome the chance to clear himself. Even the guilty may see some advantage in trying to convince the police of his innocence; and in due course the jury may draw unfavourable conclusions from the accused's refusal to give a statement to the police. It may be doubted, too, whether the average citizen realizes that the police have no compulsive power; and one can hardly expect the police to make their task harder by prefacing every invitation to come to the station with the express intimation that the citizen may please himself whether he accepts. If he should complain of this 'detention for questioning' he will of course succeed in an action for false imprisonment unless the police prove that he consented to the detention. A citizen who complied without protest with the request to accompany the officer to the station, under the mistaken impression that he had to go, would be deemed to have consented. If, however, the policeman by his statements or conduct led him to believe that he was compelled to go, the policeman would have no defence. We read of persons being detained in police stations for hours, sometimes days, without being charged, while they 'assist the police in their inquiries'. Theoretically, these persons are free to leave at any time, and certainly they can sue if they are prevented from leaving. The difficulty here is of course largely one of proof. Who will be believed, the policeman who states that the man wished to remain in the station, or the man who says that they refused to let him go until he answered their questions? The burden of proof is on the policeman : unless the court is satisfied by a preponderance of evidence that the man did stay of his own free will, he can recover damages from the policeman who detained him.

Other objectionable events occur in the police station. The police are not entitled to photograph without their consent those whom they have arrested, but they systematically collect photographs of demonstrators. So they photograph them without permission. If challenged they blandly reply : 'Be snapped and go home on bail or even without a charge. Refuse and stay overnight in the cell to face the magistrates in the morning.'

SEARCH

A policeman may search a person whom he lawfully arrests and take and detain property found in his possession which will form material evidence on his prosecution for the crime for which he has been arrested. The law has long imposed serious restrictions on the claims of the police to search private premises. A series of cases in the 1760s followed the issuing by the government of the day of general warrants to search premises, i.e. warrants in which either the person or the property is not specified. In the great case of *Entick* v. *Carrington*[6] the Secretary of State issued a general warrant to officers who broke into the house of Entick, who was suspected of editing a seditious publication, *The British Freeholder*, and seized his books and papers. The Lord Chief Justice of the day castigated the Government's conduct severely and awarded Entick £300 damages for trespass. John Wilkes was awarded £1,000 damages against an

Under-Secretary of State who entered his house and seized papers under a warrant to arrest the (unnamed) authors, printers, and publishers of the *North Briton*.[7] The courts firmly established the rule that no state official or policeman may enter a citizen's premises unless he has authority of law. This authority may derive from a search warrant issued by a magistrate under powers conferred by one of the many statutes which authorize search for particular offences, e.g., the Official Secrets Acts, or the Theft Act 1968.

In *Elias* v. *Pasmore* (1934)[8] Pasmore had a warrant for the arrest of one Hannington, who was an official of the National Unemployed Workers Movement. Pasmore entered the premises of the Movement in order to arrest Hannington and, in addition to arresting him, seized a number of documents and removed them to Scotland Yard. Elias was the lessee of the premises and was also charged with an offence. The police retained many of the seized documents even after the trial of Hannington and Elias. Elias sued Pasmore for trespass to his premises and the return of the documents and damages for their detention. It is unfortunate that a case which raised such important points for the first time in English law went no further than the judge at first instance. This judge held that Pasmore acted illegally in refusing to return the documents at the conclusion of the trial. He also held that Pasmore was entitled to seize documents which were evidence of a crime committed by anyone, whether it be of the person arrested, or of the owner of the premises where the arrest of another took place, or of anybody else. His reasoning rested on the laconic observation that 'the interests of the state' excused the seizure, a view quite out of harmony with the leading case of *Entick* v. *Carrington*.

His decision has been strongly criticized, but did not come under direct judicial scrutiny till the Court of Appeal case of *Ghani* v. *Jones* in 1969.[9] The Court laid down that if a policeman has a right to enter then he is entitled to seize any goods which he believes to be material evidence in respect of the crime for which he entered. They added that if in the course of his search he comes upon any other goods which show the suspect to be implicated in some other crime he may take them too. They rejected the principle laid down in *Elias* v. *Pasmore*. They added that *Elias* v. *Pasmore* could be justified on the ground that the papers showed that Elias was implicated in Hannington's sedition; if the papers had implicated Elias only in some other crime such as blackmail, the police would have had no right to seize them. The present position, however illogical it may be, is that if the police have a right to enter *A*'s premises they may ransack them in the search for evidence against him of any offence, whereas they may only look for and take evidence against *B* if it relates to the same offence as authorized their entry.

The facts of *Ghani* v. *Jones* were as follows. A woman had disappeared and the police suspected murder. Without a warrant they entered her father-in-law's house and had him, his wife and daughter hand over their passports. When they wanted them back to go home to Pakistan, the police refused. The Court of Appeal ordered the police to hand back the passports. The police had not shown that they were material evidence on a murder charge and they could not keep them to stop the plaintiffs from leaving the country. (The husband was later convicted of manslaughter and Mr Ghani sentenced to prison for conspiracy to obstruct the course of justice in connection with the affair.) The case highlighted the absurd point that the police cannot get a warrant to search for evidence of a murder. In cases like that, in order to detain property the police must prove that what they are looking for is either the fruit of a probable crime, or the weapon or material evidence, and that the man in possession of it is the reasonably suspected criminal or accomplice, or has unreasonably refused to hand it over. So the innocent owner of the axe which has the fingerprints of the murderer must hand it over on request. Yet under the drugs legislation police with a warrant to search premises, e.g. a shop, can then search everybody in the shop.

We have seen that the police have no general power to stop and search a suspect with a view to deciding whether to arrest him. For particular offences, suspected poaching for instance, the police have long had statutory power to stop and frisk. The most important and controversial recent addition to this list is the power of the police since 1967 to stop and search anyone whom they suspect of being in unlawful possession of drugs. Essentially the point in dispute is this. Should the police have the right to search a youth because he looks the kind of person who might take drugs, or should they be allowed to arrest him only when they already have reasonable cause to believe that he has committed the offence of possessing drugs? More objectionable is the fact that up and down the country, concealed in obscure sources like the local Waterworks Act, local police forces have stop and search powers for a wide variety of offences – we have mentioned a Liverpool example earlier. Some areas have them whereas others have not, the police give no publicity to their powers, and anyone travelling around the country has no means of knowing whether, when he crosses a borough boundary, he is suddenly exposed to arbitrary police power. There is no central compilation of these local powers, and they are steadily expanding – Edinburgh police, for example, got new powers to stop, search and detain in the Edinburgh Corporation Order Confirmation Act 1967.

ENTERING PREMISES

A case in 1964 illustrates the restrictions on the power of the police to enter premises.[10] One night policemen found some new car parts in a passage outside a factory. They proceeded along the passage to the yard outside a café in order to pursue their inquiries about the parts, which they reasonably believed to have been stolen. The café proprietor's son ordered them off the premises, but they did not leave and asked further questions about car parts, whereupon the son struck the policemen. The son was prosecuted for assaulting the policemen in the execution of their duty. The court pointed out that the policemen had no reasonable grounds for expecting to find and apprehend the thief on the premises, so that they had no right to remain once somebody acting with the authority of the occupier asked them to leave. Accordingly the son was not guilty – indeed the café proprietor could have successfully sued them for trespass.

A case three years later [11] shows that police, like every member of the public, have an implied licence to go up the garden path to the front door of a house to make lawful inquiries; they become trespassers if they refuse to leave within a reasonable time after being told to do so. If police insist on entering the land to put down a breach of the peace or to prevent one which they reasonably believe is likely to occur, they are acting lawfully.

POLICE QUESTIONING

So far we have dealt with police conduct in connection with criminal investigation outside the police station. Next we must consider what happens when the suspect is brought to the police station.

Our concern shifts to the questioning of suspects, which is controlled in two ways. The judges have formulated rules which are intended to regulate the way in which police make investigations. These Judges' Rules do not have the force of law, but whenever a statement has been taken from a man in disregard of any of the rules, the judge at the subsequent trial may at his discretion refuse to admit the statement in evidence. Secondly, the law excludes evidence of confessions which have been made involuntarily : the prisoner is entitled to demand as of right the rejection of an involuntary confession. This matter is of great importance because statements made to the police constitute the most important evidence in criminal detection – a fact which may disappoint readers and viewers of detective stories, who have been encouraged to expect something less humdrum.

The Judges' Rules (revised in 1964 after much professional and public concern about police questioning had been voiced) recognize that where a police officer is trying to discover the author of a crime there is no objection to his put-

27

ting questions to any person, whether suspected or not, from whom he thinks that useful information can be obtained. This rule applies whether the questions are being asked in the police station or elsewhere. Once a person has refused to make a statement or, having made one, declines to say any more, he must not again be asked to make a statement.

Under the pre-1964 version of the rules persons in *custody* were not to be questioned without the usual caution being first administered. Now questions may be asked without caution and whether or not the person in question has been taken into custody. Previously, the judges have pretended that the practice of detaining on suspicion pending further investigations did not exist; now they are impliedly recognizing it. A person cannot be in 'custody' unless he is arrested; the requirement stands that a person must be told why he is being arrested. For the first time a policeman may carry on questioning somebody whom he has arrested, so long as he has neither been charged nor been formally notified that a summons is to be issued. A charge in this sense is usually made by the station duty officer at the police station, who enters the charge in the Charges book – a report in 1964 by Sir Norman Skelhorn (now Director of Public Prosecutions) found it necessary to condemn the common practice of still charging a man even though he is lying unconscious on the floor at the time.[12]

As soon as a police officer has evidence which would afford reasonable grounds for suspecting that a person has committed an offence, he must caution that person before questioning him further. The caution has to be in the following terms : 'You are not obliged to say anything unless you wish to do so but what you say may be put into writing and given in evidence.' This duty to caution arises sooner than under the former rule, which required a caution only when the policeman had made up *his* mind to charge the person. The new rules also provide for the first time that when a person is formally charged he is to be given a second caution, whereupon further questions relating to the offence may be put to him in exceptional cases, where they are necessary for the purpose of preventing or minimizing harm or loss to some other person or to the public or for clearing up an ambiguity in a previous answer or statement. The Judges' Rules are vague about a prisoner's right to consult his lawyer, to be examined by his own doctor, to contact his family, to use the telephone and to have copies of any statement which he makes, rights firmly upheld in American law. Unease persists about police interrogation in practice. In the Moors Murder case, for instance, the accused were not told of their right to see a solicitor and no contemporaneous record of their statements was kept. In 1971 the police repeatedly refused to let suspects in the Robert Carr bomb case have access to their solicitors during their police interrogation.

With regard to the rule about confessions, unless the prosecution can prove that the statement was not obtained from the accused either by fear of prejudice or by hope of advantage exercised or held out by the police or other person in authority, the confession will not be admitted in evidence at the trial. If the court finds that the police told him that it would be better for him to confess – for example, that he would get a lighter sentence, or that the police would not oppose an application for bail – or that they put pressure on him to make a statement, the police will not be allowed to give evidence of the confession. The courts are motivated by two considerations : the exclusion of confessions likely to be false and the regulating of fair police practices. The second of these is furthered by removing the temptation to the police to extract a confession in the hope that it will eventually be admitted in evidence.

These then are the rules about police questioning. What happens in practice? Casual reading of newspapers is enough to indicate that persons who eventually are charged are often taken to the police station and remain there for many hours, sometimes a day or two, having no contact with the outside world, before they are charged on the basis of what they have told the police. The 1929 Royal Commission on Police Powers and Procedure [13] found no reliable evidence of confessions obtained by violence, but they found considerable

29

evidence that the police used such devices as keeping the suspect waiting for long periods (the Director of Public Prosecutions of the time defended this practice of detention in his evidence), constant repetition of the same suggestion, bluffing assertion that the police knew all the facts anyway and that a clean breast would make things easier at the trial, and so on. Much more skilful methods have been evolved since then as psychology has developed, and presumably the police have a similar tendency today to press inquiry hard against the man whom they genuinely believe to be guilty. A recent American legal text book quotes a letter from an English policeman written to an American friend in 1950 :

Though the judges fondly imagine that their Rules are carried out to the letter they in fact very rarely are. All sorts of avoiding action are taken or otherwise the percentage of detections would be more than halved. You may have gathered that the said avoidance causes policemen to commit no little perjury in the box, and that would be a true assessment. ... The ignorance of the Great British Public neutralizes the Judges' Rules. When we deal with an educated man who knows his rights, we have had it, unless we have outside evidence enough.

One often reads even in responsible newspapers that the suspect has one safeguard : that the police have only twenty-four hours from when he first enters the station in which to secure a statement. This is a myth : there is no such time limit for questioning a man. The only limit imposed is that once the man has been *charged* he must be brought before a magistrate within twenty-four hours, and that, if this is impracticable, the station officer must ordinarily release him on bail except for serious crimes. This statutory power of the police to grant bail is sometimes abused. A good example is that of Miss Mandy Rice-Davies in the 1960s. The police needed her as a witness in the Stephen Ward case. They arrested her ostensibly for stealing a television set as she was about to leave the country. As soon as she was taken to Marylebone police station in the middle of the night, the police found that they had insufficient evidence with which to charge her. They did not release her, nor did they bring her before a magistrate; instead they granted her bail in a recognizance of £1,000. This threatened charge was kept hanging over her head and the bail imposed until she had given evidence in the Ward trial, after which of course the police dropped the threatened stealing charge. The Home Secretary, when answering parliamentary questions, has never felt able to throw light on the extent of this undesirable police practice.

The mere fact that a confession is obtained by persistent and prolonged questioning of somebody under great emotional distress does not thereby render it inadmissible. But, even though there is no suggestion that violence has been used, it may be asked whether suspects should be allowed to be interrogated when suffering from lack of food or sleep, and whether they should be denied the opportunity to have their solicitor present before statements are made. The suspect who wishes to complain of unfair treatment by the police is often in this predicament : if he has previous convictions, there is a rule of evidence that by cross-examining police witnesses about their treatment of him he may make it possible for them to do what otherwise they could not do, viz., give evidence of his previous convictions, which may of course greatly prejudice the jury against him.

To set against these considerations is the overwhelming public importance of ensuring that guilty persons are detected and punished. Take *R. v. Voisin*,[14] for example : on the body of the murdered woman was a label with the words 'Bladie Belgiam' on it. Without a caution, the suspect was asked to write 'Bloody Belgian', which he did in the same spelling as on the label, and thereby ensured his conviction. It is arguable that confessions are likely to be true, and that the court can make up its mind on the point at trial. How can the police pursue their common technique of summoning all the professional criminals whose methods resemble those used in the crime under investigation to an identification parade before witnesses of that crime, if they have no power to 'detain for questioning'? The detainee is not arrested – if so he would have been left in peace in a cell – and he is glad to secure his freedom (if offered) for the price of signing a chit that he came to the station voluntarily. If a suspect is to be informed of his right to consult a lawyer, the police will get no statement, for any lawyer will counsel silence on the part of his client. Similar objections apply to the proposal that a purely voluntary interrogation should take place only before a magistrate. Do we want rules which enable guilty men to stay free and unpunished for their crimes?

No doubt with these considerations in mind a Committee of 'Justice' recommended in 1967 that interrogations of suspects should be made by magistrates only, in the presence of the suspect's lawyer, and recorded on tape, and, most important of all, that the suspect be under a duty to answer questions. These carefully thought out proposals do not appear to have received governmental consideration, and in 1970 Mr Justice McKenna publicly opposed them.[15] The main doubt to which they give rise is whether the suspect should be compelled to confess his guilt, and what punishment is to be inflicted on a silent suspect (180 days solitary confinement, as in South Africa?). Even so a proposed rule that confessions to policemen be not admissible unless repeated in front of a magistrate merits serious examination.

The *Podola* case [16] (where a man was in such a physical state after being detained in a police station for murder of a policeman that he had to be taken to hospital for a considerable period before he was fit to stand trial) raises doubts whether suspects should be left in police cells, as distinct from prisons (which are free from police control), especially where serious crimes against policemen have been committed. Cases of police illegalities come to light with disturbing frequency. In 1964, after much evasion and procrastination, and prodding by the ever-vigilant National Council for Civil Liberties, the Home Secretary had to admit that fifteen persons had been wrongly imprisoned as a result of Detective-Sergeant Challenor fabricating evidence. That officer and his fellow policemen who were sent to prison had in some instances planted incriminating evidence on innocent people, on the strength of which the court gaoled them. In 1963

Sheffield policemen were found to have inflicted grievous bodily harm on suspects in the course of questioning them in the police station.[17] In 1964 Mars-Jones, Q.C., reported that several policemen had illegally searched citizens on the highway, had taken their fingerprints without consent, had committed numerous irregularities with respect to them in the police station, and by lying had caused them to be sent to prison.[18] In 1966 two London policemen were ordered by the High Court to pay £8,000 damages for falsely imprisoning and maliciously prosecuting two Trinidadians. Damages had been awarded against one of the two policemen for false imprisonment two years earlier. The Home Secretary has resisted all attempts to have inquiries into complaints against the police regularly conducted by independent persons, despite the fact that police investigations under the Police Act 1964 into the behaviour of other policemen are conceived in practice merely as a means of disproving the allegations against the police and not as machinery for arriving at the truth. Let the police investigate the complaint initially, but make that subject to review by an independent body. The Government appears still unwilling to make that change.

The official approach to the problem of police conduct is lacking in candour. The evidence that the police regularly break the law in handling suspects is overwhelming. It may well be that their powers are inadequate, that the proper balance is not being maintained between crime detection and liberty of the subject. Still, the solution is not to countenance illegalities but to consider what further powers the police need. Many policemen believe that it is politically impracticable to increase police powers and that there is no alternative to the present system whereby the police bluff the public that their powers are greater than they are, and the Home Office turns a blind eye to that. Surely this is too pessimistic a view.

Several conclusions follow. The present law about police powers is unsatisfactory, both because it is not achieving the desired results and because it is uncertain in definition. The courts will never in their piecemeal, case-by-case way remedy these defects; a statutory code of police powers is essential. Police discretion is extremely wide and should not be free from scrutiny.

Other aspects of relations between the police and the public reveal similar uncertainties and deceptions. Complaint is often voiced that the public render insufficient aid to the police in the arrest of criminals. There is no clear legal statement of the extent of the citizen's legal duties and powers to help the police. When he complies with the request of the police to allow his car to be used as a road block to stop an escaping criminal and his car is destroyed in the ensuing crash the police authority and the Home Office deny legal liability for the loss of the car on the ground that the citizen 'consented', and in 1965 the Home Secretary refused to alter the law. The *ex gratia* arrangements for awards by the Criminal Injuries Compensation Board set up in 1964 expressly exclude happenings of this kind.[19] An inquiry into police procedures and the rights and duties of citizens is long overdue.

It is always important that innocent persons be not convicted, but especially so in Britain. For we are one of the few countries in the Western world which provides no remedy in the courts against the state by way of damages for a person who is subsequently shown to have been convicted and sent to prison for a crime which he did not commit. All he can hope for is that the Government will make him an *ex gratia* payment, as it does in a few of these cases. Of the 64 prisoners whose convictions were quashed in 1964 by the Court of Criminal Appeal none was compensated, although on the average they had spent $18\frac{1}{2}$ weeks in prison since sentence and only three had been on bail before trial. Parliamentary questions have elicited that the Home Secretary has due regard to precedents in fixing the amount of compensation.[20] The practice is for the Minister to get an opinion from a third party such as a stipendiary magistrate or a High Court official known as the Official Referee, but the Minister is not obliged to heed his advice; complaints have also been made and not met by the Minister that not only is the claimant prevented from confronting the adviser, but he is not given a full opportunity to produce evidence of his losses consequent on the imprisonment. Major Lloyd-George (later Lord Tenby) stated in the House that £300 was a normal payment to an innocent man who had been wrongly imprisoned for an offence of causing grievous bodily harm which he did not commit and who had served years of his sentence before being released with a free pardon. Indeed the Home Secretary described the amounts as generous. This rate is no more than a small fraction of the rate at which courts would award damages in actions for false imprisonment, as members of Parliament told Major Lloyd-George. Moreover prisoners cannot take legal proceedings, civil or criminal, without the Home Secretary's permission; for instance, in 1964 a prisoner, Merro, who complained that he had been assaulted while in prison was allegedly refused permission by the Home Secretary to take proceedings for the assault. There seems no reason why the Home Secretary should pre-judge matters which fall within the purview of the courts. When innocent prisoners have complained to the Parliamentary Commissioner he has refused to publish the police reports and court papers in the case on the ground that he is not allowed to investigate the activities of the police and the courts.

English law may appear inconsistent in another respect. We have seen that confessions obtained by threats or inducement are not admissible in evidence at all. On the other hand, if a policeman obtains evidence by an illegal search, e.g. if he discovers ammunition on the person searched or if he obtains fingerprints from a person in custody without a caution,[21] he is not prevented from putting this in evidence. Contrast this with the rule in United States Federal Courts that evidence obtained by illegal seizure is excluded. In a Californian case one Rochin was suspected of trading in narcotics. When police broke into his room, they saw him swallow some capsules. They promptly handcuffed him and rushed him to hospital where a doctor forced him by means of a stomach pump to vomit. The Supreme Court of the United States refused to admit in evidence two capsules containing morphine which were found in the vomit : in England the evidence would be admissible,[22] whereas the Supreme Court of the United States has since confirmed the principle that evidence unconstitutionally obtained is inadmissible in criminal proceedings.[23] (Similarly in 1966 the Supreme Court decided that a confession was inadmissible if the police had not told the accused of his right to remain silent, or if he had been denied access to a lawyer – nor will they admit evidence obtained after unlawful arrest.) In support of the English position it may be argued that if a policeman acts illegally the remedy lies in an action against him for damages which English law affords. Real evidence in the shape of bullets or morphine capsules cannot lie, and there is no sense in letting a guilty man go scot-free because the evidence has been obtained unlawfully. The case of confessions can be readily distinguished in that the illegality, i.e. the coercion, affects the truth of the evidence; the truth of the real evidence obtained by illegal means remains, notwithstanding the illegal way in which it was obtained. On the other hand Americans maintain that to tolerate this kind of police behaviour is to set course for the police state in the worst sense. Such invasions of a citizen's privacy must be stopped. There is one way to stop them : to make it no longer worth-while for the police to get evidence in such ways by forbidding them to use it when they have got it.

BAIL

Inevitably, there is a considerable interval in the ordinary course of things between charge and trial. If the criminal process is commenced by summons, the accused remains at liberty until trial : this is the normal procedure for minor offences, e.g. most road traffic offences. We have seen that when the accused has been arrested he must be brought before a magistrate within twenty-four hours if he remains in custody. The machinery of bail operates to allow many accused persons liberty pending trial. The police have power to grant bail, and so have the magistrates. If the magistrates refuse bail, they must tell the accused that he can appeal to a High Court judge – many magistrates illegally conceal this right, and worse, there is no legal aid for the appeal. Hundreds do appeal yearly, and from five to ten per cent are granted bail on this appeal. Yet each year twenty to thirty thousand people are confined to prison while awaiting trial because they have been refused, or could not provide, bail. Only one half of these are eventually sent to prison after sentence.

The accused must enter into a recognizance to surrender for trial when called upon, or to forfeit the sum named in the recognizance, which may be anything from £10 to, say, £5,000 depending on the circumstances. Often one or two other sureties in named sums will be required. The police will investigate the standing of suggested sureties, and will give evidence of their attitude to the request for bail. If the accused absconds, the accused and the sureties must pay to the court that proportion of the amount in the bond which the court decides in the particular case, and normally it will be the whole or most of that sum. Prisoners cannot have insurance companies or other paid bodies act as bondsmen.

Public disquiet at the unfairness of bail procedures resulted in changes being made by the Criminal Justice Act 1967. The discretionary power of magistrates to refuse bail has been curtailed. In less serious cases, i.e. those triable in a magistrates' court and punishable by not more than six months' imprisonment, bail must be granted subject to a list of exceptions such as no fixed abode or previous imprisonment. Bail remains discretionary in more serious cases. It is disturbing that even since the 1967 Act more than one in two of those refused bail are not sent to prison after trial. Only one in ten get bail when the police oppose it, and complaints are made that even when bail is granted the police are frustrating that decision, especially in the case of demonstrators, by unreasonably objecting to the sureties which the accused has to find as a condition of his bail. Magistrates have also been adopting a practice of doubtful validity whereby they make bail subject to an undertaking 'not to organize or take part in any demonstration any-where'. In 1969 a demonstrator, one Davoren, challenged the legality of his imprisonment by the chief metropolitan magistrate for this – the Lord Chief Justice avoided ruling on the legality of the 'no demonstration' condition by grant-ing him bail without the condition.

Bail should be granted unless the accused is likely not to appear at trial, or unless his being at large might prejudice a fair trial, as by interfering with witnesses, or unless he is likely to commit further serious crimes. The courts are not respond-ing to the liberal approach of the 1967 Act. The case of Mr William Owen, the former M.P. who was acquitted in 1970 on charges under the Official Secrets Acts, is typical. An old man of good character and poor health, he was refused bail by both magistrates and a High Court judge, so that he was in custody for three months awaiting trial. That 31 per cent of those committed for trial are still denied bail is the more serious when the delays before trial at the Old Bailey and other criminal courts are now so lengthy. There is anxiety lest magistrates refuse bail as a means of inflicting punish-ment – remands for medical reports are particularly sus-pect. Most magistrates refuse bail after a very perfunctory inquiry. And why on an appeal to a judge against bail is the prisoner refused an oral hearing unless he is legally repre-sented? The experience of Richard Neville, editor of *Oz*, in December 1970 is revealing. The London magistrate re-fused him bail without even allowing his solicitor to com-plete his argument, so that he had to disturb Mr Justice Bridge in his home to reverse the magistrate.

HABEAS CORPUS

It is curious that the most famous of all the Englishman's symbols of liberty should bear a Latin name : *habeas corpus*. It is a direction by a judge to anybody who has a person in custody to bring that person before the judge so that he can investigate the legality of the detention. It represents a vital link in the subjection of officialdom to the law. Its significance cannot be measured by the frequency with which men are set free by it. What counts is that police and others are aware that it is immediately available to prevent illegal imprisonment. The slave brought by ship into British territorial waters en route elsewhere;[24] the demobilized army officer pulled from his civilian bed for alleged military crimes over which the Army no longer has jurisdiction;[25] the Polish seamen who feared punishment for their political opinions if they were not freed from their ship in the Thames before it sailed back to Poland;[26] the foreigner who was being extradited to his own country for a political crime for which extradition was not available;[27] the inmate of a mental hospital who was illegally detained there by the hospital authorities;[28] the woman imprisoned by the Vice-Chancellor of Cambridge University for 'walking with a member of the University';[29] all these secured their release upon a writ of *habeas corpus*. Even the validity of detention by order of either House of Parliament may be challenged in this way. An application for *habeas corpus* takes precedence over all other business before the court.

Unfortunately, the Administration of Justice Act 1960 has restricted the liberty conferred by *habeas corpus*. Previously, once a court had ordered the gaoler to set the man free, the decision was final. Now, the custodian can with leave appeal from the Divisional Court of the Queen's Bench Division straight to the House of Lords against the grant of *habeas corpus*. If therefore a man is ordered to be set free by a Divisional Court in a criminal matter, he may find himself remaining a prisoner because the House of Lords reverses the decision of the lower court. In civil matters a released person is not re-imprisoned – the object of giving the custodian a right of appeal is to enable him to raise points of law before the higher court. It seems that the Government introduced these restrictions by way of retaliation for the fact that they felt constrained to release in the 1950s over three thousand mental patients after a decision of the Queen's Bench Division had established that the detention of one inmate was illegal. At one time it used to be thought that a person who

failed to secure release from one judge could apply successively to all the other judges. The Act of 1960, not unreasonably, prevents more than one application unless new evidence
is adduced. A person whose release is refused may always
appeal.

Valuable though *habeas corpus* is, its limits must be noted.
It operates only where the tribunal or person had no *jurisdiction* to detain. If some tribunal acting within its jurisdiction erroneously ordered detention, *habeas corpus* would not
secure release. It is no protection against that kind of honest
mistake in the course of legal administration.

TELEPHONE TAPPING AND INTERCEPTING MAIL

In 1956 the Bar Council were investigating a complaint of
unprofessional conduct on the part of a barrister called
Marrinan. They asked the police if they could provide any
evidence. The police had been intercepting all telephone
calls to and from a criminal suspect, Mr Billy Hill, without
his permission or knowledge, and in this way had acquired
details of telephone calls between Hill and Marrinan. Even
though Marrinan had not been under suspicion, the police
handed over to the Bar Council's secretary transcripts of
the tapped telephone conversations. The Home Secretary
authorized the handing over and the disclosure of the contents to all members of the Bar Council involved in the
investigation of the complaint against Marrinan. In due
course Marrinan was disbarred after the Bar Council's committee had made its findings, and even in 1970 his readmis-
sion was refused. In 1957, when these matters came to light,
the Home Secretary reacted to the public concern at this
revelation of wire tapping by setting up a Committee of
Privy Councillors (Lord Birkett, Sir Walter Monckton, and
Mr Patrick Gordon Walker)

to consider and report upon the exercise by the Secretary of State
of the executive power to intercept communications, and, in
particular, under what authority, to what extent, and for what
purposes this power has been exercised and to what use informa-

tion so obtained has been put; and to recommend whether, how, and subject to what safeguards, this power should be exercised and in what circumstances information obtained by such means should be properly used or disclosed.[30]

These terms of reference have that degree of obscurity which is usual when Governmental inquiries are initiated. Presumably, the terms were drawn up so as to prevent the Committee from reporting on the legality of the power, to confine that part of the inquiry to the authority under which the power had purported to be exercised. It is the usual practice to draw up terms of reference which make the public believe that the inquiry will relate to everything which the public wants to know or about which there is public disquiet, but which in fact exclude whatever the Administration does not wish to be ventilated. The Committee first looked at the practice of intercepting mail, a practice which Lord Campbell, a distinguished nineteenth-century Lord Chancellor, had found to be illegal at common law. Government witnesses pressed the Committee with the argument that these interceptions were made under the authority of the royal prerogative and that they were part of a more general prerogative power to intercept all communications. No decisions of the courts supporting the existence of such a power could be found; the one classical work of authority, written in the nineteenth century, on the royal prerogative, made no mention of such a power. The extent of the royal prerogative is a question of law, and it is not open to the monarch or Government of the day to declare its extent for themselves. The ruling of English law in *Entick* v. *Carrington*, that an official has no power to interfere with a citizen unless the official can prove affirmatively that the law confers on him such a power, will be recalled. In the Crown Proceedings Act 1947 the Government had found it necessary to make an express provision that the Crown was not to be liable in damages for anything done in relation to letters; when it is considered that the same Act also reserved existing prerogative powers of the Crown, it is difficult to maintain the view that the Crown had such a prerogative power, for, if so, why make the express provision in the Act? The alternative Governmental argument was that 'how it arose can only be conjectured because historical records are wanting, but that the power existed and was used permits of no doubt whatever'. This is relevant to the question of what powers were exercised in fact, but it is useless as a legal justification for the exercise of the power unless the Government prove that the law established the power – a person does not ordinarily derive the right to act in a certain way from the mere fact that he has from time to time done so without lawful authority. The next argument was that Parliament had recognized the power to intercept. The Post Office Act 1953 and earlier Acts exempted from criminal liability anything done in relation to postal packets and telegrams by Post Office officials acting on an express warrant in writing under the hand of a Secretary of State. The argument that such Acts validate interception is absurd; they merely state that people who commit such acts are not criminals.

The Committee then considered wire-tapping. Until 1937 the General Post Office acted on the view that anybody could intercept telephone communications, but in that year the Government decided as a matter of policy that a warrant of the Secretary of State should be obtained before a telephone communication was intercepted. Those who maintain the legality of wire-tapping have not even an Act like the Post Office Act on which to rely. If they call in aid the royal prerogative they cannot merely establish a power to intercept letters but must prove a power of interception so general in its terms as to cover forms of communication (like the telephone) unknown when the power was laid down. The only relevant Act is the Telegraph Act 1868 which made it a misdemeanour for any official, contrary to his duty, to intercept the contents of telegraphic messages, and empowered the Postmaster-General to make regulations to carry out the intention of the section. Naturally, the Committee was unwilling to accept this as proof of the power, for it suggests the unlawfulness rather than the legality of interception. The Committee reached the lame conclusion that 'it is difficult to resist the view that if there is a lawful power to intercept communications in the form of letters and telegrams, then it is wide enough to cover telephone communications as well'.

The Crown has not provided any lawful authority to support the interception of telephone communications. This does not mean that the citizen can obtain damages when his calls are intercepted, because the Post Office Act of 1969 contains a provision which is effective to exempt them from any such liability. The position may well be that the Crown has no power conferred by law to tap telephones but that the citizen has no means of redress if the Crown does authorize tapping of his calls.

The Committee then reported that it had been the practice of the Home Secretary to issue warrants for intercepting telephone calls in order to detect breaches of emergency food regulations, evasions of exchange control, posting of Irish Sweepstake tickets in violation of the Lotteries Acts, sending of letters with obscene contents, and traffic in drugs. These warrants were usually issued to the Metropolitan Police. Warrants were also issued to the Board of Customs and Excise to track smugglers, and to the Security Service. In 1951 the Home Office prepared a memorandum setting out the principles which would guide its issue of warrants. The offence must be serious, normal methods of investigation must have failed or be unlikely to succeed, and the interception must be likely to result in a conviction involving a sentence of at least three years. Customs offences must be of substantial and continuing fraud which would seriously damage the revenue or the economy of the country if unchecked. Warrants to the Security Service were to be only in respect of subversive or espionage activity likely to injure the national interest. The Committee found that the highest number of telephone taps in any one year was 241, and that the power had been exercised scrupulously and effectively.

The majority of the Committee was satisfied with the way in which interceptions were being carried out, and subject to minor changes recommended continuation of the present practice. One member would have preferred restrictions on the exercise of the power much more severe than those outlined in the Home Office memorandum of 1951. The Committee unanimously recommended that transcripts should not be passed on to persons outside the public service and called the Home Secretary's conduct in the *Marrinan* case 'mistaken'. The Government have accepted the Committee's recommendations. On the other hand, the Government will do nothing to prevent police from persuading a telephone subscriber to let them have an extension to his telephone so that they can listen in to his conversations and then hand over the information to some private body investigating complaints of breaches of professional etiquette by the person whose call was, without his knowledge or permission, being overheard. It was in this way that a Dr Fox was removed from the medical register in 1959 for unprofessional relations with a married woman patient. The Government will not regard listening-in on an extension, put in by the police for the purpose, as an 'interception', and so such listening-in remains free from the restrictions set out above.

The Government has made out a strong case on grounds of expediency for restricted use of wire-tapping. There are, however, many objections to the present arrangements. It is undesirable that Governments should indulge in practices for which there appears to be no lawful authority. Is the Home Secretary the appropriate person to decide when to issue the warrants? The overworked doctrine of ministerial accountability to Parliament does not really strengthen his claim, for no record of the use of the power will be available to the public or to members of Parliament. There was renewed disquiet in 1971 over the telephone tapping disclosed in the Rudi Dutschke deportation case. We have seen that Home Secretaries have misused their powers in the past. They refuse to answer parliamentary questions about the number of tappings or the categories of person whose lines are tapped. Most European countries require the order of a judge before an interception is permitted. Would not a High Court judge be a more suitable person here?

One of the dominant characteristics of British Governments is that they resist any legal restrictions on the exercise of their powers : at all costs they will do no more than make *ex gratia* concessions of no legal effect. So with wire-tapping: notice that the Government has not agreed to embody in legislation the restrictions on its use recommended by the Committee and accepted by it. If its contention that wire-tapping is lawful be sound, it remains legally free to issue warrants to anybody to intercept any communications for any purposes. Things are strikingly different in, say, Australia. The Telephonic Communications (Interception) Act 1960, in that country makes it a criminal offence for anybody to make an unauthorized interception or an unauthorized disclosure. Interception is permissible only where the activity threatened would prejudice the security of the Commonwealth. Moreover, the Attorney-General's warrant is required. These legal restrictions are greatly to be preferred to the freedom which British Governments enjoy. American experience points to other weaknesses in the British system. Even if the police tap telephones without a warrant, the evidence will not thereby be rendered inadmissible : the majority did not endorse the recommendation of one member of the Committee that no intercepted material should be admissible in evidence. In the United States, no evidence obtained by wire-tapping, whether by federal or state officers, is admissible in any Federal Court. The absence of all these restrictions in England is obviously calculated to make officials less careful in the exercise of these powers, which are in principle obnoxious. But British Governments so systematically avoid the imposition of legal restrictions upon their powers that it would be rash to expect them to follow the Australian and American examples.

Electronic devices such as laser beams, closed-circuit television and micro-miniaturized radio transmitters have rendered wire-tapping an old-fashioned method of overhearing conversations. Little is known about the extent to which police eavesdrop by these new methods : for example, by the use of portable radio equipment which can be hidden in a briefcase or even on a person's premises. One thing is plain : such evidence will not be rendered inadmissible merely because the police have to break into private premises in order to conceal the equipment there.[31] No doubt one day an incident involving such devices will come under public scrutiny, and public concern at the law's failure to restrict their use will show itself, although whether with any legal results is more doubtful.

In 1970 a private member's Bill sought to regulate these and other methods of invading privacy. The Bill was dropped when the Government promised to set up a departmental committee to investigate the problem. Predictably, but regrettably, when its terms of reference were published it was seen that they excluded all interferences by governmental officials and the police; the committee is left with the much less important task of examining the conduct of private individuals and business.

CHAPTER 2

MEETINGS AND DEMONSTRATIONS

HISTORICALLY, the Englishman's right of public meeting has been of great importance. The public meeting has been one of the chief methods of influencing public opinion on big issues, and the key factor in electioneering in particular. Television has greatly reduced the importance of election meetings, but has contributed to the new importance of demonstrations and public protest. In this chapter the law of meetings and demonstrations will be explained so that the contemporary theme of law and order can be kept in proper perspective. This has, however, to start with a negative.

PLACE OF MEETING

Englishmen have no *right* to hold a public meeting any-where : even if they begin to hold public meetings in their own premises they will presumably need town and country planning permission from the local authority for this change in use of the land. There is a popular belief that there is a right of meeting in such places as Speakers' Corner in Hyde Park and Trafalgar Square. This is erroneous : the Commissioners of Works have been entrusted by Parliament with control of meetings there, and they make regulations which set out the terms on which they will allow meetings. So also with parks managed by local authorities : a statute empowers local authorities to make by-laws which regulate the use of the parks, and it is usual for them to have specific by-laws about public meetings. If therefore a by-law requires police permission for meetings and forbids the distribution of literature, breaches of the by-law will be criminal offences. Exceptionally, a citizen might persuade a court that a particular park by-law was so unreasonable as to be void. (Is it reasonable to elevate the need to keep the parks clean above the claims of free expression, so as to prohibit the handing out of literature and pamphlets because many of them will be thrown down when read?) If a particular organization believed that it was being discriminated against in the matter of permission to hold a meeting, it is not clear what legal remedies, as distinct from the obvious political steps of having the matter raised in council and the local press, are available. It is a gap in the law that there is no clear-cut legal process for preventing political discrimination on the part of a local authority in controlling public meetings in its parks and open spaces. The citizen has no right to use premises belonging to local authorities for meetings, except a statutory right to use school or other premises controlled by the local authority upon payment of a reasonable fee for meetings organized by a candidate in connection with a parliamentary or local government election. Of course, many local authorities habitually let on hire meeting-halls to local associations and societies, but as the law stands this is a purely private business arrangement completely at the discretion of a local authority. A ratepayer could secure the court's intervention if the local authority charged lower fees to one political body than to another, yet it is very doubtful whether he could have any legal remedy if the local authority systematically refused to allow particular associations the use of its premises on payment of the ordinary fee. The citizen's rights seem inadequate here : the rights given in respect of elections could well be made of general application. Whereas nobody would contend that there should be a right to hold meetings on the premises of some other private person or body, there ought to be some obligation on public bodies to provide equal facilities for meetings of outside organizations.

We are all familiar with processions and indeed meetings on highways. Is this the exercise of some legal right on the Queen's Highway? We have rights on every highway, but only to pass along it in a reasonable manner. Whoever owns the surface of the highway can sue us in trespass if we use the highway for any other purpose. Local authorities usually own the surface of main roads, so that they could sue in trespass anyone who used those roads for purposes other than that of passage. Other highways are usually owned by the owner of the land fronting the highway. The racehorse trainer who objected to Press racing correspondents timing from the highway his horses' practice gallops on his adjoining land,[1] and the landed duke whose pheasant shoot was interfered with by somebody deliberately opening and shutting his umbrella on the highway,[2] had their remedy in trespass. A landowner can also eject a trespasser with reasonable force after first requesting him to desist from the trespass; whether a local authority could employ its policemen to do this is a nice question. It is a criminal offence wilfully to obstruct free passage along a highway without lawful excuse, and policemen may arrest offenders without a warrant; the courts have decided that the offence may be committed although only part of the highway is obstructed, and even though no nuisance is committed. The severity of the crime is illustrated by what happened to Pat Arrowsmith: her conviction was upheld although the area was frequently used for meetings, the police had been notified and she believed her meeting was lawful.[3] It follows that meetings on highways are unlawful : the owners of the appropriate part of the highway can always have the public removed, and any obstruction will constitute a criminal offence.

A procession will not ordinarily be a trespass to the highway because the highway is merely being used for passage. It may, however, be a criminal obstruction; obstruction is so loose a word that in practice everything turns on how the police interpret it in deciding whether to prosecute, and how the courts choose to interpret it in the event of a prosecution; certainly there may be a criminal obstruction even though passage is not completely blocked. In short the position is as uncertain, and perhaps as unsatisfactory, as that of the motorist who parks his car under the ever-present threat of prosecution for obstruction. This elasticity of the term 'obstruction' provides the police with a powerful weapon to restrict freedom of public meeting, a weapon which they do not hesitate to use. Further, the Public Order Act 1936 (which was passed to counter the outbreak of Fascist–Communist strife), empowers a chief officer of police who reasonably apprehends that a procession may cause serious public disorder to give directions imposing conditions necessary for public order and to prescribe the route (for example, he may divert the procession from a hostile district) : if he thinks the above procedure to be inadequate, he can ask the council of a borough or urban district to make an order prohibiting classes of processions for a maximum period of three months, and such an order by the local authority (or by the Commissioner of the Metropolitan or City of London Police in the London area) is effective when the Home Secretary consents to it. Some have thought that it is regrettable that there is no similar power to prohibit, or to impose conditions as to place of, public meetings in the open air. But this would surely be a dangerously wide new executive power, which the Government has wisely refused to assume.

Suppose that the organizers of a public meeting have satisfied all the above requirements about place of meeting. Are they free to go ahead with the meeting, confident that so long as they behave in a peaceable manner they will not fall foul of the law? The answer, perhaps surprisingly, is no. We now have to examine a series of decided cases. Of each of them we shall have to conclude that we do not know exactly what law they lay down. All these cases were decided by a Divisional Court of the Queen's Bench Division. The standard of judgment in that court is not normally high, but these cases perhaps fall below the usual level. Cases which decide important issues normally go to a court of higher status, where they are argued at length, and finally adjudicated upon by experienced appellate judges who adjourn the case in order to prepare considered written opinions. Judgments in the cases now to be described were delivered *ex tempore* upon conclusion of counsel's argument. Until the Administration of Justice Act 1960 no appeal was possible from these judgments of the Divisional Court. It follows that important points of law have not been given the considered and authoritative ruling which they require. If similar issues arise in the future, the Act of 1960 creates the possibility of clarification, for it provides for leave to appeal to the House of Lords where the Divisional Court certifies that a point of law of general public importance is involved in the decision.

The first of the cases, *Beatty* v. *Gillbanks* (1882),[4] was a prosecution for the crime of *unlawful assembly* : an assembly of three or more persons with intent either to commit a crime by open force or to carry out any common purpose, lawful or unlawful, in such a manner as to give firm and courageous persons in the neighbourhood of such assembly reasonable grounds to apprehend a breach of the peace in consequence of it. The Salvation Army regularly met in Weston-super-Mare and held processions in the streets. This had excited opposition from a body known as the 'Skeleton Army', and disorder had frequently resulted. Disregarding a notice by magistrates and a direction from the police purporting to prohibit their processions, the Salvation Army held another procession, and commotion ensued. The magistrates convicted members of the Salvation Army of unlawful assembly, but the conviction was reversed on appeal to the Divisional Court. In effect, the Divisional Court appeared to rule that the Salvation Army members did not commit the crime, because the disturbances were caused by other people, whom the Salvation Army did not incite, and not by the accused. The Court did not make clear, however, whether they were laying down a general rule that if others committed the disturbance those who held the meeting were not guilty, or whether they merely found on the facts of this particular case that the accused did not cause the disturbance because it was not the natural and probable consequence of their procession that the Skeleton Army should create the commotion.

In *Wise* v. *Dunning* (1902)[5] Wise led a Protestant crusade in Liverpool, holding meetings in the streets which Roman Catholics as well as his supporters attended. At these meetings, by his language and gestures Wise insulted the Roman Catholics present, who thereupon committed breaches of the peace. Wise did not himself commit breaches of the peace, and counselled his supporters not to do so, but he declared his intention to continue to hold meetings. The police prosecuted Wise, not for unlawful assembly, but for *disturbing the peace*. The magistrates exercised their power to bind over Wise to keep the peace and to require him to find sureties. The Divisional Court upheld the magistrates. They purported to distinguish *Beatty* v. *Gillbanks* on the ground that the disorder was the natural and probable consequence of Wise's conduct. Perhaps the case may decide that, where the accused is guilty of using insulting and abusive language of a kind likely to provoke others to commit breaches of the peace, he may be bound over to keep the peace. This imposition of *binding over and finding of sureties* can be a severe punishment, as the next case shows.

In 1914 George Lansbury, the Socialist leader, speaking at a suffragette meeting, urged that they should continue their policy of militancy.[6] The magistrates required him to enter into a personal recognizance of £1,000 and to find two sureties of £500 each, and ordered that in default he should suffer three months' imprisonment, on the ground that he incited others to commit breaches of the peace. This means that if the accused is, as Lansbury was, unable to provide the recognizance and sureties, he must go to prison. The Divisional Court upheld the award of the magistrates, laying down that it need not be shown that anyone was put in bodily fear; a mere apprehension of a breach of the peace was sufficient.

The continued use of binding-over powers occasions public concern. In 1969 a Metropolitan magistrate bound over a man who was charged with using insulting words, before the end of the case and without giving the accused the chance to rebut the police evidence. On appeal, the court held that he could while the case was in progress bind over the accused to keep the peace if it emerged that there might be a future breach of the peace, but not without giving him the opportunity to argue against it.[7] In the same year six persons including a woman J.P. were summoned for demonstrating

against a 6d. charge for admission to a local authority park
and garden at Havant; without even five of the six being
present when the evidence against them was given the magistrates sent them to prison for refusing to be bound over
while the case stood adjourned. On appeal, they were of
course released because of the magistrates' unlawful conduct.
In 1968 Pat Arrowsmith was gaoled for six months for
obstruction during a sit-down demonstration because she
would not be bound over. It is scarcely surprising that the
Home Secretary has now ordered a departmental review of
this practice of binding over. Meanwhile free use is made of
it in public order cases.

Duncan v. *Jones* (1936)[8] shows the police making use of a
charge which was not available to them on a summary
charge in *Beatty* v. *Gillbanks*, that of *obstructing a police
officer in the execution of his duty*, which Parliament made
an offence punishable summarily for the first time in 1885
by the Prevention of Crime Act. Duncan was told by Jones,
a police inspector, that she could only hold her meeting some
175 yards from the proposed place of meeting on the highway. When she indicated her intention to hold it at the
original spot she was arrested and charged. Merely to
obstruct a police officer is no crime; he must be obstructed in
the exercise of his duty – the prosecution must prove that the
police officer was entitled to do that which he was prevented
from doing. Did he then have the power to forbid Mrs
Duncan to hold her meeting where she wanted to hold it? A
meeting held by her at the same place fourteen months previously had been followed by a disturbance on the same day
in a training centre for unemployed workers, which was
across the road. The superintendent of this centre believed
that the meeting caused that disturbance, and that further
meetings in the same place would have the same result. It
was not alleged that she had caused any obstruction, other
than by the presence of her box and the crowd around it, or
that she or any person at the meeting had caused or provoked
a breach of the peace. The Divisional Court held that there
was evidence which would support a conviction by the lower

courts. It was also found that she must have known that a disturbance was a probable consequence of her holding the meeting, that she was not unwilling that such consequences should ensue, and that the police inspector reasonably apprehended such a breach of the peace. The Divisional Court held that on these findings she was rightly convicted of obstructing the police officer in the execution of his duty. The case certainly does not decide that whenever a policeman believes a breach of the peace likely a person who refuses to move on commits an offence; if the court finds that the policeman's belief was an unreasonable one in the circumstances no offence is committed. It is uncertain whether the offence is committed if the accused neither foresaw nor desired that others would create a disturbance.

The police regularly escape the difficulties of *Beatty* v. *Gillbanks* by prosecuting for obstructing a policeman in the execution of his duty, just as they charge persons with disturbing the peace, with its attendant punishment by way of binding over as an alternative to a fine. Yet they do still rely on unlawful assembly in clear-cut cases. There were 58 convictions in 1967, 22 in 1968 and 3 in 1969. In more serious ones they may prosecute for riot, or 'riotous assembly' as it is often colloquially named! An unlawful assembly becomes a riot when force or violence is used in the execution of the common purpose of the three or more gathered together. There were about 20 convictions each year from 1967 to 1969. The most discussed recent example is that of the Cambridge University students, five of whom were convicted of riot and two of unlawful assembly and sentenced to prison for up to 18 months for demonstrations against the Greek regime which led to damage to the Garden House Hotel, Cambridge. It was on the Director of Public Prosecutions' advice that the charges were riot and unlawful assembly.

To translate these cases into practical terms : organizers of public meetings are not safe from criminal prosecution merely because they and their supporters will behave themselves. They take a great risk if they do not seek police permission beforehand, for, if the police believe that disorder is likely and forbid the meeting, disobedience will be criminal unless the magistrates find that the police's apprehension was unreasonable (and common sense suggests that magistrates are highly unlikely to override the view taken by the police on the spot). The right of public meeting then is dependent almost entirely on the police exercising their discretion in a reasonable manner. The promoter should cooperate with the police in the expectation that they will treat him fairly : if he proceeds in defiance of their wishes, conviction is likely.

THE CONDUCT OF THE MEETING

The police have ample powers to control disorderly behaviour at meetings. They make most use of those given by Section 5 of the Public Order Act 1936 as amended by the Race Relations Act 1965 whereby it is an offence for any person in any public place or at any public meeting to use threatening, abusive, or insulting words or behaviour or to distribute or display any writing, sign, or visible representation which is threatening, abusive, or insulting with intent to provoke a breach of the peace or whereby a breach of the peace is likely to be occasioned. The Lord Chief Justice ruled in *Jordan*'s case (1963) that the offence is committed if the words are likely to provoke a breach of peace among the particular audience, even though that audience is an unreasonable one and made up of hooligans whose aim was to prevent the speaker from making an address.[9] A constable may arrest without warrant any person reasonably suspected by him of committing this offence. The increase of the maximum penalties made by the Public Order Act 1963 is sensible.

Succumbing to pressure consequent on incidents at Fascist meetings, the Government also introduced a new offence in the Race Relations Act 1965. It is a crime for a person, with intent to stir up hatred against any section of the public in Great Britain distinguished by colour, race or ethnic or national origins, to publish or distribute threatening, abusive or insulting matter, to use in any public place or at any public meeting threatening abuse or insulting words, if the matter or words are likely to stir up hatred against that section on grounds of colour, race, or ethnic or national origins. What is new and disturbing about this new offence is that the content makes the writing or speech criminal even though no public disorder results. The existing provisions of the Public Order Acts would have been wide enough to cover statements of this kind which resulted in disorder, so that the need for this new offence is questioned. A typical use of it was made in 1968 when there was a conviction for handing out anti-Vietnam leaflets to United States soldiers as they left their London service club.[10] There were fourteen prosecutions in the country in the first two years, and some heavy sentences have been imposed, including a year's imprisonment for Michael X, who made an anti-white speech at a public meeting in Reading, though there was no evidence of any likelihood of violence among his audience, and eighteen months for Colin Jordan. In the final chapter of this book the circumstances under which a citizen can appeal under the European Commission on Human Rights are discussed; when Jordan appealed the Commission held his case inadmissible.[11]

In 1932 the Home Secretary stated in Parliament that the police had no lawful right to go to a meeting unless either the promoters asked them or they had reason to believe that a breach of the peace was actually being committed. Yet, three years later, in 1935, there was decided the remarkable case of *Thomas* v. *Sawkins*.[12] A meeting was advertised in a hall of a Welsh town for the purpose of protesting against the Incitement to Disaffection Bill, which was then before Parliament, and demanding the dismissal of the Chief Constable of Glamorganshire. The public were admitted without payment. The promoter asked police officers who entered the meeting hall to leave. A constable used force on him because he believed that he was about to remove his superior officer forcibly from the hall. No crime or breach of the peace was alleged to have been committed. The promoter prosecuted the police officer for battery. The magistrates' court found that the police had reasonable grounds for believing that if they were not present at the meeting seditious speeches would be made and breaches of the peace would occur. They held that the police had a right to enter and remain in the meeting hall, so that no battery was committed. The promoter appealed unsuccessfully to the Divisional Court. What, however, did the Divisional Court decide? It will be noted that the police apprehended both sedition and breach of the peace. The case certainly decides, therefore, that the police may enter and remain wherever they apprehend both sedition and breach of the peace. One of the three judges held that they could remain if they apprehended any offence, the second if they apprehended either breach of the peace or sedition, and the third if they apprehended both breach of the peace and sedition. No subsequent case has cleared up these differences of opinion on these important questions of police power to attend public meetings. The other difficulty is whether the case applies to private as well as to public meetings. The court held that because it was a public meeting the police were entitled to be there. But there can be no doubt that, even though a general invitation is issued, the promoter can turn away particular individuals. Logically, therefore, this case would seem to imply that the police have a right to attend private meetings in private premises where they believe that the appropriate offences are likely to be committed if they are not there.

This case seems to confer tremendous powers of interference upon the police, and there is no precedent for it. Certainly, earlier Irish cases had decided that where the only means of restoring the peace is to use reasonable force a policeman has a defence to a claim of battery : for example, where a policeman removed an orange lily being worn by a lady who walked through a crowd of Roman Catholics. But *Thomas* v. *Sawkins* goes much further. Suppose the police believe that somebody at a private meeting of a few persons in a private house may say something seditious (and we shall see later how elastic is the legal definition of sedition). Apparently, the police will be entitled to enter the private house without the owner's permission and attend the meeting. They cannot disperse the meeting merely because they believe that some offence will be committed, but they can do so, remember, if they believe that a breach of the peace would otherwise be likely to ensue.

The activities of the anti-bomb demonstrators in 1961 illustrate the workings of this branch of the law. Before the advertised time of the Trafalgar Square meeting Bertrand Russell and other organizers were summoned for inciting members of the public to commit breaches of the peace, and on their refusing to be bound over to keep the peace were sent to prison. Originally, the Home Secretary exercised his power under the Public Order Act 1936 to ban processions in the Trafalgar Square area. When that ban expired on 17 September the Commissioner of the Metropolitan Police used a power available in London only given to him by the Metropolitan Police Act 1839 : he issued regulations for preventing obstruction for a further twenty-four hours in the same area, and for this, unlike action under the Public Order Act, no consent of the Home Secretary is required. Disobedience to the Commissioner's order is an offence, just like disobedience to the Home Secretary's order under the other Act, though the maximum punishment under the Metropolitan Police Act is smaller. Some of those who took part in the Grosvenor Square demonstration on Vietnam in 1968 were charged with assaulting a policeman, possessing offensive weapons, insulting, threatening and abusive behaviour, obstructing the police, obstructing the highway and footpath and malicious damage. In 1967 the police were following their usual practice of preventing all demonstrations within a mile of Westminster during parliamentary sittings. A Mr Papworth challenged his conviction for holding a peaceful and stationary vigil at the corner of Downing Street and Whitehall and was eventually acquitted. No offence is committed under Section 54 of the Metropolitan Police Act 1839 unless it is proved that the accused was likely to obstruct M.P.s or to cause disorder or annoyance.

The police are no longer able to impose a total ban on peaceful demonstrations merely because Parliament is sitting.[13]

Leaders of Spearhead, a neo-Nazi society, and of the Free Wales Army were also imprisoned under this Act in the 1960s for organizing quasi-military bodies. When a Miss Abrahams interrupted the Prime Minister to denounce the Labour Government's Vietnam policy while he was reading the lesson in a Brighton church, the Lord Chief Justice held that she was guilty under the Ecclesiastical Courts Jurisdiction Act 1860 of 'indecent behaviour'.[14] When three hooded men took part in a Ku Klux Klan rite near Rugby in 1965 they were sent to prison for contravening the Public Order Act 1936 by wearing political uniforms at a public meeting.

Suspicion has been voiced that the police exercise unfairly their choice of what offence to prosecute for when nuclear disarmament officials are involved. For example, when demonstrations took place in London in 1963 on the occasion of the visit of the Greek Royal Family, many ordinary offenders were prosecuted summarily for disobeying the Commissioner's regulations, or for obstructing a highway, offences then punishable merely by fine. An official was, however, sent to prison for inciting a crowd to commit a nuisance by unlawfully obstructing the free passage of a highway. Incitement is a common-law misdemeanour punishable by imprisonment even though neither the accused nor anybody else is guilty of the substantive offence. Obstruction of the highway is a means of committing the crime of public nuisance, but it is very rare to treat it in that way. By resorting to this almost unprecedented step of charging the official with inciting others to commit a nuisance by obstruction, the police were able to secure his imprisonment, yet if previous practice had been followed, if the official had committed the very act which he allegedly incited, he would merely have been convicted of an offence punishable only by fine.[15]

Does the law strike a fair balance between police and organizers of meetings, between public order and free speech and discussion? If a person is behaving in a peaceable way, should the police be free to take the easy way out and stop the meeting before they have first tried to control the real offenders, the rowdies who are likely to break up the meeting? Does the present law (reinforced by the 1963 decision that the speaker must take his audience as he finds it, and violates the Public Order Act if his insulting words are likely to provoke disorder by the thugs present) not afford undue temptation to a police force, and an undermanned one at that, to put their own convenience ahead of the right of free speech? In answering these questions it must be remembered that the police have a statutory power to arrest and charge those whom they think guilty of insulting or abusive language or behaviour. Those who sponsor unpopular causes from the public platform will commonly excite mutterings and hecklings from their audience; no doubt they commonly exaggerate, vilify, and distort, but should they not, nonetheless, be protected by the police against the threats of their audience? If they do not obtain this protection, and instead the police throw their weight on the side of those who would break up the meetings, do not the police become in effect the new censors of speech? Whatever one's opinion of the views of the Mosley group, one would not want to see their opponents free to break up their meetings or to prevent them from taking place by threats to use violence and thereby prevent those views from being expressed. It is also important that the police should not discriminate against certain categories of citizens in respect of matters concerning meetings and demonstrations, both when deciding whether to prosecute, and, when they have so resolved, in determining with what offences to charge them. They must act fairly and be seen to act fairly.

What, then, of the law and order controversy? We see that the powers of the police are already varied and great, that there is no absolute right to demonstrate, and that demonstrators are prone to fall foul of the law in many different ways. The existing law is more than adequate to deal with them – whether we have sufficient police or pay them enough is another matter. It is sometimes said that the law fails to deal with demonstrators on cricket and other sports grounds. Let us review the legal situation. If a spectator abuses his entry by interfering with the players or creating a disturbance, the club and its stewards can evict using such force as is reasonably necessary. The police have a common-law duty to quell or prevent a breach of the peace which they reasonably apprehend. It is therefore lawful for them to enter a ground whether invited or not, and arrest unruly demonstrators. The same is true if the unruly behaviour occurs in university administration buildings or if it is by squatters in another's premises. At the request of the owner, the courts can order squatters (whether identified or not) to leave the premises and send them to prison if they don't comply. It is not surprising that the police are satisfied with the powers the law now gives them – they need no more. The doubters ought to be convinced by the Garden House Hotel, Cambridge, case.

CHAPTER 3

FREEDOM OF EXPRESSION (1): THEATRE, CINEMA, AND BROADCASTING

In this and the following chapters the theme is freedom of expression. The law may interfere in two ways. It may prevent expression by imposing restraints before the communication is made : in short, censorship. It may punish as criminals or mulct in damages those who have transgressed by publishing. This division is not clear-cut, nor is it always possible to separate legal and administrative matters. Both here and in Chapter 4 we shall consider censorship of the principal media of communication, and in Chapters 5 and 6 discuss the ways in which the already published word may fall foul of the law.

Theatre

From the fourteenth century until 1968 the law imposed theatre censorship. The Theatres Act 1968 brought it to an end. The censor was the Lord Chamberlain under the Theatres Act 1843 and in the 1960s opposition mounted to both censorship and the way in which he exercised it. In 1967 a Joint Committee of the House of Lords and Commons unanimously recommended its abolition. Its excellent report met with widespread approval, and George Strauss, its chairman, had the satisfaction of piloting a private member's Bill through Parliament, which carried out the Committee's proposals.

The abolition of theatre censorship is total. No residual powers are left to the royal prerogative or to the local authorities which license theatre buildings for reasons of safety. In granting theatre licences local authorities are now forbidden to impose conditions about the nature of plays or manner of performing them in the licensed theatre. The Act recognizes that the criminal law must continue to operate in the theatre and that at the same time playwrights and theatrical managements must not be subject to unfair risk of prosecution. The law of obscenity now applies to theatres, but subject to those defences, especially that the play was for the public good, which as we shall see apply in respect of books. As five Manchester revue proprietors found out in 1971 in the first prosecution of its kind under the Act, those who direct filthy perverted revues can still find themselves in prison. It is forbidden to curtail this new freedom by prosecuting under the Vagrancy Acts or for the common-law offence of conspiring to corrupt public morals or to do any act contrary to public morals or decency. Those defamed in a play are protected by the new rule that defamation in the theatre, as in broadcasting, is to be treated as libel and not as the less serious wrong of slander. It is made an offence to incite to racial hatred by means of a public performance of a play. Public order is protected: a producer commits a crime if with intent to provoke a breach of the peace he presents a performance which as a whole is likely to occasion a breach of the peace, and there are penalties for the use of threatening, abusive or insulting words or behaviour. Management is immune from the risk of local or private prosecution or local variations in enforcement because no prosecutions under the Act for obscenity, incitement to racial hatred or breach of public order may be brought without the consent of the Attorney-General. (The 1970 decision not to prosecute *Oh! Calcutta!* is significant.) In practice a playwright who intends to plead the merit of his work will have trial by jury on a charge of obscenity.

The Act allows no exceptions for the royal family, plays about public figures, the recently dead, heads of foreign governments or religious themes, to mention some subjects which the Lord Chamberlain used to ban.

The Act is an admirable one. Of course, the odd producer may now risk a pornographic play, and there may be some uncertainty about the applicability of the law in particular circumstances, but there seems no reason why on the whole the Act should not greatly benefit the English theatre. Playwrights are given free choice of themes, and yet the criminal law lurks when the Attorney-General decides that the mark has been overstepped in those limited areas where prosecution is still permitted. All the indications are that the theatre, government and judiciary will ensure that the new legal regime works fairly and predictably. There is, however, anxiety lest state-aided theatres be subject to a censorship beyond the law in order, as it is put, to prevent the taxpayer subsidizing pornography.

Cinema

THE CINEMATOGRAPH ACTS

In 1909 Parliament passed 'an Act to make better provision for securing safety at cinematograph and other exhibitions'; the cinema was a new form of public entertainment and, in view of the risk of fire, clearly needed official supervision. Accordingly, the Act provided that an exhibition 'for the purposes of which inflammable films are used' required a licence : county councils and county boroughs were made the licensing authorities, and county councils were expressly authorized to delegate their powers to justices sitting in petty sessions. These licensing bodies might grant licences to such persons as they thought fit to use the premises specfied in the licence for the above purpose on such terms and conditions and under such restrictions as, subject to regulations of the Home Secretary, the licensing bodies might determine. Many had supposed that the only conditions authorized would relate to public safety and order; and that any other conditions would be void. When confronted with a power to impose conditions which on a literal interpretation seems unrestricted, the courts frequently have given that power a restricted meaning in the light of the general purpose of the Act. A former permanent head of the Home Office, which originated the Act, has written that the Home

Office never supposed that local authorities were being given a power to censor films.

However, soon after the Act was passed some local authorities responded to local pressure by refusing to allow the exhibition of films of which they disapproved. Exhibitors who challenged the legality of such action surprisingly failed, the courts holding in several cases that the licensing power did extend to matters affecting public morals.[1] Faced with the prospect of conflicting decisions on particular films the cinematograph industry pressed the Home Office to centralize film censorship. The Home Office refused to introduce legislation setting up compulsory national censorship : obviously they shirked undertaking a new duty which might expose their chief to continual criticism in Parliament and the Press. Working in close cooperation with the Home Office, the industry itself set up in 1912 a voluntary and unofficial body, the British Board of Film Censors, to certify and classify films for public exhibition. Thereupon, the Home Office, after consultation with licensing authorities, and in the light of representations from welfare organizations about the impropriety of many of the films then being exhibited, began to encourage licensing authorities to make use of the Board's work so that suitable and reasonably uniform standards of censorship might be applied. The Home Office recommended to the licensing authorities certain 'model' conditions which they might attach to cinema licences. They are based almost entirely upon the British Board of Film Censors' censorship and classification of films. Licensing authorities are not bound to adopt recommendations made by the Home Office; the Cinematograph Act leaves decisions to the discretion of the licensing authorities to accept, reject, or modify any of the decisions of the Board under the Cinematograph Act 1909 – indeed, a condition attached to a licence that the Board's rulings must always be followed has been held void because the final decision must be that of the licensing body, not of the Board.[2] The legal position, in brief, is that the British Board of Film Censors has no official statutory existence; it is a private body set up by the cinematograph industry, which derives its authority from the fact that when the local authorities license cinemas they usually stipulate that the films ordinarily conform to the Board's rulings – a stipulation which a court of first instance has surprisingly held to be valid and which has gone unchallenged ever since.[3] The only important legal change since 1909 is the passing of the Cinematograph Act 1952. This for the first time extended the powers of licensing bodies to non-inflammable films. It also put on a firm legal basis the power of licensing bodies to make conditions or restrictions on the admission of children to films designated as unsuitable for children and indeed imposed a duty on them to consider such restrictions. In all other respects the legal position about licensing set out above remains unaltered.

CENSORSHIP IN PRACTICE: THE BRITISH BOARD OF FILM CENSORS AND LOCAL LICENSING AUTHORITIES

What then happens in practice? First, the power to delegate to justices has been widely exercised, so that more than half of the country's seven hundred cinema-licensing bodies are justices. Many other local authorities have delegated the powers to their watch committees, and one even to its health, sewerage, and cemeteries committee. Of 487 licensing bodies which answered a canvass all but 32 had adopted the Home Office's model conditions.

The main provisions of the model conditions are as follows. No film shall be shown, and no poster or other advertisement of a film in or outside the premises shall be displayed, which is likely to be injurious to morality or to encourage or incite to crime, or to lead to disorder, or to be offensive to public feeling, or which contains any offensive representation of living persons. If the licensing body serve a notice on the licensee that they object to the exhibition of any film on any of these grounds, that film shall not be shown. No film which has not been passed by the Board shall be exhibited without the express consent of the licensing body. The next provisions refer to the Board's classification : U, children under 5 not admitted, whether accompanied or not; A, like U, except that it conveys a warning that the film contains some material that some parents might prefer their children not to see; AA, children under 14 not admitted, whether accompanied or not; X, those under 18 not admitted. These categories, revised in 1970, were settled after consultation with the Cinema Consultative Committee, a body on which local authorities and all sections of the film industry are represented. A licensing authority, even though it has adopted the model conditions, is free to reject the Board's classification either by refusing to permit the exhibition of a film in accordance with that classification, or by allowing its performance in disregard of the Board's refusal or restricted classification. Conditions sometimes imposed by authorities which do not follow the model conditions include : specific permission to be sought before exhibiting X films on Sundays; synopses of all X films to be submitted in advance so that the authority may, if it chooses, view any such film before deciding whether to permit its exhibition.

How does the British Board of Film Censors go about its work? The President of the Board is selected in this way : the Council of the Incorporated Association of Kinematograph Manufacturers, of which the Secretary to the British Board of Film Censors is *ex officio* secretary, makes a recommendation to a joint committee which consists of representatives of the British Film Producers' Association, the Federation of British Film Makers, the Association of Specialized Film Producers, the Kinematograph Renters' Society and the Cinematograph Exhibitors' Association. Prior to this meeting there will have been consultation with the Home Office, the Association of Municipal Corporations and the County Councils Association. The Incorporated Association makes the appointment. The President appoints examiners (three men and two women at present) who, together with the President and the Secretary (who is now appointed by representatives of that committee which appoints the President), constitute the Board. None of the Board's members is connected with the film industry, and its revenues are derived from fees charged for all films submitted for censorship. In the past the Home Office has exercised some influence on the Board. Some appointments, both to the presidency and to the influential secretaryship, have been of persons with Home Office connections. There are authenticated examples of governmental interference before the Second World War. In 1939 the Home Secretary admitted under questioning in the House of Commons that the Board had consulted him about certain films before deciding whether to recommend them for exhibition. In 1938 the Secretary of State for India arranged with the British Board of Film Censors to prevent production and exhibition of a film about the Indian mutiny at Lucknow. Again, in 1935 a pacifist film of the Peace Pledge Union was refused a certificate on the ground that it might lead to disturbances, whereas in the following year a Territorial Army film was approved and widely exhibited. *Professor Mamlock*, a Russian film which attacked the Nazis' anti-semitism, was banned in 1939; the ban was lifted as soon as war was declared later that year. In recent years the Board has attained strength and independence. Neither its present President, Lord Harlech (formerly British Ambassador in the United States), nor its present Secretary has Home Office antecedents. The Home Secretary was at pains to protest in the House of Commons his inability to prevent the exhibition of *Rommel.*[4] There is no reason to believe that the Board now consults government departments on any decisions, and still less that it ever submits to governmental pressure. Each film is seen by two or more examiners; films in which important problems occur will also be seen by the Secretary or President, or both, and matters involving important changes of policy will usually be discussed by the President with all the Board's examiners – all seven Board members saw *Ulysses*. Sometimes the Government has interfered with the exhibition of films without attempting to exert pressure on the Board. In September 1938, at the time of Chamberlain's visit to Hitler, four out of the five cinema news companies exhibited films favourable to the Government – the fifth, Paramount, included interviews with persons opposed to appeasement : the Foreign Secretary successfully stopped exhibition of this newsreel by persuading the American Ambassador to intervene with Paramount. In 1959 the Foreign Office advised the British participants in a Moscow Film Festival not to exhibit *Carlton-Browne of the F.O.* on the ground that it might be misunderstood.

The practice of the local licensing bodies varies widely. Films are sometimes exhibited despite the Board's refusal : Cambridge and Maesteg, for instance, allowed the playing of Brando's *The Wild One*. Under Manchester's Chief Constable there is an Entertainments Department, with functions such as are performed in some other towns by the fire service. Its members read the cinema trade newspapers in order to decide which trade shows of films in the city to attend, and they will at least attend all X, AA and A films. They prepare for the Chief Constable a report on any film which they think ought not perhaps to be shown in the city. This report is forwarded to the watch committee, who will have a private viewing of the film and then decide whether to allow it to be shown. For example, Manchester refused to allow *The Savage Eye* to be exhibited, although it won an award at the Edinburgh Festival. It also banned *The Killing of Sister George*, but it was screened in neighbouring Stockport and Salford. If an application is made to exhibit a film which the Board rejected, the committee will view that also. By arrangement, Manchester police circulate their reports on films to many north-western towns. Whatever Manchester has approved without reservation these other towns will approve ordinarily without further check ; in the remaining instances they will usually view and decide for themselves. London and the Midlands have more formal consultative arrangements. Birmingham has delegated the task to the licensing justices, who have appointed women inspectors for the discharge of both cinema- and theatre-licensing functions. These inspectors attend shows, and, if they make unfavourable reports, two nominated justices attached to whichever of the city's five police districts is affected visit the cinema within twenty-four hours. These justices also attend trade shows if the local cinematographers' association so request them because they are doubtful about booking a particular film. Occasionally they change the Board's classification. Birmingham has an arrangement with Walsall, Wolverhampton, West Bromwich, Warwick and other West Midland boroughs, to invite representatives from all of them whenever it views a film in consequence of having received a complaint. Although each authority reserves liberty of action, in practice uniformity is achieved, so that exhibited films do not acquire notoriety through being banned in neighbouring towns – there will be no 'Banned in Birmingham' posters. The administrative county of Warwickshire is not a party to this arrangement : thus, in 1961, it banned *Saturday Night and Sunday Morning*, which Birmingham and the other boroughs allowed to be exhibited in accordance with the Board's X certificate. The Greater London Council joins forces with the county councils of Surrey, Berkshire, and Essex and some other neighbouring boroughs in viewing films which have been the subject of complaint or have not been passed by the Board, but these bodies do not necessarily make uniform decisions. Some local authorities always accept the Board's rulings; others never vary them without asking the Board to give reasons for their decision. Manchester, Oxford and Brighton (on the decision of its fire brigade committee) banned the uncut version of *Ulysses* – the Board gave an X certificate subject to cuts – whereas the Greater London Council and Warwickshire approved it. Cases like that show how film companies sometimes use local authorities as a court of appeal against what they regard as harsh decisions of the Board.

The British Board of Film Censors does not follow the former American practice of publishing a detailed code of rules for the production of films, e.g., 'open-mouth kissing' is not to be shown, 'pansy', 'S.O.B.', 'son-of-a', and other listed expressions were forbidden. Its task is also easier because in Britain there are very few unofficial powerful pressure groups systematically viewing and censoring films, whereas in the United States dozens of organizations such as the General Federation of Women's Clubs, the National Legion of Decency (a Roman Catholic organization) and the Daughters of the American Revolution publish regular reports to their members and the trade. Contrary to popular belief, violence and horror, not sex, is the Board's primary concern. The Board rejects films for other reasons, too. It denied a certificate to the film *Operation Teutonic Sword* because it believed that it contained matter defamatory of a living person, General Speidel of the German armed forces. Its judgement was vindicated in the sense that, when certain local authorities allowed the film to be shown despite the Board's refusal, the General successfully sued the distributors for libel. At the same time one wonders whether the Board should not leave it to the ordinary courts to protect a man's reputation. The situation is the more disquieting in that the Board was also influenced in its decision to reject by the fear that the Board might itself be liable for defamation if it authorized the exhibition of a defamatory film. It would surely be undesirable if the Board were to deny a certificate to every film which it thought might be defamatory of some living person; the courts can be relied on to afford remedies for libel victims. The Board encourages the growing practice of submitting the scripts of films to it in advance of production. Where the Board cannot approve a film in the form submitted, cuts are usually suggested, and if these are substantial, if they involve reductions in scenes rather than definite eliminations, or if there are other good reasons, re-submission of the appropriate reels is required. Sometimes cuts are made at the request of a film company in order to avoid the restriction of a film to the X or A categories, since there are often financial advantages in U or A as compared with X films.

GENERAL OBSERVATIONS ON FILM CENSORSHIP

How is one to appraise this system of cinema censorship? It seems to be generally agreed that the Board tackles the task in an intelligent manner, and that, particularly with the development of the X certificate since 1951, few sincere and serious films are now denied public exhibition. For example, this category has permitted such films as *Room at the Top, La Ronde, Death of a Salesman*, and *Baby Doll* to be seen in unabridged versions by the adult British public. On the other hand, because it has sometimes been thought commercially unprofitable to exhibit solely on an X classification, some serious films have never been made at all, or else like the school film *Spare the Rod* (1961) have been produced in a watered-down version. It has been criticized for not allowing a shot of a woman's pubic hair in *Hugs and Kisses*, and for banning drug films such as *The Trip* which its psychiatric consultants advised to be harmful. On the whole the Board is sensitive to public opinion, and Mr John Trevelyan (its Secretary until he resigned in 1971) had a high reputation.

Obviously, if the statutory system of local licensing is to continue, the Board fulfils an essential function in making unnecessary the submission of all films to all licensing authorities. But why have local censorship at all? It is responsible for much local expenditure, and argument that local bodies know the peculiar quirks and susceptibilities of their own folk seems thin in a small homogeneous country. It seems a waste of public funds that conferences of local authorities and the Board have to be convened so that the local authorities and the Board can understand the reasoning underlying each other's decisions. It is perhaps significant that in one area of control that is inescapably local, film advertising, there is dissatisfaction with local authorities because there is so much offensive advertising material at cinema entrances.

There is another objection to the present system of local licensing. It is the practice to make the licence revocable for breach of condition : consequently local authorities have a much wider power to close down cinemas than theatres. Moreover, local authorities (with the laudable exception of the Greater London Council) do not usually give a licensee the right to appear personally and to be legally represented before them when a licensing decision is taken. Licensing justices usually do afford this facility – in Liverpool, for example, the justices listened to counsel's arguments before refusing the usual twelve months' renewal to a cinema which had persistently published offensive posters – and licensees are seriously prejudiced when the licensing is carried out by local authorities. Fortunately their lot is to some extent improved by the Act of 1952, which gives those aggrieved by the revocation of a licence the right of appeal to Quarter Sessions.

If local censorship were abolished the choice would then be between putting the Board on a statutory basis, thus giving its decisions legal effect, and leaving the industry free to continue to operate a Board which would be shorn of the indirect legal sanctions which at present attach to its rulings. If the Board were legally recognized, there would be a strong case for widening its membership and ensuring its judicial independence. In order to keep the decisions out of the political arena, it would also be desirable to enact the grounds on which rejection and classification are to be based. Its decisions should be unchallengeable in Parliament and only subject to judicial review if the powers were exceeded. Perhaps such a body should listen to any arguments in support of a film made by its sponsors and be required to give reasons for its refusal to comply with the sponsors' requests. Some of the grounds on which films have apparently been censored should be excluded. Take the treatment given in 1954 to *The End of the Affair*, of which its director, Edward Dmytryk, complained in the *New York Herald Tribune* : the censor refused permission to include a newsreel shot of the royal family on the balcony of Buckingham Palace on V.E. Day on the ground that to associate the royal family with the film could be improper – yet Dmytryk stated that a representative of the royal family itself eventually permitted the shot.[5] There has also been complaint that the British Board is hypersensitive on religious matters : parts of the script of *The Left Hand of God*, which passed the Code of the Motion Picture Association of America and the Legion of Decency, were either altered or deleted at the behest of the British Board. In short, the Board may be subject to criticism (though to a lesser extent) in largely the same areas as the Lord Chamberlain used to be. In its regulation of obscenity, horror, and violence it will have widespread support, but not in an interpretation of 'offensiveness' which appears to be unduly deferential to monarchy, the Church, and similar institutions. No doubt censorship of this latter kind is infrequent, but it would be better to make its exercise impossible.

It is not inconsistent to have abolished theatre censorship and yet to retain national censorship of films, either legal or unofficial. Factors like the large attendance of children and the facility for portrayal of horror justify making a distinction between the two media.

Broadcasting

B.B.C. AND I.T.A. – THE LEGAL POSITION

The British Broadcasting Corporation is a body incorporated by royal charter. There are nine governors (including the chairman and the vice-chairman) who are appointed by the Crown on the advice of the Prime Minister : three of the governors are 'national' governors, representing Scotland, Wales, and Northern Ireland. The powers of the B.B.C. to provide sound and television broadcasting services and the controls to which they are subject are to be found in the Licence and Agreement of 7 November 1969.[6] The key figure is the Minister of Posts and Telecommunications; he grants the licence, and without it there can be no broadcasting. The Licence and Agreement requires the publication of various programmes; for instance, Clause 13(2) orders the broadcast of 'an impartial account day by day prepared by professional reporters of the proceedings in both Houses of the United

Kingdom Parliament'. Clause 13(4) of this Licence provides that 'The Minister of Posts and Telecommunications may from time to time by notice in writing require the Corporation to refrain at any specified time or at all times from sending any matter or matter of any class specified in such notice.' In pursuance of this power, the Minister has sent the following memoranda to the B.B.C. The B.B.C. is not to broadcast its own opinion on current affairs or on matters of public policy, and in 1927–8 was directed not to broadcast matters of political, industrial, or religious controversy. In 1964 the B.B.C. was also directed for the first time to maintain standards of good taste and decency and to maintain a high general standard in respect of the content and quality of programmes, a proper balance and wide range in their subject matter, and a proper proportion of British-produced programmes. And what if the B.B.C. were to disobey a direction from the Minister? Clause 23 provides for the revocation of the licence by the Minister of Posts and Telecommunications upon non-compliance with a direction of his – and the approval of Parliament is not required either for the cancellation of the licence to broadcast or indeed for the revocation of the royal charter. Clearly these are water-tight legal controls.

The Independent Television Authority was set up directly by the Television Act 1954 in order to provide television broadcasting services additional to those of the B.B.C.: the operative Act is now the Television Act 1964. The I.T.A. has a chairman, deputy chairman, and at least five (at present nine) other members, appointed by the Minister of Posts and Telecommunications, three of whom represent Scotland, Wales and Northern Ireland respectively, and is assisted by a General Advisory Council. The Act contemplates that programmes shall be provided, not by the I.T.A., but by programme contractors under contract with the I.T.A. Surprisingly enough, the 1954 Act laid down no procedures for the award of these highly lucrative contracts. This contrasts with the American prescription of procedures of a judicial kind calculated to ensure that these decisions are arrived at fairly and impartially. In fact when the first contracts were allotted the I.T.A. interviewed some applicants but not others – presumably it interviewed those whom it appointed. In the event, two of the first four contracts were allocated to companies backed by right-wing newspapers. When contracts came up for renewal in 1964 and 1967 all applicants were each interviewed secretly for an hour or so, but no public hearings were held. The Act contains several rules about the content of programmes, which will be examined later. Programme contractors are required to submit programme schedules to the I.T.A. and must not broadcast programmes which do not form part of an approved schedule. One year the I.T.A. refused to accept the contractors' schedules because they had too many American crime and Western films during the peak viewing period from 8 p.m. to 9 p.m. No doubt this refusal was justified in view of the statutory duty to ensure that the programmes maintain a high general standard in respect of their content and quality and a proper balance and wide range in their subject matter, having regard both to the programmes as a whole and also to the days of the week and times of the day at which the programmes are broadcast. The I.T.A. may also direct the inclusion or exclusion of particular items, and may require the production of scripts in advance. The contracts must contain such provisions as the I.T.A. thinks necessary for ensuring that the programme contractors comply with the requirements of the Act and the restrictions imposed under the Act by the I.T.A. The contracts must also include power for the I.T.A. to determine or suspend the duty to transmit programmes by a contractor who has three times been in breach of his obligations : any dispute whether there is such a breach is to be settled by arbitration. Suppose that the I.T.A. fails to enforce its contract against a defaulting programme contractor. The Act merely provides that 'it shall be the duty of the Authority to satisfy themselves that, so far as possible, the programmes broadcast by the Authority comply with' the requirements of the Act. These words were deliberately drafted in this loose discretionary form so as to impose no enforceable legal duty on the I.T.A.; they have no legal effect, they are merely words of exhortation which the I.T.A. can disregard without any legal consequences. Programme contractors have been freely allowed to ignore the promises on the strength of which they were awarded contracts, and no action is taken by I.T.A. It is therefore not surprising (though regrettable) that the Government has refused to enact legislation which would require hearings in public, reasons for allocating contracts, and the publication of the successful applicants' memoranda to the I.T.A.

By notice in writing the Minister of Posts and Telecommunications may at any time require the I.T.A. to refrain from broadcasting any matter or classes of matter specified in the notice. Unlike the similar power with respect to the B.B.C., non-compliance does not threaten the power to broadcast (although the I.T.A., like the B.B.C., has a licence from the Minister of Posts and Telecommunications, this licence differs from that of the B.B.C. in that it is silent on programme content and therefore makes no express provision for revocation on non-compliance with directives) : the Act merely adds that it shall be the duty of the I.T.A. to comply. At most, the Minister could obtain in court an order of mandamus requiring the I.T.A. to comply : in the unlikely event of matters going so far, perhaps the members of the I.T.A. could then be committed for contempt of court if they still did not comply with the Minister's notice after he had obtained the order of mandamus against them.

The Minister has the power to prescribe the actual hours during which broadcasting shall take place. It was because the Postmaster-General, acting under his power, limited the number of hours of Outside Broadcasting Time that Granada was prevented from carrying out its plan in 1965 of transmitting continuously in the day the party political conferences. Both the B.B.C. and the I.T.A. are required to broadcast any Government announcement at the time specified by a Minister : this refers not to statements about Government policy, but to official announcements; for example, the calling up of certain classes of reserves in the armed forces. In practice police messages and the like are broadcast without a direction. The biggest safeguard against political abuse of this Governmental power is that the B.B.C. and I.T.A. are entitled to say that the broadcast is being made at the request of the Government.

We have been discussing the legal obligations of the B.B.C. and the I.T.A. contained in the Licence and statute respectively : the matters to be discussed next do not for the most part rest on the law.

BROADCASTING AND POLITICS

This is a subject of great and often unnecessary complexity, which is best dealt with under a number of sub-heads.

Ministerial Broadcasts

These are broadcasts for which the initiative comes from the Government and in which the speaker is a Minister. The rules are contained in an agreement between the Conservative Party, the Labour Party and the B.B.C. of 3 April 1969 (usually referred to as the 'aide-mémoire', and which is not made available to the public). The agreement creates two categories as follows :

The first category relates to Ministers wishing to explain legislation or administrative policies approved by Parliament, or to seek the co-operation of the public in matters where there is a general consensus of opinion. The B.B.C. will provide suitable opportunities for such broadcasts within the regular framework of their programmes; there will be no right of reply by the Opposition.

The second category relates to more important and normally infrequent occasions, when the Prime Minister or one of his most senior Cabinet colleagues designated by him wishes to broadcast to the nation in order to provide information or explanation of events of prime national or international importance, or to seek the cooperation of the public in connection with such events.

The B.B.C. will provide the Prime Minister or Cabinet Minister with suitable facilities on each occasion in this second category.

Under the original aide-mémoire of 1947, the B.B.C. alone decided whether the Opposition should be allowed a reply to a broadcast of the second category. Under the 1969 aide-mémoire, the Opposition now has the right of reply. When the Opposition exercises this right to broadcast, there follows a third programme, a discussion of the issues between a member of the Cabinet and a senior member of the Opposition nominated respectively by the Government and Opposition. The aide-mémoire continues :

An opportunity to participate in such a discussion should be offered to a representative of any other party with electoral support at the time in question on a scale not appreciably less than that of the Liberal Party at the date of this Aide-Mémoire.

The effect of the 1970 General Election is to deprive the Liberal Party (now that it has fewer M.P.s) of participation unless the aide-mémoire is altered.

Although, as we shall see, parts of the aide-mémoire are treated as applying to the I.T.A. as much as to the B.B.C., the I.T.A. is in a different position from the B.B.C. in regard to these Ministerial broadcasts. The I.T.A. is bound by the Television Act, which overrides, for the I.T.A., whatever is in the aide-mémoire. That Act requires the I.T.A. to satisfy itself of the impartiality of any series of programmes respecting matters of political or industrial controversy or relating to current public policy. Before a Minister is permitted to make any broadcast it is the duty of the I.T.A. to examine the script in order to decide in advance whether it is in fact impartial; if it is not, it must arrange beforehand for a broadcast by the Opposition.

The B.B.C. regularly avoids the constraints of the aide-mémoire by inviting a Minister to broadcast; the B.B.C. is then free to allow replies by the Opposition. Of course Ministers and M.P.s of all parties regularly appear on discussion programmes and the like on both B.B.C. and I.T.A., although steps are taken to ensure that a fair balance over a period is maintained between appearances by the various political parties.

Budget Broadcasts

Time is offered to the Chancellor of the Exchequer and a spokesman nominated by the Opposition to broadcast on T.V. and radio on successive evenings in Budget week.

Party Political Broadcasts

The 1947 aide-mémoire provided :

A limited number of controversial party political broadcasts shall be allocated to the various parties in accordance with their polls at the last General Election. The allocation shall be calculated on a yearly basis and the total number of such broadcasts shall be a matter for discussion between the parties and the B.B.C.

The broadcasting authorities provide the time but the parties decide on its allocation, which they have based on the number of votes the parties secured at the previous general election. Subjects and speakers are chosen by the parties, and any party may use one or more of its quota to reply to a previous broadcast. In addition to national broadcasts by the three main parties, the Scottish and Welsh Nationalists are allotted broadcasts in Scotland and Wales respectively.

The B.B.C. is prohibited by direction under its licence from sending out any other controversial party political broadcasts. The I.T.A. is not legally bound to relay these broadcasts, and in practice the parties have to fall in with the I.T.A.'s own suggested times, which of course will exclude the peak advertising revenue-earning hours. All channels take them simultaneously despite the fact that the opinion polls show that two-thirds of the people oppose that. In 1961 one of the programme contractors announced that it would not relay party political broadcasts unless the parties indemnified it against all damages and costs awarded against it in libel actions arising out of such broadcasts – no doubt the attempt by Mrs Barbara Castle to obtain damages for libel from Mr Christopher Chataway occasioned this attitude. The contractor was correct in saying that it would be answerable for any such libels, because, as we have seen, it is by agreement and not compulsion that these broadcasts are made. On the other hand, if the libel were contained in a Government announcement, i.e. a broadcast which the Government can compel the B.B.C. and I.T.A. to make, the B.B.C. and I.T.A. would probably not be liable. The I.T.A. but not the B.B.C. is precluded by the Television Act 1964 from putting out subliminal messages. When Mr McWhirter believed that a 1970 Labour party political broadcast was subliminal it was against I.T.A. alone that he issued a writ.

General Election Broadcasting

Arrangements for party election broadcasts are made by the Broadcasting Committee, which consists of two representatives each from the B.B.C., I.T.V. and the three main parties. In practice the broadcasting representatives allow their views to be overridden by the political members. In the 1970 election I.T.N.'s *News at Ten* had to be cut down to make way for politicians' speeches; audience participation shows in which politicians were questioned by the audience were banned, and confrontation of opponents and evaluation of party speeches by political commentators were prohibited. In short everything the viewing and listening public wanted was denied them by the politicians, and what they abhorred was foisted on them. What is worse is that the agreement is a classified document which is never published; its contents are not disclosed even to producers, so that *Panorama* in 1970 did not know that Mr Wilson could insist on Healey talking about defence when it wanted Stewart on foreign affairs. The head of B.B.C.-T.V. Current Affairs later confessed in the *Listener* his ignorance of the agreement's details and added that, 'whatever actually happened, there was the appearance of an agreement to restrict the ability of television journalists to cover the election, an agreement in which the public took second place'.

Why the broadcasting authorities are so craven is hard to understand unless they fear next year's taxes or refusal of increase in licence fees. Certainly the *Sunday Times*'s explanation that the law requires the B.B.C. to be impartial so that any party can veto examination of any issue by withholding a spokesman is false. The impact of the law is slight. It is an election offence for anyone not authorized by the candidate to incur expense with a view to promoting his candidature by presenting his views or disparaging his opponents. Newspapers have always been exempt, but the Representation of the People Act 1949 required candidates to include broadcasting expenses in their returns of electoral expenses. During the 1964 General Election campaign the B.B.C. and I.T.A. had allowed Sir Alec Douglas-Home to appear in five party political broadcasts. One of his opponents sought to unseat him on the ground that there had been a corrupt practice under the Act. In consequence this provision was repealed by the Representation of the People Act 1969 so that broadcasting now has the same wide exemption as the Press with respect to electoral expenses. The same Act introduces an ambiguous provision the effect of which might be to make it an illegal practice for a candidate to broadcast an item about his constituency in which any other opposing candidate neither takes part nor consents to its going forward without him. Uncertainty about its meaning led Mr Wilson on his television-covered constituency tours of the 1970 campaign not to allow local Labour candidates to participate.

Parliamentary Matters

One controversial aspect of relations between Government and broadcasting authority in the 1950s was discussion of matters being debated in Parliament. During the war, when of course there was no effective Opposition, a Minister prevailed on the B.B.C. to let him make a broadcast, on a subject unconnected with the war effort, the night before it was to be debated in the House of Commons. Repenting of this weakness in face of Governmental pressure, the B.B.C. then itself made a rule for its own protection that it would not allow broadcasts by anybody in anticipation of parliamentary debates. This was incorporated in the aide-mémoire of 1947 without discussion, and almost by accident. Again the B.B.C. had second thoughts and became irked by its own rule. The

Beveridge Report on Broadcasting (1951)[7] recommended its repeal, but Sir Winston Churchill's Government rejected this proposal by the Beveridge Committee. Then the B.B.C. showed commendable courage. When the parties turned down its proposal that the governors should decide how much discussion of political issues would be broadcast, on an undertaking that no members of Parliament would be allowed to broadcast within fourteen days before parliamentary debates, it refused to renew this provision of the aide-mémoire and thereby forced the Government to take upon themselves the odium of imposing it. Without consulting Parliament, the Postmaster-General in 1955 issued directions in the same terms as those contained in the aide-mémoire, to both the B.B.C. and I.T.A. (which, as we have seen, are legally binding) : that they should not

on any issue, arrange discussions or *ex parte* statements which are to be broadcast during a period of a fortnight before the issue is debated in either House or while it is being so debated, and that when legislation is introduced in Parliament on any subject, they shall not, on such subject, arrange broadcasts by any member of Parliament which are to be made during the period between the introduction of the legislation and the time when it either receives the Royal Assent or is previously withdrawn or dropped.

The responsible Press, commendably putting on one side its own interests, was unanimous in its condemnation of this Governmental policy. In 1956 a Select Committee was set up to consider the matter. It found that any restrictions should be reduced to the smallest extent that is practicable (and would have gone further had not its terms of reference precluded it) and that the only justification which could be claimed for any policy of restriction was the necessity of upholding the primacy of Parliament in debating the affairs of the nation. The Government refused to implement the Report, but instead agreed to suspend the fourteen-day rule for an experimental period of six months. The price exacted was an undertaking by the B.B.C. and I.T.A. that they would continue to act in a way which would not 'derogate from the primacy of Parliament' as the forum for debating the affairs of the nation.[8] Subsequently, the fourteen-day rule was suspended indefinitely, and remains suspended today. Both bodies are free to arrange discussions and talks on any political matters – they are themselves to be the judges of what derogates from the primacy of Parliament. They are both forbidden to televise parliamentary proceedings. For the time being then, the I.T.A. may, without the encumbrance of the direction, include programmes relating to matters of political controversy or current public policy; the only statutory duty is to take care that due impartiality is preserved considering, when there is a series of programmes, that series as a whole.[9] Programmes like I.T.A.'s *This Week* and B.B.C.'s *Twenty-Four Hours* can pursue their course of political discussion, by either members of Parliament or others. Whether the whips will allow M.P.s to broadcast freely is another matter – Lord Boothby has told how, when a member of Parliament, he received orders from the Tory whips restricting his T.V. appearances in particular programmes to a specific number.[10] Whereas, however, the B.B.C. could invite a public figure to speak on a controversial issue, the I.T.A. could not, unless it was satisfied that to do so was consistent with its statutory duty to preserve 'due impartiality'.

It may be that the above discussion has not covered every aspect of Governmental interferences with programmes. The Press and the Opposition accused the Government of attempting backstairs interference at the time of Suez. It is now said that Eden instructed Kilmuir to prepare an instrument to take over the B.B.C. altogether; the omission of any reference to this in the Eden and Kilmuir memoirs is not regarded as significant. On another occasion South Africa's Minister for External Affairs complained that a *Panorama* feature on apartheid had been broadcast in the face of an express request of the United Kingdom Government that it be postponed. Apparently in the 1960s *Panorama* did not broadcast an interview with Bidault at the time it was filmed because the Government requested its postponement so as not to jeopardize Common Market negotiations, although it did broadcast it seven weeks later, after the Common Market talks had broken down.

So far we have been examining relations between the broadcasting companies and the Government of the day. Parliament itself also exercises supervision, although the Government is not responsible to Parliament for the day-to-day running of the B.B.C. and I.T.A. and has denied, for instance, any obligation regularly to monitor programmes. At question time in the House of Commons the Minister of Posts and Telecommunications is often asked about the B.B.C. and I.T.A. Questions about the alleged failure of the I.T.A. to enforce compliance by the programme contractors with the requirements of the Television Act are frequent, and are usually countered by denials of responsibility for such day-to-day activities of the I.T.A. The daily motion for the adjournment of the House of Commons is sometimes used to air grievances : an allegation of excessive Welsh nationalism in Welsh B.B.C. broadcasts led to the setting up of a Select Committee, which cleared the B.B.C. of the charges levelled against it. Similar accusations of bias in treatment of the Suez crisis were made, to be refuted by the B.B.C. governors after a full inquiry. Occasionally a motion of censure on the B.B.C. is put down, as when the B.B.C. was alleged to have made statements contradicting facts found by a Parliamentary Select Committee about methods of slaughtering horses. Sometimes, the B.B.C. submits to threats of parliamentary action. When a member of Parliament threatened to raise on the adjournment a projected broadcast by an ex-Queen's Scout who had been expelled from the movement for being a Communist political officer, the Director-General cancelled the recorded broadcast within two hours.

OUTSIDE PRESSURE ON BROADCASTING AUTHORITIES

Other forms of informal pressure influence the B.B.C. A documentary about sending a worker to Coventry was cancelled, consequent upon Trade Union Congress comment; when on Easter Sunday the B.B.C. put on a play (*Family Portrait*, previously licensed by the Lord Chamberlain) which presented a Christian doctrine acceptable to some denominations but not to Roman Catholicism, the Director-General apologized to Cardinal Griffin for his 'grave error' : no doubt this approach would rule out many of the miracle plays, at least at periods like Easter and Christmas. Public bodies, too, restrict the freedom of the B.B.C. – British Rail withdrew a promise of facilities for a television Special Inquiry into railways in which there would be raised such matters as dirty lavatories and unpunctuality; Salford City Council resolved never to allow broadcasts about the city without its express permission because of a television programme on the city's health services. When the police objected to a *Cause for Concern* programme in 1968 the B.B.C. cancelled it. In 1969 Tyne Tees T.V. made a film about NATO. Some NATO officials then changed their minds about the film and asked that it be not shown. Without even seeing the film, the heads of I.T.A. thereupon banned it. *Mrs Wilson's Diary*, which had had 255 West End performances, was banned by I.T.A. on the ground that it was offensive. Programme contractors regularly consult I.T.A. before screening controversial programmes. For instance, Granada obtained I.T.A. clearance for a piece on methods of sanction-busting in Rhodesia.

INTERNAL CONTROLS

Editorial control within the B.B.C. is largely in the hands of programme producers. Written directives on specific matters are issued – there is a detailed one on violence from the Controller of Television Programmes.[11] Light entertainment producers have lists of forbidden subjects, such as royalty and the Church. There are 71 paragraphs of rules for current affairs programmes, and when in doubt producers refer to their superiors or sometimes to their equals. For example, religious allusions in a non-religious programme would be referred to the Head of Religious Broadcasting.[12] Like other censors whom we have considered, the B.B.C. in its self-censorship is at great pains to avoid upsetting susceptibilities. It will ban a record by Petula Clark entitled 'The Sky' because it finds offensive a veiled reference to God. It will remove Malcolm Muggeridge and Lord Altrincham from its programmes because they have written magazine articles which criticize the monarchy. It will ban records of Noel Coward's musical *Sail Away*, which American audiences have listened to unrestricted for years. In 1967 it banned the Beatles record from Sergeant Pepper, 'A Day in the Life'. It is difficult to resist the conclusion that the tendency within the B.B.C., especially before commercial television, was to lean over backwards so as not to give offence to any 'important' section of the community. The B.B.C. denies that it has any code and maintains that its key personnel merely instinctively understand what is expected of them by the governors and Director-General. But it is believed that lists of forbidden subjects have been compiled from time to time for producers. The fullest official statement of its internal censorship is in the Appendix to the Report of the Joint Committee of both Houses of Parliament on Censorship of the Theatre (1967).[13]

By the Television Act it is the duty of the I.T.A. to satisfy itself that, so far as possible, nothing is included in the programmes which offends against good taste or decency, or is likely to encourage or incite to crime or to lead to disorder or to be offensive to public feeling. It has to draw up a code giving guidance as to the rules to be observed in regard to the showing of violence, particularly when large numbers of children may be expected to be watching. It may include other matters in the code, especially having regard to programmes broadcast when large numbers of children may be expected to be watching. The I.T.A. must secure observance of the code, and it may also impose further prohibitions or restrictions on any programmes as respects matters going beyond the code where it decides to impose requirements as to standards and practice for such other programmes. The Code on Violence which was published in 1964 stresses that violence must be kept within the needs of the dramatic context in which it occurs, and it specifies ways in which scenes of violence must avoid causing harm to children who are viewing. In 1969 I.T.A. protested to Granada about scenes in a gang-war series, *Big Breadwinner Hog*. The detailed workings of this system are found in the 1967 parliamentary report mentioned above.[14]

No religious service or propaganda may be broadcast without the I.T.A.'s approval. The I.T.A. used to be required to comply with the recommendations of its religious advisory committee. By the 1964 Act the functions of the committee, like the B.B.C.'s religious advisory committee, have been made merely advisory. The I.T.A. committee is to be 'representative of the main streams of religious thought in the U.K.'.

One matter peculiar to I.T.A. is the control of advertisements. The Television Act empowers the programme contractors to insert advertisements in their programmes in consideration of payment to them. The Act contains many requirements on advertising: they include the rule that advertisements must be clearly distinguishable as such and recognizably separate from the rest of the programme. The I.T.A. is required to draw up a code governing standards in advertising and prescribing the advertisements and methods of advertising to be prohibited. It is also the duty of the I.T.A. to secure that these requirements are complied with. An advisory committee composed of representatives of the advertising industry and the public is set up under the Act in order to keep the code under review and to advise the I.T.A. with a view to the exclusion of misleading advertisements and generally as to the principles to be followed in connection with advertisements. Yet it is the I.T.A. which takes decisions on advertisements, and its decisions are not subject to appeal to any court or tribunal. Detailed comment on television advertising will be made in Chapter 4.

The Act imposes another restriction on I.T.A. No programme may offer 'a prize or gift which is available only to persons receiving that programme, or in relation to which any advantage is given to such persons'.[15] Some may rejoice that this prevents our following the American habit of playing Bingo on television. A few naïve souls were under the delusion that it prevented the giving of prizes to quiz contestants; but it is those 'receiving' the programme, not the participants, who must not be offered prizes. The I.T.A. does, however, have to approve the amount of prizes awarded in relation to a particular programme.

A COMPARISON WITH CINEMA CENSORSHIP

How does broadcasting compare with film censorship? The B.B.C. refused to televise *The War Game*, a film about nuclear raids, but the British Board of Film Censors then granted it an X certificate. Films may be exhibited on television even though the British Board of Film Censors has refused a licence : one example was *The Warsaw Ghetto*. Frequently X films are televised without notification of their classification. All this is undeniably legal. It seems pointless to require television to heed British Board of Film Censors classifications unless there is similar treatment of other plays and features. There is pressure from the film industry for uniform treatment in cinema and television. At least, it should be possible to keep X films off peak family viewing periods and to require that the programme announcements and *T.V. Times* and *Radio Times* state their British Board of Film Censors classification. The broadcasting bodies believe that they do enough if they postpone X films until after 9 p.m. In 1971 there has been parental protest at the Board's allowing trailers for X films to be shown at children's matinées.

CHAPTER 4

FREEDOM OF EXPRESSION (2): THE PRINTED WORD AND ADVERTISING

The Printed Word

HISTORY OF THE FORMER CENSORSHIP

FROM the sixteenth century the Crown assumed the prerogative power to grant printing privileges and thereafter treated this power as its monopoly. The Crown was concerned at the threat to the established order of Church and State presented by unrestrained printing. Philip and Mary therefore granted a charter to the Stationers' Company in 1556 which confined printing to members of the Company and its licensees. In return the Company undertook to search out and suppress all undesirable and illegal books. The censorship was political and religious, not moral. The system continued thoughout the Tudor and Stuart eras. The Licensing Act of 1662 illustrates how it worked. All printed works had to be registered with, and licensed by, the Stationers' Company. A licence was required to import and to sell. Printing presses had to be registered, too. Wide powers to search for and seize suspected printed matter in shops and houses (except those of peers) were given.

In 1695, when the current licensing statute expired, the House of Commons refused to renew it, although the House of Lords voted for its renewal. Thus, the licensing system lapsed, never to be re-introduced. The end came, not through any decision of principle, but merely through complaints at abuses in operation and the difficulty of devising a workable machinery of control. Since that time there has been no legal censorship of books – Milton's *Areopagitica* (1644) was written in a successful attempt to ward off a parliamentary threat to reinstate the licensing of printing –

although until 1855 newspapers were subject to a tax designed to make them too expensive for the masses. Freedom of the Press from licensing restriction was soon seen as a vital common-law right, as this quotation from the leading eighteenth-century jurist shows :[1]

The liberty of the press is indeed essential to the nature of a free state; but this consists in laying no previous restraints upon publications, and not in freedom from censure for criminal matter when published. Every free man has an undoubted right to lay what sentiments he pleases before the public; to forbid this, is to destroy the freedom of the press; but if he publishes what is improper, mischievous or illegal, he must take the consequences of his own temerity.

During the Second World War, Defence Regulation 2D empowered the Government to suppress a newspaper without previous warning if it was systematically publishing matter calculated to foment opposition to the prosecution of the war. Thus, the *Daily Worker* was suppressed in 1941, and the *Daily Mirror* was officially threatened with suppression in 1942 because it published a cartoon allegedly calculated to cause unrest in the armed forces and merchant navy : the cartoon depicted a shipwrecked seaman, and implied that the petrol which he and his shipmates were trying to bring across the Atlantic was being used for non-essential purposes. At the end of the war censorship was at once removed.

OTHER PRESENT-DAY RESTRAINTS

There is, then, no official censorship of printed works. Until 1966 there was, however, one form of unofficial censorship of books, the Index of the Roman Catholic Church. The rules were contained in the papal code of canon law. Certain classes of books were banned without inclusion in the Index, such as translations of the scriptures by non-Catholics, and books attacking religion or morals, or upholding the validity of divorce. The twelve categories of forbidden books were considered more important than the Index of specific books.

The Pope could also ban particular books throughout the world, and each bishop might do so in his own diocese. Books on the Index included all the works of Balzac, Stendhal, and Zola, Richardson's *Pamela* and Gibbon's *Decline and Fall of the Roman Empire*, and totalled some four to five thousand in all. The Index was revised periodically by a small congregation of cardinals and priests, although one wondered how efficiently that revision was done. Dusty polemical tracts by obscure seventeenth-century and eighteenth-century writers abounded, but there was no mention of Marx, Lenin, or Freud, for instance. Some restrictions remain. No Catholic may publish a work of a religious character without the prior approval of one of the diocesan censors appointed by the bishops. Priests and members of religious orders need permission before publishing a book or article on any subject whatever.

Selection of books – even though it falls short of censorship – must also have a restrictive effect. In this connection, the decisions taken by the library committees of the local authorities, and by the persons responsible for choosing school books, are of interest. In the absence of detailed surveys, it is difficult to assess their effect. Two points are relevant : there seems little publicly expressed dissatisfaction; and although a hundred years ago there were active and powerful societies for the prevention of vice, library selection committees now seem as free from external pressures as our cinema censors. True, there is the Public Morality Council, with high-ranking membership of the the main religious denominations, but it does not appear to attempt that kind of detailed interference with the work of elected representatives on local government bodies. Commercial distributors, too, can exercise a restrictive influence : for example, W. H. Smith & Son, which has a monopoly at various points of distribution, such as railway stations, refused to sell a pamphlet by Randolph Churchill which criticized the Press. In 1971 we have seen, too, Birmingham education committee's ban on the film *Growing Up*.

In 1949 the Royal Commission on the Press reported its

findings.[2] The Press has no statutory duty to be impartial politically in the way that, say, the I.T.A. has, and we have seen that Parliament even exempted it from the provisions of Section 63 of the Representation of the People Act 1949. The Commission found evidence of the Press's 'willingness to be satisfied with what at best corresponds only roughly to the truth and of readiness to make statements on inadequate evidence'.[3] 'Through excessive partisanship, or through distortion in the interests of news value' all the popular papers and certain of the quality papers fell short of the requirements of truth and fairmindedness. The Report abounds with examples, and no doubt the reader will add his own. For example, the *Daily Express* reported a speech by Marshall, the United States Secretary of State. The Commission found its report 'not merely inadequate; it was a travesty', the exact opposite of the true impression of the speech was given – 'it was a case ... amounting virtually to suppression, which appeared to be associated ... with the political views of the proprietor',[4] Lord Beaverbrook, with whose policy the speech was made to conform by being distorted. Another typical example was an article in the *Observer*, published while the Commission was sitting, which made categorical statements about the Commission's proposals : many of these statements were 'not only untrue but devoid of any resemblance to the truth'.[5] The Report condemned this practice of dressing up uninformed guesses as facts. Of course the Report also found evidence of triviality and sensationalism in the popular Press.

The Commission found evidence that advertisers occasionally seek to influence the policy of a newspaper, but none of concerted pressure to induce a newspaper to adopt a particular policy. It thought that only newspapers which were financially less strong avoided policies detrimental to advertisers' interests. A Scottish newspaper, for example, refused to insert any advertisements for auction sales of property on which there appeared the name of solicitors who had successfully sued them on behalf of clients for libel. Instances of similar conduct have occasionally come to light since the

Commission reported. When, some years after the Commission had reported, the Classics Club complained to the General Council of the Press that the leading music magazines refused to advertise its records because they were price-cutting the large record companies, the Press Council replied that it is a recognized principle in journalism that an editor has the sole and absolute right to reject any advertisement which is submitted to him, and nobody can question his decision.

The Press Council also defended the refusal by *The Times* to publish advertisements of Dr Marie Stopes's book, *Married Love* and in 1971 the refusal of the national Press to advertise a magazine for lesbians. On the other hand, it condemned, in 1962, the Society of West End Theatre Managers for an attempt to influence editorial policy when most of its members withdrew advertisements of their productions from the *Observer*, which refused to discontinue a weekly 'Quick Theatre Guide' containing potted criticism of the shows.

The Commission uncovered one instance of Governmental pressure. The *Glasgow Herald* opposed appeasement at the time of Munich : the editor and proprietor were invited to see a senior member of the Cabinet, who pointed out to them their shortcomings and indicated the Government's dislike of their editorial policy : the pressure was resisted successfully, and the *Glasgow Herald* adhered to its editorial view. One recalls also that the Press was persuaded not to mention the relationship between Edward VIII and Mrs Simpson (organized by Beaverbrook through the Newspaper Proprietors' Association), and the application by Prince Philip for British nationality. When the Government is attacked in the Press on false grounds it can of course utilize Parliamentary time to defend itself. For instance, some of the inaccurate statements in Koestler's articles on capital punishment in the *Observer* reflected on the Home Office : a parliamentary question and answer were used as a vehicle for the Government's denial of the assertions contained in the articles.

The Commission thought that the system by which the Press took news from Government departments through Public Relations Officers needed careful watching, because of the obvious dangers of totalitarianism if the Press relied on them instead of making independent inquiry. They might have said more about the Government's practice of giving non-attributable information to accredited lobby correspondents. There is a Services, Press, and Broadcasting Committee of five officials and eleven representatives of Press and broadcasting which unofficially agrees on the draft of 'D' notices, i.e. information about defence matters. In this way agreement is reached on the amount of information to be published about specific matters. The workings of this committee are examined more closely in Chapter 8.

THE PRESS COUNCIL

Perhaps the most important recommendation of the Commission was that there should be set up a General Council of the Press. This Council was in no sense to be a Government organ, but a voluntary body set up by the Press. A lay chairman entirely unconnected with the Press and a twenty per cent lay membership were recommended. The Commission recommended that a body set up along these lines should endeavour to safeguard the freedom of the Press and to encourage the growth of a sense of public responsibility and public service among journalists.

In 1953 the organizations of the Press did set up a General Council of the Press with functions broadly similar to those recommended. But it consisted entirely of persons engaged in full-time journalism. The Royal Commission on the Press, 1961–2, recommended that if the Press did not establish, within a specified time, an authoritative General Council with a lay element as recommended by the 1949 Commission, the Government should introduce legislation for the establishment of such a body.[6]

The work of the Council can be assessed in the light of its annual reports which are available to the public and which contain an account of the cases adjudicated. Broadly speaking, it has concerned itself with matters affecting the freedom of the Press to obtain information and with complaints from the public about both the methods used and standards of reporting. For instance, the *Daily Sketch* smuggled a girl reporter into the grounds of the Duchess of Kent's home in the boot of a car in the hope of her attending the Duke's twenty-first birthday party. She had to be escorted off the premises by the police when her statement that she was a personal friend of the Duke who had mislaid her invitation was challenged. The Council severely condemned the editor's conduct. Frequently the Council has criticized newspapers for intrusion into private lives or for failing to correct inaccurate statements in subsequent editions when their attention was drawn to them. It also criticized what it regarded as the unwholesome exploitation of sex in articles by Diana Dors in the *News of the World*.

The Press Council used to be criticized on the ground that its procedures were unfair and that it defended the Press at the expense of the citizen. In 1964 the force of these criticisms was acknowledged when a lay chairman (Lord Devlin, now succeeded by another judge, Lord Pearce) took over, and a further lay element not exceeding twenty per cent of its voting membership was introduced through co-option by the chairman and the professional members. Lord Devlin lost no time in devising fairer procedures and in explaining them to the public. Complaints by the public are now handled by a Complaints Committee, which investigates every case where it thinks that there is a case to answer, and then recommends to the Council. It normally arrives at its recommendation upon written evidence, but it takes oral evidence when it appears desirable, for example if there is a conflict of evidence about a material fact. Any journalist who expresses a wish to appear in person before the Council will be allowed to do so. Legal representation is not permitted, and hearings are in private. The Council's statement did not say expressly that an affected newspaper would always be notified of a complaint, and would always be shown all supporting evidence considered by the Council; one hopes that it would treat newspapers in this way.

After prolonged examination the Council published a useful general statement on 'cheque-book journalism'. It condemned the practice of paying criminals for the disclosure of their deeds as public entertainment. It objected to any tactics which deprived competitors of legitimate access to facts that the public ought to know, and especially to body-snatching or public brawls between competing newspapers over the body, i.e. the person whose exclusive story was being bought. In 1966 after judicial and governmental protest at the *News of the World*'s entering into a contract with the principal witness at the Moors murder trial before the trial began to serialize his full story after the trial ended, the Press Council issued a Declaration of Principle. It said that witnesses should not be offered payment before criminal proceedings had ended and that no payment should be made for feature articles to persons engaged in crime or other notorious misbehaviour when the public interest does not warrant it; it deplored publication of personal articles of an unsavoury nature by persons who have been concerned in criminal acts or vicious conduct.

The effect of these new procedural rules which Lord Devlin introduced in 1964 has been wholly beneficial. At first they produced a big increase in the number of complaints; the public had sensed that under the old regime their complaints would not get an unbiased hearing from an exclusively Press body. Because the Council has been affording more protection to the citizen the Press has reacted by raising its standards. Consequently the Council is now making fewer adjudications, and the number of serious intrusions, misrepresentations or other ethical wrongs on the part of the Press is declining. Adjudications are now running at fewer than 100 a year. Even now serious lapses occur : in 1969 the Council criticized a newspaper which had received a 650-word article for publication because, without consulting the author, it extracted 90 words from it and published that as a letter.

The procedure could still be improved. Take the complaint that the *Daily Express* published photographs of the Queen in bed soon after the birth of Prince Edward. The complaint was not upheld, but the *Daily Express* understandably protested that the Press Council announced on the day of publication that it was taking action without waiting for complaints, and did adjudicate although the Queen never objected. The early efforts of Lord Pearce have been unhappy. In 1969, before the Council had read them, it condemned the *News of the World* for printing the Christine Keeler memoirs, and without specifying the details of the complaint. More serious, the following month it upheld the right of the *Daily Telegraph* (which knew that all other newspapers were withholding names) to publish, in the face of the express request of the relatives and the hospital on health grounds, the names of the recipient and donor of a transplanted heart. In its decision the Council gave far more weight to the newspaper's case than to the relatives'. Later, when the wife of one of the train robbers published her memoirs it did not institute inquiries, and when complaints were made it did not uphold them, the Declaration of Principle notwithstanding.

The criticism is made that the Press Council has no teeth : editors cock a snook at it, continue to intrude into people's private lives, and fail to correct statements whose falsity the Press Council has exposed. All this is true, but it is difficult to see how the Council could be given greater powers. To give a private body powers of fining or suspension seems impracticable. No doubt newspapers are guilty of unwarranted and offensive invasions of private lives; no doubt they should correct errors. But is it not the function of the ordinary law of the land to deal with such matters, just as the law of defamation is a weapon against the Press? We shall consider later whether the law confers adequate protection on the citizen against the Press in these matters. It may be that the slogan 'Freedom of the Press', which properly connotes freedom to publish without prior restraint, has been deliberately and cynically used by the Press to give them unjustified powers of obtaining information. Of course what is a trespass by an ordinary citizen should be and is an actionable wrong by a journalist too – the Press is not above the law. The question for later consideration is whether the Press as a pressure group has moulded the law into a form which inadequately protects the citizen against activities in which the Press particularly engages.

In some areas the law imposes a prohibition on publication : some aspects of this are dealt with in the section on Contempt. Mention might be made here of the Judicial Proceedings (Regulation of Reports) Act 1926. This makes it a crime to publish in relation to any judicial proceedings any indecent matter or indecent medical, surgical, or physiological details which would be calculated to injure public morals. In particular, the Act makes it an offence to publish in relation to proceedings for divorce or nullity any particulars other than the following : the names, addresses, and occupations of the parties, the charges, legal argument, and the judge's summing up and verdict. The Press must not publish the 'juicy' details of the evidence.

*

Advertising

LEGAL CONTROLS

Advertising presents a sharp conflict of competing interests. The advertiser of the product wishes above all to sell his product and to beat his competitors. The agent whom the advertiser employs has to prove his ability to sell the product. The owner of the medium through which the product is advertised, whether newspaper or periodical, poster or television, requires the advertising revenue in order to stay in business. Massed against this powerful trio are the general public. The trio rest their case on the virtues of freedom of expression, and freedom of business competition. The opposing interests are more complex : that the consumer should have full, frank, and accurate statements of the quality of the product advertised; that public safety, public amenities, and public morals should not be imperilled; and that business competitors should not be subject to unfair trade practices.

Is the individual member of the public adequately protected against false advertising? Sometimes he used to have an action for breach of contract. For example, in 1891, the Carbolic Smoke Ball Company, the makers of a 'Carbolic Smoke Ball', advertised in the *Pall Mall Gazette* a reward of £100 to any person who contracted influenza or a cold after having used the balls as directed and stated that they had deposited £1,000 in a named bank to show their sincerity. Mrs Carlill read the advertisement, bought the balls, and contracted influenza. The Court awarded her £100 damages for breach of contract.[7] But advertisers do not fall into this trap nowadays. The company was liable because its lodging £1,000 in the bank suggested that the advertisement was no mere puff. Today's advertisers take care that their advertisements are mere puffs which do not subject them to contractual liabilities. 'X's slimming pills, guaranteed to reduce your weight' will give no remedy to the unfortunate purchaser who remains as fat as ever. The law ordinarily allows him to recover compensatory damages against anybody who has fraudulently made a false statement to him on which he has acted to his loss. In practice, however, no one who has been taken in by a false advertisement has very much chance of recovering damages. The courts are guilty of muddled thinking about fraud : they think that to charge somebody with fraud is so serious that such a finding should be made only in a very clear case. But the issue is not whether the advertiser should be sent to prison, when such an attitude would be justified, but whether a member of the public who is out of pocket through relying on a seller's false statements should recover his loss from him. In the United States, the law of fraud is much more comprehensive than in England, although even there it is recognized that it does not in itself afford adequate protection to the consumer against the wiles of the advertiser. Suppose that the advertiser has not been fraudulent, but merely negligent. Normally of course, victims of negligence can recover compensation. English law has in the past been most reluctant to hold that there was any liability for causing financial loss to others by making negligent *statements*. It is true that the House of Lords has sometimes recognized that in some circumstances there might be a liability. Nonetheless, in all probability it remains the law that advertisers will not ordinarily be liable for their false statements, however carelessly made. Only in the rare case where the victim could show that the advertiser had such special skill or knowledge that he would know that the victim was relying on his statement, so that the advertiser would assume responsibility for its accuracy, would the victim have a remedy against the advertiser.[8]

Nor is the law of contract of any use to the consumer. If the person from whom he buys the product tells lies about it, those misrepresentations will in some cases form part of the contract, so that when they are not made good an action lies for breach of contract. English law, however, has a firm rule that those who sue for breach of contract must be parties to the contract. Advertisements of products are made by the manufacturer, but the purchase is normally made from the retailer. The customer's contract is with the retailer, not with the manufacturer, so that he can never sue the manufacturer for breach of contract on the basis of false advertising. Some American judges, on the other hand, are extending the benefit of a manufacturer's warranty to the eventual consumer, although he has no contract with the manufacturer-advertiser.

Nor does the ordinary law adequately protect the business competitor. Suppose that an advertiser makes false statements about his product so that sales of his rivals fall off. English law gives damages only in the rare case where the rival can prove that his customers were misled by the advertisement into believing that they were buying the rival's product. This relief is not adequate : we are concerned with the case where the advertisement makes no reference to the rival's product, but tells lies about the product sold, so that its sales increase at the expense of its rivals. English law has no remedy, whereas in the United States the injured rival tradesman could recover damages against the lying advertiser.

The courts then have failed to protect the public against false advertising. Spasmodically Parliament has over the years stepped in by making particular advertising abuses criminal offences. Betting circulars cannot be sent to those under twenty years of age; money-lenders are restricted in advertising; hire-purchase advertisements must indicate the size of deposit and the number and amount of instalments; unrestricted advertisements for the sale of company shares are forbidden; indecent or obscene hoardings are prohibited. Most important have been the restrictions on advertising some medicines, food, and drugs. Commercial advertisements which prescribe cures for cancer, venereal disease, tuberculosis, diabetes, epilepsy, Bright's disease, cataract, glaucoma, and paralysis are forbidden. It is a criminal offence to publish an advertisement which either falsely describes any food or drug or is calculated to mislead with regard to its nature, substance, or quality. It would be fair to say that until 1960 Parliament too had failed to safeguard the public adequately against advertising defects. The Merchandise Marks Acts were a case in point. Although they were concerned to restrain false descriptions of goods, they had never been phrased so as to cover advertisements. The advertising industry itself practised a degree of self-regulation which helped a little to compensate for the law's weaknesses. Various advertising organizations had codes which sought to maintain standards. These arrangements have been greatly strengthened recently – those now in force will be examined later – but ten years or so ago they did not effectively control advertising.

Matters have improved greatly in the last decade. Important legislation has been passed, and regulation within the industry has been tightened. The reason is the increasing concern for the protection of the consumer. These changes of the 1960s will now be described.

The most important has been the Trade Descriptions Act

1968 which replaced the Merchandise Marks Acts. This makes it a crime to publish advertisements which make false or misleading statements about goods or houses, or facilities. The hotel can no longer be advertised as two minutes from the sea when it is a mile inland, the cruise brochure cannot have a picture of a de luxe cabin without indicating that it is not one of the ordinary cabins on the ship, the car cannot be advertised falsely as one owner or 5,000 miles if the mile-ometer has been turned back from 40,000 miles. The adver-tiser, the advertising agent, the owner of the newspaper or poster or whatever the advertising medium used may all be guilty of offences, although there are ample defences for those who did not know of the falsity. So assiduously have the weights and measures inspectors of local authorities carried out their duty of enforcing the Act that with the exception of used cars the media now carry few lying advertisements. Most of the convictions for false advertising now arise out of advertisements at the point of sale. Two recent cases will illustrate. The North Western Gas Board had a notice in their Warrington shop window which read '£3 allowance when you buy any two gas fires at the same time'. A customer who went in to buy two portable fires was told that the offer applied only to fixed hearth fires, the only fires near the notices. The Lord Chief Justice upheld the conviction of the Board. Beechams advertised Ribena at '2s. off'. The fine print added 'your next purchase. Details overleaf', and in fact the customer had to buy two other bottles of Ribena to get 2s. off. The company was fined £50. Premium offers of this kind con-tinue to give trouble, especially where the offer is for some product which the supplier does not manufacture himself. The customer buys the product relying on the offer adver-tised to sell him something else on production of the coupon at a reduced price, only to be told later that the stocks of the other product are now exhausted. Advertisers in such cases will fall foul of the Act. One of the defects of the old Mer-chandise Marks legislation was the failure of the Board of Trade to enforce it. It is sad that one of the most notable failures under the new Act must be attributed to the Department of Trade and Industry. The Act empowered the Department to order that certain information be given about named goods. Not a single order has been made. Why shouldn't the life of an electric light bulb, the size of sheets (what size is 'double' or 'single'?) be stated, and why should motorists continue to be imperilled because tyres are not identified as tube or tubeless, radial or cross ply?

Parliament has recently been active in other directions. Thus, the Civil Aviation (Licensing) Act 1960 makes it a crime for an aircraft to advertise while in the air over the United Kingdom or territorial waters in such a way that the advertisement is visible from the ground – sky-writing is now prohibited. The Noise Abatement Act of the same year prohibits the use of loudspeakers on the street for advertising purposes, except that between noon and 7 p.m. sounds other than words may be made in an inoffensive way from a vehicle to inform the public that perishable goods for human consumption are on sale from that vehicle : thus the chimes of the ice cream van are inoffensive. The Medicines Act 1968 has tightened up advertising of medicinal products generally. The Act makes it a crime to issue false or misleading advertisements; the manufacturers now need a licence from the Government before they can function, and the further threat of licence revocation will obviously make them take care over their advertising material whether in the Press or sent through the post to the medical profession. The purposes for which a medicine may be advertised for use are limited to those specified in the licence. The Minister of Health and Social Security is also empowered to restrict advertising, and to restrict the use of specific words with regard to particular products. New regulations under food and drugs legislation have also been promulgated.

Comprehensive regulations made in 1969 under the Town and Country Planning Acts now effect widespread restrictions on poster and other outdoor advertising. The planning authorities, that is, the Minister of Housing and Local Government and the local government authorities, are empowered to regulate all outdoor advertising displays except those on vehicles such as buses or minicabs, or within buildings and enclosures such as football grounds which are not visible from outside. They are to have regard to both amenity and public safety in exercising their powers. 'Amenity' is recognized to have a varying content, so that certain areas of natural beauty such as the Peak and Lake Districts (in all about one-fifth of the country) are defined as areas of special control where large-scale commercial advertising is prohibited. It would obviously be impossible to require every advertisement in the rest of the country to be considered by a planning authority. Advertisements are, therefore, divided into two groups, those which must have individual approval and those where consent is deemed to have been given. Even in a 'deemed consent' case a notice to discontinue a specific advertisement may be issued. Whether an advertisement is of the kind that ordinarily requires individual approval or of the challenged 'deemed consent' kind, the decision on it is normally taken by the local planning authority, acting in the interests of amenity and safety. From that decision an appeal lies to the Minister, some member of whose Department will in fact decide – there are usually about 1,500 to 2,000 appeals a year. In any event all advertisement sites must be clean, tidy, and safe, and a 'deemed consent' one must be no hindrance to traffic. Most important of the 'deemed consent' category are advertisements on business premises or their forecourts. These may be displayed with deemed consent if they conform to certain requirements as to size of lettering, height from the ground, and the like, and refer wholly to the business or trade conducted on the premises, the goods sold or services provided, or the qualifications of the person carrying on the business. It is generally agreed that planning authorities have struck a fair balance between advertiser and public, and that the standards of outdoor advertising have improved in consequence.

REGULATION WITHIN THE INDUSTRY

There is a vast complex of controls within the advertising industry. They must be both described and evaluated.

Many businesses which regularly advertise their products or services have their own trade associations formulate standard advertising codes. One example is the Association of Unit Trust Managers. Almost never do questions of infringement receive publicity. One exception, and an illuminating one, occurred in 1970. Jessel Securities were told that their proposed newspaper advertisement of Jessel Investment Trust Unit Trust violated the code. Jessel Securities went ahead and published the advertisement unaltered; the Association took no effective steps. The Association of the British Pharmaceutical Industry has its own code with a committee to police its members. It holds its meetings in secret, and does not publish names of offenders, but it is believed that in a recent year more than one-tenth of its members were found by its committee to have contravened the advertising code. It is scarcely surprising that when the Sainsbury Committee set up by the Government to examine the drug industry reported in 1967, it found the existing arrangements inadequate and recommended that a committee with an independent legal chairman should investigate alleged infringements and should require undertakings to withdraw offending advertisements; this recommendation was not implemented in the Medicines Act which followed the Report.

The advertising media themselves have their own separate committees and codes. For example, the British Poster Advertising Association has a censorship committee for posters, the Newspaper Publishers Association and the Newspaper Society have a joint committee and their own advertising code. Other committees cover cinema advertising, and clutter on business premises. London Transport publishes a code – it refuses advertisements which advertise contraceptives, or attack a member or policies of the Government or are otherwise of a political nature, which 'knock' other firms or products, or which 'are likely through possible defacement to offend the general travelling public'. It is difficult to describe these committees in operation because they do not publicize their detailed workings, and the Press apparently seldom learns what is going on.

Then there is the most important code of all, the British Code of Advertising Practice (4th edition, 1970). That code is supported by seventeen organizations representing every aspect of the advertising industry. They include the British Direct Mail Advertising Association, the British Poster Advertising Association, the Independent Television Companies Association, the Newspaper Publishers' Association, the Newspaper Society, the Periodical Publishers' Association, the Proprietary Association of Great Britain and the Solus Outdoor Advertising Association. Many of the most objectionable features have been removed by the 1970 version, thanks to pressures outside the industry. An advertisement is no longer prohibited because it makes comparisons with competing products; of course the comparison must be capable of being substantiated. Attempts are made to control 'free' offers, use of the word 'guarantee', and the confusion of advertising and editorial matter in newspapers. Part B deals solely with medicines, treatments and appliances in an effort to deal with the British public's long-standing gullibility where patent medicines are concerned. There are twenty prohibitions : for instance, no advertisements for bust developers, inducing miscarriages, promoting sexual virility, hypnosis, restoring hair, natural remedies, no 'money back if not satisfied' offers. There is also a list of some seventy-five diseases for which treatment by medicine, appliance or advice must not be advertised : these run through the alphabet from anaemia (pernicious) to whooping cough. The seventeen sponsoring bodies are all represented on the British Code of Advertising Practice Committee, whose function is to secure consistent interpretation of the code by all involved.

Of course a code is useless unless it is enforced. Therefore the advertising industry was also induced in 1962 to set up the Advertising Standards Authority. The Advertising

Association (a trade association) appoints the chairman and he appoints the members. Five of the eleven members are directly and professionally concerned with advertising, and no representatives of consumer organizations were appointed or invited to be represented. The Authority concerns itself with advertising standards generally; its chairman, Lord Tweedsmuir (succeeding Lord Drumalbyn), and its members – the London and Home Counties weighting is excessive – are part-time and are paid out of funds provided by the Advertising Association. It has concerned itself with such problems as switch-selling, advertisements presented in the style of editorial and news, and unsolicited and premium offers, and now publishes annual reports. It would not initiate any changes in the general principles of advertising without consulting the Advertising Investigation Department of the Advertising Association and the British Code of Advertising Practice Committee. If there is a complaint that a particular advertisement infringes the Code of Advertising Practice it will investigate and if necessary raise the matter with the medium concerned. It never gives a hearing to a complainant, although it hears the representatives of the media concerned. It never publishes any details of a product which has been advertised in breach of the code. It does not employ staff to investigate breaches, and it attempts no pre-publication scrutiny whatever. (Since 1964 the Code of Advertising Practice Committee has looked at samples of advertising in particular categories such as cigarettes and slimming diets.) It is significant, for instance, that the Press Council, not the Authority, detected and criticized in 1967 the *Manchester Evening News* for publishing in its editorial columns matter which was found to have been written to support an accompanying advertising display of the named product referred to. The Authority has no power to fine offenders or to require media who are members of a constituent body to desist from accepting advertisements. It relies on the fact that members are pledged to observe the codes. Control of newspaper advertising is reinforced by the fact that an advertising agency could be removed by the Newspaper Publishers' Association and the Newspaper Society from the official list of agencies to whom the newspaper will pay a commission of fifteen per cent for each advertisement accepted for publication.

In essence the Advertising Standards Authority stands for a voluntary system of advertising control. It has not set itself up as a mediator between the industry and the public; it is prepared to attempt to improve advertising standards by working behind the scenes in the advertising industry. It has not the financial resources with which to unearth and penalize infringements of the Code. Not all media fall within its scope (many provincial newspapers and the new free local newspapers which contain mostly advertising material, for instance, are not included), and it relies on indirect persuasion to secure conformity in due course by those media which are within its jurisdiction. Although it has effected improvements in advertising standards, this is not enough. Its procedures have hitherto lacked the fairness and openness of a comparable body, the Press Council, despite the fact that the problem is more serious than that of the Press in the sense that infringements directly affect the pockets of poorer sections of the community. Its basic weakness has been that its approach is insufficiently independent of the advertising industry; it could learn much from the vast improvement which Lord Devlin effected in the workings of the Press Council.

TELEVISION

Television advertising, where there is a blending of legal and self-regulating controls, demands separate examination.

The Television Act 1964 authorizes the inclusion in programmes broadcast by the I.T.A. of advertisements inserted in consideration of payments to the relevant programme controllers. Schedule 2 of the Act contains certain rules about advertisements which the Minister of Posts and Telecommunications may amend by regulation with the approval of each House of Parliament. The I.T.A. is required to draw up a code giving standards and practice in advertising. In 1969 the I.T.A. published the second edition of its Code of Advertising Standards and Practice. The Code also had to prescribe the advertisements and methods of advertising to be prohibited : section 7(5) of the Act requires the I.T.A. to consult the Minister of Posts and Telecommunications on these two points and to carry out any directions given by him. The booklet in which the Code appears states that the I.T.A. consulted the Minister on the rules in the Code and that he has accepted those to which section 7(5) is applicable. It also draws attention to the fact that the Act expressly reserves to the I.T.A. the right to impose requirements as to advertisements and methods of advertising which go beyond the requirements imposed by the Code; this right is reinforced by a power for the I.T.A. to give directions to programme contractors on these matters.

The first six restrictions in the Code are also in the Act itself. The advertisement must not imply that an advertiser has sponsored any programme (in practice the I.T.A. approves of an advertiser booking space at a time when he knows that a particular programme is being televised). Advertisements must be clearly distinguishable as such, and recognizably separate from the programmes : this confirms in statutory form the Minister's ban in 1962 of advertising magazines such as *Jim's Inn*. In 1971 the I.T.A. stopped a company from confusing viewers by calling an advertisement a 'News Flash'. Subliminal advertising is prohibited. Advertisements must not offend against good taste or decency or be offensive to public feeling. That is why advertisements for the *News of the World*'s Christine Keeler Memoirs were banned in 1969. No offer of a prize of significant value which is available only to viewers may be made. Audible matter must not be excessively noisy or strident. The Schedule to the Act, but not the Code, prohibits unreasonable discrimination in the acceptance of advertisements.

The Code then follows Schedule 2 in precluding advertisements on behalf of anybody whose objects are mainly political or religious. Under this head the I.T.A. refuses advertisements for the *Morning Star*. The Code and Schedule also prohibit advertisements directed towards any religious or political end or related to any industrial dispute. The I.T.A. in 1971 banned a series of advertisements for the Common Market issued by the Government. The National Farmers Union's campaign for a fair deal for agriculture came under this ban. In 1970 an advertisement for a part series, *The Bible*, was banned but a parson was allowed to advertise margarine.

The remaining provisions of the Code go beyond the restrictions in the Act, although they are lawfully made under the power to frame a Code given by the Act. Many advertisements are forbidden : for instance, of breathalyzers, cigarettes, and tobacco, inertia selling, those from moneylenders, matrimonial agencies, fortune tellers, undertakers and tipsters, and those concerned with betting (including pools). There are special restrictions on advertisements for homework schemes, hire purchase, and instructional courses. Other provisions are similar to Part A of the British Code of Advertising Practice.

Three matters are regarded as so important that each is in a separate Appendix to the Code. The first relates to advertisements likely to be seen by large numbers of children. Nothing detrimental to their safety, good behaviour, or morals is allowed, and advantage must not be taken of their credulity and sense of loyalty; an advertisement must not suggest that a child who does not use a certain product is inferior or lacking in loyalty. So an appeal to buy chocolates for Mother's Day was prohibited. The second is financial advertising. Many formerly banned, for example unit trusts, are now authorized subject to stringent conditions set out in the Appendix, such as that no celebrity shall recommend the investment. The third concerns the advertising of medicines and treatments. In accordance with the Act, the I.T.A. consulted the medical advisory panel set up under the Act before adopting the provisions contained in this Appendix. The rules are similar to those of Part B of the British Code of Advertising Practice, which is reproduced in the Appendix to the Code. Additionally, the Appendix forbids advertisements for contraceptives, contact lenses, and cures for smoking and alcoholism.

The day-to-day acceptance of advertising is in the hands of the programme contractors, who have formed the Independent Television Companies Association (I.T.C.A.). All advertising scripts other than purely local ones are referred to the I.T.C.A.'s copy clearance group. There is close liaison between that Committee and the I.T.A.'s advertising control office, especially through the Joint Advertisement Control Committee composed of I.T.A. and programme contractors' representatives under the chairmanship of the I.T.A.'s head of advertising control. The I.T.C.A. publishes several volumes of *Notes of Guidance*, which supplement the Code and also govern the decisions of the I.T.C.A. copy clearance group. They are in the nature of more detailed rules for advertising agencies. Typical of these rules are : 'Foundation garments : In the use of live models care should be taken to ensure that no embarrassment is caused by over-exposure of the body.' 'Deodorants : ... shots of armpits or references to "sweat" or "smell" should be avoided.' 'No advertisement for a medicinal product should feature a well-known personality endorsing the product on the basis of his or her own personal experience.' In children's advertisements 'The word FREE should be used in its literal sense only.'

Schedule 2 requires that the amount of time given to advertising shall not be so great as to detract from the value of the programmes as a medium of information, education and entertainment. In *ITV 1970, A Guide to Independent Television*, the basic rules are set out :

'1. The total amount of time given to advertising may not exceed six minutes an hour averaged over a day's programmes.

2. Normally there may not be more than seven minutes of advertising in any one clock-hour.'

The Schedule also enacts that 'advertisements shall not be inserted otherwise than at the beginning or the end of the programme or in natural breaks therein'. It is submitted that this means that advertisements may be inserted only at the beginning or the end, *or* in natural breaks. *ITV 1970* allows advertisements *both* in breaks *and* at the beginning and end of programmes.

The Schedule requires the I.T.A. to obtain the agreement of the Minister of Posts and Telecommunications on rules specifying the programmes which must not be interrupted by advertisements and prescribing the interval which must elapse between those programmes and any previous or subsequent advertisement : if no agreement is reached, the Minister can decide the issue. In fact, the following rules were agreed with him, and are in *ITV 1970*. No advertisements shall interrupt a religious service or programme, a formal royal ceremony, or that part of a programme which covers the incidental appearance of a member of the royal family : there are also to be no advertisements within two minutes before or after such programmes. In 1966 the two-minute rule was generally abandoned for religious programmes but it remains for royalty and religious services. School programmes must also be uninterrupted by advertisements; the periods of separation from advertising shall be at least two minutes before and one minute after those programmes. The Minister may, after consulting the I.T.A., impose rules as to the minimum interval between advertising periods : it is stated in *ITV 1970* that he has imposed no such rules. He refrained, 'having regard to the limiting effect of the rules on the number of advertising intervals an hour'; this is a reference to other rules on which he was consulted (though the Act does not require it) stipulating how many natural breaks are permitted for advertising for each programme according to its length. The Act authorizes the I.T.A. to give directions to the programme controllers about all the matters discussed in this and the preceding paragraph.

The I.T.A. must appoint an advertising advisory committee. This used to be representative only of the advertising industry, but the 1964 Act now requires it also to be representative of the public as consumers. It has no statutory part in the making of the I.T.A. Code, but has the duty of keeping it under review and submitting recommendations for amendment. Its chairman is Mr S. Howard; it consists at present of four members representing the public, including the secretary of a large consumer group, an officer of the Federation of Women's Institutes, and Jean Robertson, a journalist on consumer affairs, four from organized advertising bodies, and four experts concerned with medical advertising. It exercises day-by-day supervision of advertising; no advertisements are required to be submitted in advance to it.

There can be no doubt that the system just described is a great improvement on that set up under the Television Act 1954. The I.T.A. is plainly concerned that advertising should be respectable. Yet the nature and extent of the legal controls should be understood. The duty of the I.T.A. to secure that the rules of the Schedule and its Code are observed is mandatory, not discretionary. Therefore, while, as we have seen earlier, the law cannot interfere with the merely discretionary functions regarding programme content contained in the Act, the law could operate if the I.T.A. failed in its duties with respect to advertising. Many lawyers believe that the private citizen is powerless to secure performance of these duties. It may well be that he could not obtain from the High Court an order of mandamus (with its sanction of punishment for contempt upon disobedience) commanding the I.T.A. to carry out its duty. Yet the Court could probably grant an injunction to the citizen restraining the I.T.A. from violating it. Many lawyers deny this. It is true that the citizen could not bring these proceedings of his own initiative unless he could show that the I.T.A.'s breach of the Act damaged him particularly – he could himself sue, for example, if the I.T.A. refused his own advertisements but accepted those of a competitor (it is doubtful whether he could ever sue for a breach of the Code only, for the Code has no legal sanction other than the duty of the I.T.A. to enforce it, and confers no legal rights on the citizen). It is submitted, further, that in any event a citizen can sue for an injunction if he obtains the Attorney-General's consent. Suppose that an interested citizen believes that religious advertisements are being broadcast in violation of the rules, the Attorney-General may himself sue, or, if he consents, the citizen may bring a relator action, for an injunction. (It is a weakness of the Act that the citizen is helpless if the Attorney-General refuses his consent. The citizen is not entitled to know the reasons for refusal – they may be party-political – and cannot appeal to any body against that refusal.)

The I.T.A. has no duty to heed the recommendations of the advertising advisory committee and is not required to consult it on any specific matter. The medical advisory panel must be consulted on medical advertisements, but the I.T.A. is free to disregard its advice. The *I.T.C.A. Notes of Guidance* have no legal effect. On the other hand, the rules about classes of programmes which must not be interrupted, or immediately preceded or followed by advertisements, have legal effect, although they are only to be found in an unofficial source, *ITV 1970*. Presumably, the I.T.A. must secure their observance, whereas the rules set out in the same part of *ITV 1970* about the number of natural breaks are extra-legal because the Minister of Posts and Telecommunications has not exercised his rule-making power under that head.

The I.T.A. is conscientiously trying to work fairly the improved provisions of the Television Act 1964. There has, for example, been no prosecution under the Trade Descriptions Act in respect of a television advertisement. In its first report on the working of that Act the Institute of Weights and Measures Administration states that there were thirty times more complaints (many, of course, either trivial or not justified) about Press advertisements than television ones. Is the viewer properly protected? If he feels that those powers of the Act which are for his protection – restrictions on advertising time, for example – are violated, what can he do? There is no machinery for his complaint to be heard personally. There is no independent body charged with the task of monitoring programmes on his behalf : this is not a function of the advertising advisory committee, and indeed that body would be acting beyond its legal powers were it even to complain about non-observance of natural breaks, for its advisory powers with respect to particular programmes are restricted to the inclusion of misleading advertisements. Some advocate independent machinery for deciding whether particular advertisements violate the law. It is a serious matter of complaint that television advertising law is so inaccessible and so complex. There really is no excuse for the labyrinth of statutes, codes, rules of practice, Ministerial directions having the force of law, and rules not having the force of law, to be gleaned from (and nowhere else) a miscellany of Acts of Parliament, the I.T.A. Code of Advertising Standards and Practice, the annual reports laid before Parliament by the I.T.A., and *ITV 1970*. Nobody without all those sources of information can know the bare bones of television advertising law.

The B.B.C. is precluded by its licence from broadcasting commercial advertisements. The Director-General has issued an internal directive which in some twenty detailed rules prescribes how the B.B.C is to avoid giving publicity to any person or organization, except where this is necessary for providing a full service under its Charter.[9] The difficulties which the B.B.C. experiences in practice through trying to be consistent are obvious to viewers and listeners.

THE FUTURE

The scales are still weighted in favour of the advertiser against the consumer. The defects are obvious. The common law affords inadequate protection in actions for damages by aggrieved citizens : the fault here is with the judges, who have failed to use the opportunities open to them to maintain a fair balance between citizen and advertiser. Secondly, the legislation which imposes criminal sanctions, greatly improved as it is, is too diffuse and haphazard.

Have we gone far enough in safeguarding the interests of the citizen? The critical question is whether the advertising industry should be left alone to regulate itself. It might be persuaded with prodding by the Government and the public to put its own house in order. Need the Advertising Authority compare so unfavourably with the arrangements in commercial television? After all, it has responded substantially in the last decade. Would the industry ever be willing to finance an authority truly independent of the advertising profession? Would it allow effective sanctions, publication of offenders' names, and blacklisting of them from the media? Would it allow oral hearings to members of the public who make complaints? Would it finance adequate investigatory and monitoring staff so as to carry out checks both before and after publication? All these changes are necessary in the public interest.

What is the alternative if advertising itself refuses to make these internal reforms? The Federal Trade Commission of the United States points the way. This Governmental body has the investigation staff to unearth for itself illegal advertising practices : it examines half a million every year. These illegalities include false advertising which constitutes an unfair method of competition, and deceptive or misleading practices which are contrary to the public interest. It punishes misrepresentations of composition and character of products wherever advertised, claims to cure, and false disparagement of products. Its standard weapon of control is the cease-and-desist order. When, after a hearing, it declares a practice illegal, it issues an order to the offender requiring him to abandon the illegal practice, and large fines are imposed for failure to comply with this cease-and-desist order. A case in the 1960s is typical :[10] an advertisement stated that the product was capable of preventing 'the common type of baldness'. After taking expert evidence, the Commission found that 95 per cent of cases of baldness were caused by endocrine, hereditary, and age factors, in which the product was useless. Even though the product might benefit the remaining 5 per cent of cases, the failure positively to disclose this limitation in the efficiency of the product was a ground for a cease-and-desist order : a Federal Court confirmed this decision by the Commission.

The former Consumer Council and the Advertising

Inquiry Council and the 1966 Report to the Labour Party of the Reith Commission of Inquiry into Advertising all favour a body with powers similar to those of the Commission. If it did become necessary to set up such a commission, it would be best also to cut down the jungle of legal and unofficial controls of the I.T.A. and subject television advertising to the commission. Admittedly, such a body might not always prevent the harm from being done before its order became operative. To impose legal censorship of all advertising would be too sweeping a move; if the fines were large enough they would effectively discourage deliberate violations. Better still, the deliberate offender could face the risk of being denied an outlet in the media. In those areas such as television where pre-publication scrutiny is both desirable and practicable it would be wise to entrust the task to the commission. It was in line with the general level of the Molony Report of the Committee on Consumer Protection in 1962 that its only reason for rejecting a body like the Federal Trade Commission was that 'we do not find the model ... a congenial one'.[11]

The single biggest advantage of having such a commission would be the systematic inspection of advertising matter. Even though there would be no censorship in advance of display, the knowledge that staff were employed full time throughout the country in scrutinizing advertisements would be a most potent factor in restraining illegalities on the part of advertisers.

CHAPTER 5

FREEDOM OF EXPRESSION (3): OBSCENITY AND DEFAMATION

FREEDOM OF EXPRESSION

So far we have been examining those restraints on freedom of expression which operate before publication. We must now consider the ways in which the law intervenes with regard to publications already made. First there is the law of obscenity.

Obscenity

THE LEGAL POSITION UNTIL 1959

Our starting point is the prosecution of Sir Charles Sidley in 1663 for his behaviour after a drinking orgy. In the words of the report :[1]

> He was fined 2,000 marks, committed without bail for a week and bound to his good behaviour for a year, on his confession of information against him for showing himself naked in a balcony and 'throwing down bottles (pist in) *vi et armis* among the people in Covent Garden, *contra pacem* and to the scandal of the government'.

To hold this conduct criminal was an innovation. There was however more than mere obscenity here – there was an element of public indecency towards a captive audience, and the case certainly did not purport to declare a separate crime of obscenity. Nonetheless this case was made the basis for convicting in 1727 one Curl for publishing a pornographic book. Curl's case firmly established the crime of publishing obscene libels.[2] From time to time afterwards prosecutions for pornography followed regularly, but growth of the trade led to the passing of the Obscene Publications Act 1857 which empowered magistrates to order the destruction of obscene books and which made this procedure the more effective by authorizing the grant of warrants to the police to search suspected premises. Its sponsor, Lord Campbell, assured the House of Lords that he had no desire to interfere with works of art such as those of Ovid or the Restoration dramatists, Wycherley and Congreve :

The measure was intended to apply exclusively to works written for the single purpose of corrupting the morals of youth and of a nature calculated to shock the common feelings of decency in a well-regulated mind.[3]

In 1868 there was decided *Hicklin*'s case,[4] the leading case on obscenity, which arose out of an order by Wolverhampton magistrates for the destruction of 'The Confessional Unmasked', a Protestant tract which contained obscene extracts from allegedly Roman Catholic publications and which purported to expose the iniquity of the confessional. The Queen's Bench Division upheld the magistrates' order, Chief Justice Cockburn stating that 'the test of obscenity is this : whether the tendency of the matter charged as obscenity is to deprave and corrupt those whose minds are open to such immoral influences and into whose hands a publication of this sort may fall.'

In 1923 the United Kingdom signed an international convention for the suppression of the circulation of and traffic in obscene publications, and shortly afterwards, upon Sir William Joynson-Hicks becoming Home Secretary, there was an increase in prosecutions for obscenity. There was a new development now : a burst of prosecution of serious works of literature. The *cause célèbre* was the Government's application in 1928 for a destruction order in respect of *The Well of Loneliness* by the widely praised Radcliffe Hall. Norman Birkett, counsel for the defence, had assembled forty expert witnesses, including Desmond MacCarthy, E. M. Forster, and Julian Huxley, but the Bow Street magistrate refused to admit their evidence about the book, on the ground that he alone was to judge whether it was obscene, and ordered its destruction. In the ensuing twenty-five years there was a gradual cessation of prosecutions in respect of literature, but in 1954 came a sudden revival. Hutchinson, Heinemann, Secker & Warburg, Werner Laurie, and Arthur Barker were all prosecuted for publishing allegedly obscene novels, and, most notorious conviction of all, *The Decameron* was ordered by Swindon magistrates to be destroyed (although this destruction order was reversed by Quarter Sessions on appeal). In the prosecution of Secker & Warburg for *The Philanderer*, Mr Justice Stable summed up to the jury in a manner which received great praise in the Press :[5]

Turning for a moment to the book that you have to consider, it is, as you know, in the form of a novel. Remember the charge is a charge that the tendency of the book is to corrupt and deprave. The charge is not that the tendency of the book is either to shock or to disgust. That is not a criminal offence. The charge is that the tendency of the book is to corrupt and deprave. Then you say: 'Well, corrupt and deprave whom?' to which the answer is: those whose minds are open to such immoral influences and into whose hands a publication of this sort may fall. What, exactly, does that mean? Are we to take our literary standards as being the level of something that is suitable for the decently brought up young female aged fourteen? Or do we go even further back than that and are we to be reduced to the sort of books that one reads as a child in the nursery? The answer to that is: of course not. A mass of literature, great literature, from many angles is wholly unsuitable for reading by the adolescent, but that does not mean that a publisher is guilty of a criminal offence for making those works available to the general public. I venture to suggest that you give a thought to what is the function of the novel. I am not talking about historical novels when people write a story of some past age. I am talking about the contemporary novelist. By 'the contemporary novelist' I mean the novelist who writes about his contemporaries, who holds up a mirror to the society of his own day. The function of the novel is not merely to entertain contemporaries; it stands as a record or a picture of the society when it was written. Those of us who enjoy the great Victorian novelists get such understanding as we have of that great age from chroniclers such as Thackeray, Dickens, Trollope, Surtees, and many others of that age.

In the world in which we live today it is equally important

that we should have an understanding of how life is lived and how the human mind is working in those parts of the world which are not separated from us in point of time but are separated from us in point of space; and that we should have this understanding (particularly at a time like today when ideas and creeds and processes of thought seem, to some extent, to be in the melting pot and people are bewildered and puzzled to know in what direction humanity is heading and in what column we propose to march). If we are to understand how life is lived in the United States of America, France, Germany, or elsewhere, the contemporary novels of those nations may afford us some guide, and to those of us who have not the time, opportunity, money or, possibly, the inclination to travel, it may even be the only guide. This is an American novel written by a citizen of the United States of America, published originally in New York, purporting to depict the lives of people living today in New York, and to portray the speech, the turn of phrase, and the current attitude towards this particular aspect of life in New York. If we are going to read novels about how things go in New York, it would not be of much assistance, would it, if, contrary to the fact, we were led to suppose that in New York no unmarried woman or teenager has disabused her mind of the idea that babies are brought by storks or are sometimes found in cabbage patches or gooseberry bushes?

This is a very crude work, as you may think. You will consider whether or not it does seek to present a fair picture of aspects of contemporary American thought in relation to this problem. You will, no doubt, further consider whether or not it is desirable that on this side of the Atlantic we should close our eyes to a fact because we do not find it altogether palatable. . .

The jury, who had been told previously to take the book home and read it as a book, not picking out bits here and there, found the accused Not Guilty.

The prominence and praise rightly accorded to this passage are calculated to deceive. After all, it was only one judge's summing up. Contrast it with the trial of Hutchinson in respect of *September in Quinze* at the Old Bailey three months later. The judge, Sir Gerald Dodson, told the jury, who convicted :

A book which would not influence the mind of an Archbishop might influence the minds of a callow youth or girl just budding into womanhood. . . . It is a very comforting thought that juries from time to time take a very solid stand against this sort of thing and realize how important it is for the youth of this country to be protected and that the fountain of our national blood should not be polluted at its source.[6]

Indeed, such judgments were more characteristic of the judiciary as a whole than was that of Mr Justice Stable.

This outburst of activity prompted the Society of Authors to set up a Committee presided over by Sir Alan Herbert. This Committee produced a Bill for reform of the law which was introduced in the House of Commons in March 1955 by Mr Roy Jenkins, M.P., under the Ten Minute Rule, although it got no further.

Contemporaneously with the doings of the Herbert Committee, the Government introduced a Bill to deal with horror comics. Despite its lukewarm reception in the national Press on the ground that it was a piecemeal solution of a larger question, it was enacted as the Children and Young Persons (Harmful Publications) Act 1955. The Act applies to any book or magazine of a kind which is likely to fall into the hands of children or young persons and consists of stories told in pictures, being stories portraying the commission of crimes or violent, cruel, repulsive, or horrible acts or incidents in such a way that the work as a whole would tend to corrupt a child or young person into whose hands it might fall. It is an offence to print, sell, publish, let on hire, or possess for those purposes any such work. The 1966 experience of the Chester Consumer Group in their attempt to prevent horror cards from being put in bubble-gum packets sold to children explains why the Act is ineffective. The Chief Constable of Cheshire refused to act on the ground that it was the national responsibility of the Home Office; the Home Office refused to act on the ground that the duty lay with the Cheshire police. There has never been a prosecution under this Act.

Obscene publications furnish an outstanding example of how difficult it sometimes is to frame laws to attain objectives on which there is general agreement. In, say, 1955 most people would have agreed that the law should punish and prevent pornography, but that it should not interfere with serious literary works. What, then, was wrong with the law of obscenity?

The overriding problem is, What do we mean by 'obscene'? The standard answer was that of *Hicklin*'s case, a 'tendency to deprave and corrupt', which unfortunately Chief Justice Cockburn did not define with any precision. Is its meaning obvious? He gave us a clue to what he meant by his view that the book in question 'would suggest to the minds of' the reader 'thoughts of a most impure and libidinous character'. But when is a thought 'impure'? Only when it relates to sexual passion? To normal sexual intercourse? In the marriage bed, or outside? To perversions? Do books on sex in marriage corrupt or deprave? What degree of causal relationship must there be between the book and the sexual thought? Do we know when and how and to what extent the reading of a particular book will arouse sexual passions, either in itself or with the aid of other stimuli, and, if only with the aid of the latter, is this sufficiently causal? In any event, should the law concern itself with men's thoughts? It is no answer that lustful thoughts are sins according to religious doctrine. Or is the law really looking to the depraving and corrupting *consequences* of stimulating sexual thoughts, i.e. forms of sexual conduct condemned by contemporary society? Is this what the courts mean when they speak of corrupting 'the morals'? The difficulty here of course is that nobody, judges included, can measure the effect of a book on the sexual behaviour of the reader. Or are 'deprave and corrupt' not limited to sex? Do they extend to that bane of the cinema, the emphasis on horror and violence?

A related question is whether the courts are to fulfil a social function. Why used Ibsen's *Ghosts* and Shaw's *Mrs Warren's Profession* to be regarded as obscene? Surely on the social ground that they attacked existing conventions in discussing venereal disease and prostitution. Is a book obscene because it is calculated to bring about a change in the accepted moral standards of society? From this it is not a big step to condemn the offensive, the vulgar, the shocking as obscene.

So far the charge against the law of obscenity is that it failed to face up frankly to the difficulties of defining obscenity. We now pass to more specific grounds of complaint.

The law did not require the courts to consider the work as a whole. Prosecuting counsel were encouraged by many judges to select the 'highlights' from the book, to quote them with emphasis out of context and thereby convince the jury of the obscene character of the work. One can imagine what counsel could do with James Joyce's *Ulysses*, for example.

We have seen that English law soon turned its back on the promise given by the sponsors of the Obscene Publications Act 1857 that an allegedly obscene work would be judged, for the purposes of that Act, by its effect on the ordinary person. *Hicklin*'s case talked of the effects on the minds of the young : in Mr Justice Stable's words, the test of the fourteen-year-old schoolgirl. Should not the standard be that of the normal person, unless the abnormal or the young are shown to be the probable readers? It is true that judges occasionally mentioned the relevance of the circumstances of the publication. In *Hicklin's* case itself Chief Justice Cockburn said :

A medical treatise, with illustrations necessary for the information of those for whose education or information the work is intended, may, in a certain sense, be obscene, and yet not the subject for indictment; but it can never be that these prints may be exhibited for anyone, boys or girls, to see as they pass.

There is no clear judicial guidance of when and for what purposes 'circumstances of publication' were relevant. One would have desired at least a finding that the probable readership should be judged by considering such circumstances of publication as the nature of the advertising material, the publisher's reputation, the channels of distribution, the price and quality of the books sold; but nothing explicit emerged.

We pass naturally from this last point to the relevance of

the literary, scientific, and educational values of the work. There was no authoritative decision on whether these were defences to a charge of obscenity. Certainly the judges refused to hear evidence from expert witnesses on them, so that in practice the defence could not be established.

The position of the author was a difficult one. Under the Act his books could be destroyed without his being made a party to the proceedings. His works could be castigated as obscene without his knowledge. But let us suppose that the accused bookseller or other publisher communicated with him. The courts would not hear him as a witness. Were they right? Is the author's purpose in writing the book material either to the literary value of the work or even to the question of whether it is 'obscene'? This is not the same question as one with which it is often confused : should a man be guilty of obscenity even if he had no intention 'to deprave or corrupt'? Remember that quite often the accused is not the author, but the bookseller or the publisher. Should a judge say : 'You have published the work; it is obscene, therefore you are guilty, regardless of whether you intended to corrupt or deprave'?

ATTEMPTS AT REFORM

With these comments on the law of obscenity in mind, we now turn to the efforts made to reform it.

In 1955 and 1956 Mr Hugh Fraser, M.P., and Lord Lambton, M.P., made two further attempts to launch the Bill previously introduced by Mr Roy Jenkins. In March 1957 the Bill was referred to a Select Committee on the second reading. This Committee took a great deal of evidence but was unable to complete its inquiry by the end of the parliamentary session. Another Select Committee carried on in the next session and reported to the House of Commons in March 1958.

This Report was a first-class document reflecting the thorough examination made of the problem. The Committee were impressed with the existence of a sizeable and lucrative trade in pornography, in both books and postcards. In 1954 167,000 books and in 1957 22,000 postcards had to be destroyed. The number of books and postcards destroyed greatly exceeds the number of articles the subject of prosecution because, as the Director of Public Prosecutions explained to this Committee, a system of 'disclaimers' is operated whereby the possessors of obscene books are given the opportunity to agree, without proceedings being instituted, to their destruction. The Committee made proposals for facilitating its suppression. Their proposals sought also to clarify the law of obscene publications. Briefly, they approved Mr Justice Stable's approach to the definition of obscenity, proposed that the effect of the work as a whole be considered, that a defence of literary or artistic merit be afforded, and that the author have a right to be heard. In November 1958 Mr Roy Jenkins introduced a Bill designed to implement these recommendations. The Committee's report was debated in December 1958, when the Government expressed its agreement with many of the recommendations, but dissented from some, especially the defence of artistic merit and admission of expert evidence thereon. The Bill proceeded on its way but had a stormy passage in the face of considerable Government opposition and amendments. Ultimately, after some Government concessions and compromises (some possibly stimulated by Sir Alan Herbert's characteristic decision to oppose the Government's candidate at a by-election on the stand of the Government's unwillingness to promote legislation) there emerged in July 1959 the Obscene Publications Act, which must now be examined.

THE OBSCENE PUBLICATIONS ACT 1959

The Act incorporated many of the Select Committee's proposals for strengthening police powers to suppress pornography. Previously the police could not obtain a search warrant without evidence of previous sales : the mere fact that the books were stored by some disreputable wholesaler in a Soho attic was not enough. Under the Act a warrant can be had on evidence that they are being kept 'for publication for gain'. There is also a power to search stalls and vehicles, and to seize business documents which might uncover the wholesaler and producer concealed in the background. Although the Act repealed the Obscene Publications Act 1857 it retained the power of Justices of the Peace to order the destruction of the obscene works.

Section 1 of the Act provides that an article is obscene if its effect is, 'if taken as a whole, such as to tend to deprave and corrupt persons who are likely, having regard to all relevant circumstances, to read, see or hear the matter contained or embodied in it'. This section contains many good features. The book must be considered as a whole. What matters is the effect on those who are the probable readers in the circumstances. Section 2 confers a desirable defence on those charged with the crime of publishing obscene matter : they are not guilty if they prove that they 'had not examined the article .. and had no reasonable cause to suspect' that it was obscene.

Section 4 provides that no offence is committed 'if it is proved that publication of the article in question is justified as being for the public good on the ground that it is in the interests of science, literature, art, or learning, or other objects of general concern'. Moreover, the opinion of experts as to the 'literary, artistic, scientific, or other merits' is admissible evidence. The Act also meets the objection that an author's reputation and royalty-earning power may be taken away from him without his knowing. Even though he is not summoned, he is now entitled to show cause why his books should not be forfeited. Moreover he can appeal against a forfeiture order made by justices although he did not appear at the trial before justices; this enables an author who first learned of the proceedings when the forfeiture order was made still to challenge the order.

We can further evaluate the Act by considering the important prosecution of Penguin Books Ltd for publishing *Lady Chatterley's Lover* by D. H. Lawrence.[7] At the trial Mr Gerald Gardiner, Q.C. (now Lord Gardiner), Penguin Books' counsel, argued that since the purpose of the Act was to suppress pornography, but not to censor literature, it was of paramount importance to consider the intention of the author. The difficulty with his argument, however, is that D. H. Lawrence was not the accused. Be that as it may, Mr Justice Byrne ruled 'that it is not open to the Defence to call evidence to prove that there was no intention to deprave or corrupt', and his ruling presumably meant that no evidence of Penguin Books' intentions, as well as those of D. H. Lawrence, was admissible on this issue. One other point about intention : a publisher is not guilty if he had no reasonable cause to know the work to be obscene; and he is not guilty unless the jury find that the work did tend to deprave or corrupt. Mr Justice Byrne also held that in connection with the defence of literary or other merit 'one has to have regard to what the author was trying to do, what his message may have been, and what his general scope was'.[8]

Prosecuting counsel in his opening address tried to follow the pre-Act practice of reading the 'juiciest' parts to the jury. Mr Justice Byrne rightly stopped him; the Act requires the jury to view the book as a whole, although Lord Radcliffe has stated that this rule will not protect society from being contaminated by what it reads, since it does not read books as a whole.[9] The trial was adjourned so that the jury could read the book in the jury room : the judge refused to let them take it home to read.

The case also threw light on the defence of public good. The judge explained to the jury that, if they found the book not to be obscene, then the accused were not guilty. If the book were obscene, then the jury had to decide whether publication was for the public good. Because the jury merely recorded a verdict of Not Guilty it is impossible to know whether they found the book not obscene, or for the public good, or both. Indeed it may be that some thought it obscene but in the public good, and others both not obscene and in the public good. The judge told the jury that the publishers of a book which has literary merit do not always have a defence : the Act provides that they are not guilty if the publication, although obscene, is justified as being for the public good, in deciding which the opinion of experts on its literary and other merits is admissible.

Two other rulings by the judge seem sound. The first is the interpretation of the 'literary, artistic, scientific, or other merits' of which the Act permits expert evidence : he held that 'other merits' covered evidence by the Bishop of Woolwich on the *ethical* merits, because this is a merit tending to establish that the publication was for the public good. Secondly, he would not let the expert witnesses say whether the book was published for the public good; they were experts on literary or other merits, but not on public good, which it was for the jury alone to evaluate. He further ruled that the onus was on the defence to prove public good; the Act is not explicit about this, but the ruling was to be expected. The effect of all these rulings is to make the expert evidence – both sides can offer it, although, for reasons unknown, the prosecution did not in the *Penguin* case – very important. It will be difficult to prevent the astute witness from interpolating, with his legitimate opinions on the author's intention and the book's merits, his own views on the author's intention in the context of obscenity and indeed on the rendering of public good.

We said earlier that the old test of 'deprave and corrupt' was vague. The Act merely repeats the words and provides no definition. Mr Justice Byrne had to tell the jury what they meant.[10]

... to deprave means to make morally bad, to pervert, to debase, or corrupt morally. The words 'to corrupt' mean to render morally unsound or rotten, to destroy the moral purity or chastity of, to pervert or ruin a good quality, to debase, to defile ... just as loyalty is one of the things which is essential to the well-being of a nation, so some sense of morality is something that is essential to the well-being of a nation, and to the healthy life of the community ... and accordingly, anyone who by his writing *tends* to corrupt that fundamental sense of morality is guilty of an obscene libel...

This is the only help he gave them apart from explaining

that it was not enough to shock or disgust. One wonders what the jury made of it. Does this direction suggest that there was no need for special legislation about horror comics?

There have been other important decisions on the 1959 Act. In one it was held that a display of articles in a shop window with prices on them was not an offer for sale, so that a prosecution against the shopkeeper failed – the Act would still have permitted the obtaining of a forfeiture order.[11] In another it was held that when articles were bought by policemen who would not themselves be corrupted no offence under the Act was committed in the absence of evidence that others were either corrupted or likely to be corrupted.[12]

In the *Ladies Directory* case,[13] the accused, Shaw, published a periodical, the *Ladies Directory*, in order to assist prostitutes to ply their trade when, as a result of the Street Offences Act, they were no longer able to solicit in the streets. It was a booklet of some twenty-eight pages, most of which were taken up with the names and addresses of women who were prostitutes, together with a number of photographs of nude female figures; the matter published left no doubt that the advertisers could be got in touch with at the telephone numbers given and were offering their services for sexual intercourse, and, in some cases, for the practice of sexual perversions.

One of the offences charged was of publishing an obscene article in breach of the Obscene Publications Act 1959. Shaw was convicted on this and appealed to the Court of Criminal Appeal, on the ground that the judge failed to direct the jury that Shaw's honesty of intention was relevant. The Court rejected this plea. Shaw also contended that, since the persons likely to read the *Ladies Directory* were persons who had come to Soho and Paddington to look for prostitutes, they would be already depraved and corrupt, so that the magazine would not deprave and corrupt them. The Court would have none of this argument : they said that 'the fallacy in this argument is that it assumes that a man cannot be corrupted more than once, and there is no warrant for this'.

Another offence with which Shaw was charged is perhaps more important in connection with freedom of expression. This was conspiracy with the prostitutes to corrupt public morals on the ground that the advertisements would induce readers to fornicate and indulge in perversions. The Court of Criminal Appeal affirmed his conviction on this charge, but gave him leave to appeal on this charge to the House of Lords, since a point of law of general public importance was involved – they refused leave on the obscenity charge presumably on the ground that it was clear that intention was irrelevant.

The House of Lords held that it was a crime to conspire to corrupt public morals, and that it was rightly left to the jury to decide whether these advertisements did corrupt public morals. The gravity of this decision can be measured by some of the views of Lord Reid, who dissented in the House of Lords. He pointed out that there are wide differences of opinion on how far the law ought to punish immoral acts done in private, that Parliament, not the courts, should decide this, that men will not know in advance whether their conduct is going to result in their imprisonment, which will depend on how juries choose to interpret expressions like 'to corrupt public morals'. The House of Lords did not decide that any act which corrupted was a crime; they said that a conspiracy to corrupt was – all rested on the conspiracy between Shaw and the advertising prostitutes. (In 1970 the publishers of *IT* were given suspended prison sentences for the same crime when they inserted advertisements by males soliciting men or boys for homosexual activities – the court rejected their defence that they were providing a public service for a victimized harassed minority.)

The case has serious implications for other cases like the *Lady Chatterley* one. The Act prevented prosecutions under the old common-law rules of obscene publication by providing that 'a person publishing an article shall not be proceeded against for an offence at common law consisting of the publication of any matter contained or embodied in the article where it is of the essence of the offence that the matter is obscene'. Shaw pleaded that he could not therefore be charged with conspiracy since the conspiracy relied on was the obscene publication. The House of Lords rejected this plea : the offence of conspiracy 'did not "consist of the publication" of the magazine, it consisted of an agreement to corrupt public morals by means of the magazines which might never have been published'. This seems a highly technical point. There will always be sufficient agreement for conspiracy whenever author and publisher sign a contract : all the protection given to the accused by the Act can be side-stepped if the police choose to prosecute for conspiracy to corrupt public morals. And Viscount Simonds said that it was desirable that this charge of conspiracy should be brought where a doubt existed whether a conviction of obscenity under the Act could be obtained. A perusal of the report of the Select Committee and of Hansard shows that nobody ever thought of this – not surprisingly since it was not realized before this decision that there was a general crime of conspiracy to corrupt public morals. But when Parliament talked of 'the essence of the offence that the matter is obscene' did they not intend to cover conspiracies of this sort, or at least would they not have framed the wording widely enough so as to catch it had they addressed their minds to it? Be that as it may, nothing short of a new Act could override the decision in the *Ladies Directory* case. The protection given by the Act is in practice now seen to be much more restricted than had previously been thought.

The most publicized case has been that concerning the eighteenth-century work of John Cleland, *Fanny Hill*. It had been assumed that if works with literary pretensions were suspected of being obscene there would be a prosecution, with the consequent right to a trial by jury, as in the *Lady Chatterley* case. Instead forfeiture proceedings were brought before a single Metropolitan magistrate, thereby preventing trial by jury. He found that *Fanny Hill* was obscene, and that its publication was not shown to have been for the public good. Because the proceedings were for forfeiture, he had to decide the issue of obscenity with reference to the circumstances of the seizure. The relevant copies of *Fanny Hill* were seized in 'The Magic Shop', a shop to which children had ready access, and which offered for sale a variety of works. If the police had seized copies in a well-known book store the result might well have been different.

THE OBSCENE PUBLICATIONS ACT 1964

Some of these decisions were so unsatisfactory that it was no surprise when the Government introduced a new Bill in 1964. The need was the more pressing since the abolition of currency controls together with the failure of the U.S.A. to sign the 1923 Convention had led to a vast importation of pornography from the U.S.A. (seizures in Britain were running at a million a year). The 1964 Act created a new offence of being in possession of an obscene article, a provision much wider than was necessary to punish the man who was proved to have displayed the article with a price tag in his shop window or to convict him for selling to policemen. The Government refused to alter the effect of the *Ladies Directory* case – it remains possible for the prosecution to circumvent the Obscene Publications Acts altogether. The police have not been slow to take advantage. In 1970 they prosecuted the directors of the *International Times* at the Old Bailey for conspiracy. The allegation was that they conspired to corrupt public morals by inserting in their magazine advertisements whereby homosexuals were enabled to make contact with one another. The Government would not in the 1964 Act meet the outcry over the *Fanny Hill* case by allowing the right to trial by jury in forfeiture proceedings. They refused to interfere with the regular police practice of seizing books and holding them for many months without bringing forfeiture proceedings. The power to fine without upper limit which the Government refused to modify in the 1959 Act remains intact. In short, the Act gives greatly increased powers to suppress pornography, but does nothing to meet justified criticisms of the law's harshness by reputable authors and publishers.

A 1965 decision has widened the scope of obscenity under the 1959 Act.[14] The Lord Chief Justice held that a book entitled *Cain's Book* by Alexander Trocchi, which contained no objectionable passages on sex, but which advocated drug-taking, was obscene. This was the first time that obscenity had been extended beyond matters related to sex, and opens up the prospect of a very wide application of the definition of obscenity. The court also held that it was entitled to hold that the publication was not for the public good, although the expert witnesses called unanimously testified to its literary merits.

In 1966 Sir Cyril Black, M.P., successfully brought forfeiture proceedings before a London magistrate in respect of *Last Exit to Brooklyn*. The publishers were next prosecuted and their conviction quashed by the Court of Appeal.[15] The issue was whether the trial judge had misdirected the jury. (He exercised his statutory power to bar women from the jury.) The court held that the trial judge had rightly left it to the jury to decide for themselves what 'obscene' meant. He had rightly said that the intention with which the book was written was irrelevant. He did, however, err in not saying to them that 'persons who are likely . . . to read' in section 1 meant 'a significant proportion of those likely to read the book'. But a more serious error was his failure to put the publishers' defence on obscenity to the jury. The publishers admitted that the book would shock and outrage readers, but said that it would not deprave and corrupt any but a lunatic fringe. Yet the jury should have been told to decide the tendency of this book for themselves, without any help from expert evidence : ordinary adults on a jury can assess the tendency of a book read by adults. A case the previous year had decided that a psychiatrist could give evidence about the likely effect of bubble-gum picture-cards on children readers.[16] The jury should also have been told how, if they found the book obscene, they were to decide whether its publication had nevertheless been proved by the defence to be for the public good. The test is :

The jury must consider on the one hand the number of readers they believe would tend to be depraved and corrupted by the book, the strength of the tendency to deprave and corrupt, and the nature of the depravity and corruption; on the other hand, they should assess the strength of the literary, sociological or ethical merit which they consider the book to possess. They should then weigh up all these factors and decide whether on balance the publication is proved to be justified as being for the public good.

The court added :

The corruption may also take various forms. It may be to induce erotic desires of a heterosexual kind, or to promote homosexuality or other sexual perversions or drug-taking or brutal violence.

PROCEEDINGS FOR OBSCENE PUBLICATION

The Criminal Justice Act 1967 provides that only the police or the Director of Public Prosecutions (and not a private individual) can initiate forfeiture proceedings. This was to stop a private prosecutor from depriving the accused of a trial by jury. The vast majority of prosecutions for obscene publications are undertaken at the instance of the police, although there is nothing to prevent a private individual from prosecuting, as distinct from taking forfeiture proceedings.

If the police (as distinct from a private individual) contemplate prosecution, they are required by the Prosecution of Offences Regulations 1946 to report to the Director of Public Prosecutions. The Director is empowered to advise the police whether to prosecute and, if he thinks the case sufficiently important, to take over the prosecution himself. The department of the Director classifies all works reported to it into (a) material in respect of which destruction orders have previously been made, (b) material in respect of which destruction orders have been refused, (c) fresh material which it considers should be put before the court, (d) fresh material which it thinks not to be obscene. In doubtful cases, the Director seeks advice from the Treasury Counsel before prosecuting : no doubt this happened in the case of *Lady*

Chatterley's Lover. At one time the Home Office used to circulate to police forces lists of books condemned by the courts, but it no longer does this. The Select Committee recommended that the functions of the Director should not stop at advising on prosecutions, but that obscene publications should be added to that list of crimes which cannot be prosecuted without his consent. The Committee was anxious to promote uniformity, and thought that, since the Director had all the tabulated information on which to advise, it would be little extra administrative labour for him to decide whether to allow prosecution. It pointed out that consent is needed for prosecution under the analogous Children and Young Persons (Harmful Publications) Act 1955. The Government resisted this recommendation on the ground that the definition of obscenity is necessarily so imprecise that it would be improper for the Executive to usurp the court's task of deciding what is obscene by screening all prosecutions. When the Bill was in Parliament the clause requiring consent of the Director for prosecutions had to be dropped under Governmental pressure. Yet the Attorney-General has often answered parliamentary questions by explaining Government policy with regard to obscenity. He has said that proceedings would not be taken in respect of Norman Mailer's *The Naked and the Dead* and Henry Miller's *Tropic of Cancer*, that the *Ladies Directory* case would not be used to circumvent the 'expert evidence' provisions of the 1959 Act; he has sought to justify the use of forfeiture proceedings against *Fanny Hill*; and he has stated that prosecutions, as distinct from forfeiture proceedings, would be resorted to only where there was evidence of a deliberate breach of the law, accompanied by determination to persist in the breach. None of these parliamentary statements is binding on the Government, as the latest discussions of the Official Secrets Acts will show, but they illustrate how closely involved the Government is in obscenity proceedings.

The case of the Bradford bookseller, Arthur Dobson, shows the system at work. In 1965 his shop was raided and the seized books considered by the Director of Public Prosecutions. The latter thought some obscene, and Dobson was convicted and sentenced to two years' imprisonment. The Director of Public Prosecutions returned to Bradford police others which he told them were not considered obscene – copies of *Bawdy Setup* were among them. In 1966 Dobson was freed on appeal to the Court of Appeal, and his other books returned to him. In 1967 the police again seized *Bawdy Setup* in his shop; he was convicted of possessing it, and again sentenced to two years' imprisonment, and given a fine and costs amounting to £3,000, to be released once more by the Court of Appeal after serving ten months of his sentence. In 1971 the police seized on warrant *The Little Red School Book*. They seized the entire stock while the D.P.P. decided whether to prosecute. The publishers of this allegedly educational work complained that the police were in effect censoring the book.

The Home Office is the Government department concerned, as part of its responsibility for enforcing the criminal law, with the supervision of matters relating to obscene publications. The police forward reports of all convictions and detention orders to the Home Office, which maintains records and statistics. Similarly, the Home Office is notified of seizures by H.M. Customs and the Post Office. The Home Office acts as a liaison between the Post Office, H.M. Customs, and the Director of Public Prosecutions for the purpose of advising on action to be taken. It is also the authority, designated by the United Kingdom under the international convention for the suppression of pornography, for informing other states of obscene matters being distributed. In practice it even reports books which it believes to be obscene although no prosecution has been launched in the United Kingdom. The best known is *Lolita*, an American novel which had never been the subject of prosecution in England when the Home Office went beyond the Convention by writing to France about this 'highly obscene' book so as to secure the suppression of an English language version being printed in France. Of course, since that time, *Lolita* has been published in England. When Durham County Education

Committee complained about the pin-up girls on chewing gum imported from the United States, the Board of Trade stated that it fell outside the control of import licences to censor wrappers, and the Home Office ruled that they were not obscene in the accepted sense.

There have, from time to time, been waves of prosecutions for obscenity. Who, if anyone, has initiated them? The question is hard to answer. Attempts to pin the blame on the Home Secretary have not succeeded beyond doubt. There may be several factors : stepping up of the pornographic trade, enthusiastic officials in the departments concerned or in Scotland Yard's Obscene Publications Squad, hints thrown out by the Lord Chief Justice in cases concerning other obscene publications. In 1969 there were 128 prosecutions under the Obscene Publications Acts (49 in 1965), and between $2\frac{1}{2}$ and 3 million books and magazines were seized or forfeited.

CUSTOMS AND POST OFFICE

The Customs Consolidation Act 1876 prohibits the importation of indecent or obscene works. Customs officers are empowered to seize them. They are armed with a black list compiled by the Commissioners of Customs and Excise, a list which includes books which have not been the subject of prosecutions and which the Commissioners do not treat as comprehensive, but merely as a working guide. In 1964 there were 165 titles on this list. If a person asks to see this list in order to know which books he may buy abroad and import, he will be refused.[17] He must take his chance of seizure on his return home. A well publicized example was the seizure of Genet's works in French which the Birmingham Corporation had bought for their reference library – although it was pointed out in a debate on the motion for the adjournment of the House of Commons that the British Museum and Reading University stocked the books, the Financial Secretary to the Treasury defended the seizure. In 1969 the Customs seized over two million novels and magazines with over 1,000 different titles. A person whose books are seized has a month in which to notify the Commissioners that he objects – the Customs officers do not tell him this – after which the books are automatically forfeited. If he objects within the month, the matter goes to court. The Customs authorities refuse to return the book so that he can read it and thereby prepare his defence. They treat the sadistically violent as obscene. If he successfully challenges the Commissioners of Customs and Excise in the High Court, that is not the end of it as in a prosecution for obscenity – here the Commissioners can appeal all the way to the House of Lords. Those dissatisfied with the seizure of books by the British Customs authorities might reflect that Irish Customs seized the *Observer* because it contained an article on family planning, that Australian Customs seized *Portnoy's Complaint*, and that South African Customs seized the children's classic, *Black Beauty*. The Customs officials can also prosecute for the offence of importing obscene articles, though they seldom do so. The Customs witness before the Select Committee stoutly and successfully resisted, on the grounds of administrative convenience and expense, a proposal that no destructions be made without court order. It is important to notice that the Act of 1959 does not apply to these customs offences; therefore all the old defects of the law remain here : literary merit is no defence, expert evidence is probably inadmissible, selected 'juicy' parts of the book may be read, and so on. In 1964 Sir Dingle Foot, later Solicitor-General, bought Sir Richard Burton's *The Perfumed Garden* at a London Airport bookstall when outward bound, and had it seized by the Customs on his return.

The Post Office Act 1953 makes it an offence to send a postal packet which encloses obscene or indecent matter, and authorizes officials to detain and destroy such materials. Once again the protections of the 1959 Act do not extend to offences under this Act. In 1971 Paul Ableman's *The Mouth* was held not obscene at the Old Bailey, but its publisher was convicted under the Act of sending 'indecent' advertising brochures through the post. In 1959 the Post

Office was seizing *Lady Chatterley's Lover*, yet in 1960, before the trial, the Customs officers were allowing it to go through. The Post Office has no power to open sealed packets in order to see whether their contents are obscene or indecent. Cases of seizure average about 800 a year, mostly from overseas. There have been frequent complaints that unsolicited material advertising obscene literature is sent through the post. Consequently the Unsolicited Goods and Services Act 1971 has made it a crime to send unsolicited material which describes or illustrates sexual techniques.

OTHER STATUTES

Some other statutes also deal with obscenity. Until recently they have been little used, but now the police are taking advantage of the fact that they also are not limited to 'obscene' matters and do not have the defence of public good. Several art galleries have been prosecuted under the Vagrancy Acts of 1824 and 1838. When the Director of Public Prosecutions obtained a conviction against the director of a gallery exhibiting John Dine paintings, he admitted in court that they were not obscene, but relied on the accused having exposed to public view an indecent exhibition. When the Obscene Publications Squad seized the John Lennon prints in 1970 under the Obscene Publications Act they prosecuted not on that Act but on the Metropolitan Police Act 1839 so as to deprive the accused of trial by jury; the charge was of exhibiting indecent prints – they need not be obscene under this Act. The prosecution failed because of the vigilance of the accused's lawyer. He convinced the magistrate that the prosecution had wrongly omitted 'to the annoyance of passengers' from the charge. He then dismissed the charge because a gallery exhibition did not annoy 'passengers'.

In the same year, the grandson of a High Court Judge was charged under the Venereal Diseases Act 1917 and the Indecent Advertisements Act 1889 with distributing leaflets : he was advertising where V.D. treatment was available.

He was acquitted under the Venereal Diseases Act but convicted under the Indecent Advertisements Act. The latter Act appeared to make it criminal for local authorities to advertise V.D. clinics in their public lavatories; they therefore had to be exempted by the Indecent Advertisements (Amendment) Act 1970. The magazine *Black Dwarf* has been attacked by prosecutions under the Metropolitan Police Act and the Indecent Advertisements Acts 1889 and 1970, which make it an offence to deliver any obscene or indecent matter on a public highway. The Theatres Act, 1968, is much better. It has the defence of public good, it prohibits evasion by relying on these other Acts or on conspiracy, and the Attorney-General's consent is needed for any prosecution. The Post Office Act 1969 makes it an offence to send a message or other matter grossly offensive or of an indecent, obscene or menacing character.

LOCAL AUTHORITIES

Some local authorities – Bradford, for example – have local Acts of Parliament, making certain conduct relating to obscene publications offences within their area. Prints by the Victorian artist Beardsley were forfeited, and the shopkeeper fined, by an Edinburgh magistrate in 1967 under a local Provisional Order. It is not generally realized how widespread local Acts are; there is no readily available compilation of these offences, and the citizen has inadequate opportunity of knowing what the law is. It is perhaps for this reason that the Home Secretary pursues a certain course on a related matter. Some local authorities have by-laws referring to obscene publications, but for a long time now, when local authorities submit, as they must, by-laws for his approval, he has refused approval if they deal with obscenity. Local authorities exercise power in other unofficial ways : it is the practice for many seaside towns to have unofficial approved lists of comic picture postcards, which it is agreed shall not be the subject of prosecutions. Blackpool, for instance, has an unofficial censorship committee. It is of interest that the

Postcard Association, which represents most of the manufacturers and wholesalers in the trade, has been pressing the Home Office to set up an independent national censorship board : the Association has complained that what one local authority approves will be prohibited elsewhere. There was a curious episode in 1963. The Metropolitan Police as taxi licensing authority banned a taxi advertisement for a travel agency which depicted two girls in bikinis, on the ground that it could be offensive to public morals.

PROPOSALS FOR LAW REFORM

The law of obscenity remains unsatisfactory. 'Obscene', 'deprave and corrupt', which are the basic definitions of all the criminal law on the subject, are ambiguous terms, yet the jury must not be helped to interpret them. It is not enough that the words shock or disgust, yet it seems that taking drugs, and violence, are depravity as well as sex. Where do we stop? What of 'Guinness is Good for you' or 'Players Please'? Is depravity anything that in the opinion of the courts of the day promotes anti-social consequences? Even when the jury have defined 'obscene' they have to decide whether it will corrupt 'a significant proportion' of the likely readership. How many is too many? May the standard sometimes be the fourteen-year-old schoolgirl? Can the jury be expected to discharge that task of balancing the corruption against the public good which the *Last Exit to Brooklyn* case requires of them?

There are question marks about enforcement, too. Should twenty policemen in 1970 be occupied in raiding the cinema where the film *Flesh* is being shown, demanding the names and addresses of those watching, depriving the owners of the film for a month while the Director of Public Prosecutions decides not to prosecute, and giving them no compensation for their business loss? Should the Brighton police in 1968 have kept over 3,000 books of a Brighton bookseller, many learned periodicals destined for university libraries, before prosecuting in respect of only a few titles?

It is easy to suggest improvements in the law. The task at present imposed on a jury is impossible to discharge satisfactorily. We should follow the United States Supreme Court when in 1966 they held that, even when material is shown to be obscene, the prosecution must also establish that it is utterly without redeeming social value.[18] We should scrap the separate prosecution-biased rules which operate for Customs, Post Office and the like and have a set of uniform rules. If the 1959 Act is restricted to 'obscene', other Acts should not also apply to the 'indecent'. The conspiracy escape route should be denied to the police. When the police seize materials they should be liable in damages for failure to return them within twenty-eight days unless proceedings have been instituted.

These proposals are designed to confer immunity on work of value, however slight, and to minimize financial loss, but without protecting the dealer in hard-core pornography. There are many who would go further and abolish the offence of obscenity altogether, although accepting that the law should still protect those who are affected by offensive displays in public places. This case has been put best by a working party of the Arts Council which reported in 1969. They argue that nobody has proved that anybody is depraved or corrupted by what they read, hear or see, not even Pamela Hansford Johnson with her assertion that the Moors killers were affected by the sadistic books they had read. Why, for instance, did not the prosecution bring forward those depraved by *Last Exit to Brooklyn*, which had sold 13,000 copies before proceedings began? Denmark has abolished the offence without harmful results. If one believes that the criminal law should not interfere until the to-be-prohibited conduct has been shown to have caused harm, they are right. But we have traditionally had a different attitude : that one purpose of the criminal law is to support and maintain various standards of acceptable conduct, standards which are flexible and must follow in the wake of public opinion. The Suicide Act and the Sexual Offences Act abolished crime when the time was ripe. On this view a substantial body of opinion regards the cruder kinds of pornography as socially harmful, and so it is too early for us to remove the crime of obscenity. Meanwhile, all we can do is to prepare the ground by making the changes we have suggested above.

For a quarter of a century some American states, with Massachusetts in the lead, have operated a different kind of legislation. The aim is to avoid the publisher being treated like any other criminal in the dock every time a book may be obscene and to make the key issue 'Is the book obscene?' and then by court order restrain its future publication everywhere. The system has obvious snags : it may matter whether the book is sold to medical students or to children for instance. Before the Government embarks on legislative reform, it should also have this American system studied at first hand.

Defamation

This branch of the law gives money damages to those whose reputations have been harmed by disparaging and defamatory statements. The law is complex, both in substance and in procedure, and only its outlines will be given here. It is a story of competing interests. The Englishman (and the Irishman) attaches a great importance to reputation. Put him on a jury in a libel case and he will often award more damages than a judge will give to the permanently incapacitated victim of a road accident. For instance, when a film of Rasputin might have implied that a Russian princess, an *émigrée* in Britain when the film was made, had been seduced by him, the damages awarded in 1934 were £25,000 – say £100,000 at today's values of the pound.[19] Opposed to this tendency is the powerful pressure group of the Press, concerned, of course, to restrict the scope of libel and damages awarded as much as possible – witness the ex-proprietor of the *Daily Mirror* saying that the liberty of the Press is drastically curtailed against the public interest because excessive damages are awarded by juries to the libel victims. The Press has always been so willing to pay very high fees to counsel in libel actions that the subject has never failed to attract highly skilled lawyers; in consequence there has been woven into the subject a degree of technical and procedural subtlety not to be found in any other comparable branch of law. (This view, expressed for the last eight years in this book, and severely criticized by the legal profession, is presumably respectable now that a law lord has endorsed it.) Involved in this is the effort to keep as much away from the jury as possible in the hope that matters which the judge must then decide will receive a decision more sympathetic to the Press. The judge has the last word on all the complex *legal* questions : only if the plaintiff has succeeded in all of them is the jury allowed to consider whether on the *facts* the plaintiff's case is proved. For instance, it is often said proudly that in England the jury decides whether a statement is defamatory. But if the judge rules that the statement is not capable of being defamatory the jury never has the chance to decide the point. And even if the trial judge does let the jury decide, the Court of Appeal can still overrule the jury's verdict that the statement was libellous by holding that the trial judge should never have left the issue to the jury because the statement could not be defamatory. Reinforcing these attempts to shape the judicial process are even more successful attempts to persuade Parliament to cut down the liabilities of the Press in libel. The Defamation Act of 1952 gave the Press many important exemptions from liability which it had previously never enjoyed. These exemptions have been substantially augmented by the Civil Evidence Act 1968. When the Legal Aid and Advice Act 1949 introduced a widespread scheme for affording financial aid in bringing law suits, defamation was one of the few types of litigation left completely outside the scheme. The paradox is that newspapers who are largely responsible for paying high fees in libel suits now complain of the high cost of these actions; they say that the legal costs for an ordinary libel trial total at least £10,000, so that their insurers are always pressing them to settle out of court. How much greater then are the pressures on the victims to settle for sums well below the loss sustained! How many private citizens, unsupported by legal aid, can afford to put at hazard £10,000 in a battle with a financially powerful Press backed by Lloyds? Moreover the Press can set off all these expenses against profits for tax purposes; the citizen cannot.

THE MEANING OF 'DEFAMATORY'

A statement is defamatory whenever it would tend to lower the plaintiff in the estimation of right-thinking members of society generally. It is not enough that the plaintiff is made to look ridiculous or a laughing-stock; the statement must be an attack on his character or reputation. *That Was The Week That Was* could indulge in its satire without saddling the B.B.C. with heavy libel damages. Even if a right-thinking person would not shun him it is enough if most would do so – for this reason it is libellous to call a man 'insane'. It may be that if a substantial and respectable proportion of society would think less well of a person, provided that this reaction is not plainly anti-social or irrational, then a statement is defamatory. On this view, it would be actionable to say that a man is a non-unionist or works during strikes. On the other hand, the Court of Appeal would be right in having held that it was not actionable to allege that a member of a golf club had sneaked to the police about an illegal fruit-machine in the clubhouse.[20] What was libellous yesterday may be harmless today – it would have been defamatory to call a man a German in 1940 but not in 1970. In order to be libellous the attack must be on the character of the plaintiff. One of the excuses of the Press for not criticizing the products of manufacturers has been that it would expose it to libel actions. Of the many reasons why this is a false view, the first is that to find fault with goods is not to attack the character of the maker. To say that X's cooker is slower to heat, harder to clean, has less usable oven space, than Y's cooker is not to defame X, the maker of the cooker. (Nor is it normally that other wrong, injurious falsehood, because only those who act from malice are liable for that.)

A statement may be innocuous on its face, and yet have a secondary and defamatory meaning : this lawyers call an innuendo. To put a top-flight singer's name third, instead of first, on an advertising bill for a concert was actionable;[21] a caption under a newspaper photograph to the effect that it was Mr C and his fiancée was defamatory of the plaintiff, the wife of Mr C;[22] to include a cartoon of an amateur golfer in an advertisement for chocolate implied that he was prostituting his amateur status.[23]

PUBLICATION

The libel must be published to somebody other than the plaintiff : a man's reputation cannot suffer unless third parties hear something to his discredit. The plaintiff must also show that the statement is about him. For this reason the civil law is powerless to interfere with group libels : for instance, attacks on Jews or Roman Catholics as a class : when no particular members of the group are pointed at, no individuals can sue.

LIBEL AND SLANDER DISTINGUISHED

The difference between libel and slander is generally unimportant. Anything communicated in a permanent and visible form is libel, anything temporary and audible is slander. Thus books and letters may convey libel, whereas spoken words (except on radio and television) will usually be slander. To place the effigy of the plaintiff near effigies of convicted murderers in Tussaud's waxworks exhibition was a libel.[24] Libel may be also a crime where the publication is likely to endanger the public peace; slander is not a crime. The distinction is relevant for one other reason : sometimes, in order to win in slander, the plaintiff must prove that he has suffered some material loss in consequence of the defamatory statement. There is not even this difference between libel and slander in the following cases : where the slander imputes a crime; where it imputes that a person has venereal or some other contagious disease; where the words are calculated to disparage the plaintiff in any office, profession, trade, or business; and where the words impute unchastity or adultery to any woman or girl.

DEFENCES

When somebody consents to a publication of defamatory matter he cannot sue. The Racing Calendar published the report of an inquiry by the Jockey Club into the running of a horse trained by the plaintiff; although this report stated that the horse had been doped, and that the plaintiff was warned off, he was held to have no action on the ground that by taking out a Jockey Club trainer's licence he had impliedly consented to publication in the Racing Calendar of any reports by the Jockey Club on his conduct as trainer.[25]

There is no liability whenever the statement made is substantially true. The expert who has made an accurate scientific assessment of the manufacturer's products can report his findings confident in the knowledge that he has nothing to fear from the law of libel. Until 1952 every material statement had to be justified. By the Act of that year 'a defence of justification shall not fail by reason only that the truth of every charge is not proved if the words not proved to be true do not materially injure the plaintiff's reputation having regard to the truth of the remaining charges'. The completeness of the defence of justification must be emphasized. Even if the defendant be inspired by malice, or even if, when he made the statements, he did not believe them to be true, if in fact they are true, his defence is good. This makes the consequences of the failure of the English law to protect privacy so serious. Newspapers are free in this country to rake up a man's forgotten past, and ruin him deliberately in the process, without risk of incurring tortious liability.

Even if the statement is false, there may still be no liability. Some statements are said to be absolutely privileged. Thus an M.P. can in the House of Commons say whatever he likes about anybody; he may use the occasion deliberately to blacken a business rival in order to divert profitable contracts to his own company, knowing that everything he says is completely false, and positively desiring to ruin his rival : he is completely exempt from libel, and so are the Press and television when they accurately report his speech. Hence the frequency with which M.P.s spurn the challenge to repeat outside the House the disparaging remarks which they have made in it. Communications passing between senior civil servants are also absolutely privileged, but not, say, letters exchanged between directors of Imperial Chemical Industries Ltd. Statements made in court, whether by judge, lawyer, litigant, or witness, enjoy the same privilege : fair, accurate, and contemporaneous reports in newspapers and broadcasts of judicial proceedings can also never be the subject of libel actions.

Whenever it is in the public interest, or in the interest of the person making the statement and the person to whom it is communicated, that the statement be made, the maker of the statement, even though it be false and defamatory, has the defence of qualified privilege so long as he makes it without malice. There is malice if the maker does not believe in the truth of his statement, or if he is actuated by some improper motive, such as spite or ill-will. A newspaper may report that an athletics body has deprived an amateur of his status on the ground that he has been paid to run; it will not be liable even though the athlete can prove that he received no payment, provided that it has accurately reported the body's decision. Fair and accurate newspaper and broadcasting reports of proceedings of local authorities, public bodies, and company meetings are also qualifiedly privileged. The manager of a company may inform his directors of his suspicion that the cashier is falsifying the accounts – however untrue, this is no libel if done without malice; for it would be an instance of a common interest between the maker and the recipient of the statement.

It is also a defence to make a fair comment on a matter of

public interest. The defence covers the public conduct of persons holding public office or of those engaged in local government or management of religious institutions. Plays, broadcasts, the work of an architect, are other examples. Publishers may be annoyed at the scathing reviews of their books, but are remediless when the comment is one that an honest man, however biased and prejudiced his views, might have made. This is one more reason why the Press could freely criticize products offered for sale to the public. One House of Lords decision on fair comment arose when Lord Kemsley sued Michael Foot as editor of *Tribune*.[26] *Tribune* attacked a newspaper (with which Kemsley, the newspaper proprietor, was not connected) by publishing an article headed 'Lower than Kemsley'. The House of Lords held that Foot would have a defence of fair comment if an honest man would have complained that the Kemsley Press was low : after this ruling Kemsley dropped the proceedings. Whenever qualified privilege or fair comment is pleaded, no written questions about the defendant's sources of information or grounds of belief are allowed. When the *Daily Telegraph* published an allegedly defamatory letter about a radio show it did not lose the defence of qualified comment when it emerged that the letter was written anonymously from a false address and therefore the newspaper could not prove that the writer was not actuated by malice.[27]

Sometimes a libel may be published innocently. Thus, a newsagent will not be held answerable for the libel in the magazine which he sells, for he is a mere distributor who could not ordinarily be expected to know of the libel. Before the Act of 1952, newspapers were held answerable in the following cases : the *Sunday Chronicle* published a fictional article about 'Artemus Jones'; the writer of the article did not know of the plaintiff, of that name, who was a former contributor to the newspaper, but the managing editor, on reading the article in proof, had thought at first that the plaintiff was intended.[28] In another, the *Daily Express* published an account of the trial for bigamy of 'Harold Newstead, thirty-year-old Camberwell man' : the reporter had included the address and occupation of the Harold Newstead of whom this was a correct report, but the sub-editor deleted it; this want of particularity caused readers to think that the plaintiff, another Harold Newstead of Camberwell, of about the same age, was meant; it was held to be no defence that the words were true of, and intended to refer to, another, and the jury was held to be justified in finding that the words referred to the plaintiff.[29] The Act of 1952 has for the first time given newspapers a defence when they unintentionally defame a person.

In practice, therefore, those who take reasonable care about what they say have little to fear from the law of defamation. When newspapers (or those with whom they insure for libel) are caught by the law of libel, it is usually either because their reporters and proof-readers have been careless in not detecting the offending material, or because in the interests of circulation they have taken a calculated risk.

There is little to support the Press view that the law of libel prevents newspapers from commenting on many matters about which the public should know. The Press cannot, for instance, hold the law responsible for its inept and cowardly showing in the Profumo affair; a newspaper which publishes the truth cannot be held liable to the victim, whether he be a Minister or a nonentity. It used to be true that the plaintiff might be awarded damages on a very generous scale, because the Court of Appeal would rarely reduce the jury's assessment. In 1965 the Court of Appeal changed its policy; it decided that if it were satisfied that a jury award was so high that it must have been not only compensating the victim for his loss but also punishing the defendant for his wrong, it would always set aside such awards because they would be too high.[30] Since 1965 no high awards against the Press have been approved by the Court of Appeal; yet the Press campaign for lower damages persists as if this radical change in their favour had not occurred.

In 1965 Lord Shawcross with the support of the Press began a campaign in public addresses for the Press to be given further protection from the law of libel. They seek to deprive libel victims of trial by jury since they know the unfavourable view which the public takes of much Press behaviour. They also underplay the extent of the defences now available to the Press. It is true that on one or two points of detail not important enough to be discussed here the judges have unnecessarily fashioned the law of defamation in a way which is unfair to defendants; all of these Lord Shawcross and his supporters have ruthlessly exposed. They have made almost annual attempts to effect these alterations by private members' Bills. All these have failed in the face of Government opposition. No doubt what they would like is a law on the American pattern : that a newspaper may publish with impunity a full report of public interest unless they know its falsity or show reckless disregard for the truth. Any such amendment would destroy the equilibrium between protecting reputation and preserving free speech which must be the aim of libel laws.

The Press have often complained that they are muzzled when a person whom they attack issues a libel writ, even though he does not pursue the case. This is not and never was the law; the Press is free to continue its attacks after a writ has been issued; as the Court of Appeal has recently confirmed, that is not contempt of court.[31]

As a result of both legislative changes and judicial decisions the law of defamation has in the last few years become increasingly favourable to the Press so that the obstacles in the way of plaintiffs are greater than they have ever been in the modern history of the law of libel. The general verdict must be that the law is now unfairly weighted against the victim of false attacks on his character by the Press.

CHAPTER 6

FREEDOM OF EXPRESSION (4): CONTEMPT OF COURT AND CONTEMPT OF PARLIAMENT

Contempt of Court

IN this section we are concerned with the restrictions imposed upon those who wish to comment on judges and trials. There are two issues : whether the law embodied in these restrictions is sound, and whether, however good in itself, it is liable to work unfairly if judges are allowed to judge in their own causes. The power of restriction arose in this way : it used to be the law that in some cases a man who hindered another from having a fair trial (whether criminal or civil) could be indicted for a crime (called a contempt of court) and tried by a jury in the usual way. In the early seventeenth century the Star Chamber assumed jurisdiction to punish these contempts. Soon after the Star Chamber was abolished in 1641 the ordinary judges themselves began trying these contempts summarily. When this was challenged in 1765 the court held that the practice was lawful ;[1] since that date this summary method has continued unchallenged, whereas trial by jury for such contempts is now obsolete. The judges now act as if the law has always conferred on them this summary power. There can now be no doubt that they used not to have such a power, that they usurped it on the dissolution of the Star Chamber, and that the authorities relied on in the decisive case of 1765 did not warrant that decision. The power (which cannot be exercised by county court judges or other judges in inferior courts, such as magistrates) is now too entrenched to be altered except by Act of Parliament. (One might ask : why does it matter that a crime is tried summarily by a judge instead of on indictment in the usual way? First of all, the accused is denied a jury; there is nothing to stop the judge who is himself the victim of the alleged contempt from trying the charge. In some courts the accused has no right to a personal hearing on the charge; he is allowed only to swear an affidavit. The judge can impose a fine of unlimited amount, he can impose a term of imprisonment of any duration he chooses, or indeed send the accused to prison and leave him there indefinitely, and until October 1960 the law gave the accused no appeal.)

CONDUCT WHICH INTERFERES WITH THE FAIRNESS OF A TRIAL

Any conduct that tends to bring the authority and administration of the law into disrespect or to interfere with litigation is a contempt of court. We are concerned here only with those contempts which concern freedom of expression. The Press and broadcasting are obviously the most important media, but theatrical productions, cinema newsreels, sermons, and speeches have all fallen foul of the law of contempt.

It is obviously of the first importance that every accused should have a fair trial. Important though freedom of speech and freedom of the Press be, a 'freedom' which deprived prisoners of a fair trial could not be countenanced. In the United States, the Press is free to assist in detection of crime, to interview witnesses and suspects and report their observations, to comment on trials as they proceed, and to give opinions on the guilt of suspects. Englishmen should be proud of the fact that none of these things can happen in England : the law of contempt stands in the way.

This is not to say that the British Press has not tried to interfere. For instance, in the early 1920s national newspapers used to assign teams of their staff to investigate crimes. In 1924 the *Evening Standard* published misleading information about discoveries in a murder case. The newspaper also obtained from a witness information and a promise not to speak to anybody but themselves about the case, but, doubting whether she would resist the wiles of other newspapers, they arranged that she should stay out of the way with the wife of a sub-editor.[2] The proprietors were fined £1,000 for contempt, disabused of the notion that they were fulfilling a public duty, and sternly informed that any future offences of that kind would be dealt with by imprisonment. This put a stop to that type of activity on the part of the British Press.

The overriding aim of the law of criminal contempts is to ensure that the jury enters upon its task free from bias. For example, after a criminal trial where the jury disagreed, and the accused published an article before the re-trial in which he attacked the reliability of one of the leading witnesses in the case, members of the jury at the re-trial might well have been prejudiced by recalling what they had read in his article, and accordingly the accused was punished for contempt.[3] The English method of criminal prosecution creates a particular risk of prejudice. A person who is charged by the police with a crime is not tried at once. The matter is first referred to examining magistrates who decide on the evidence of the prosecution whether there is a *prima facie* case for committing him for trial. As we shall see, this investigation is normally carried out in open court. At the eventual trial journalists are free to report the proceedings contemporaneously. But it does not follow that these proceedings consist of the same evidence as that heard by the magistrates. The following cases illustrate what sometimes ensues.

In 1954 an *Evening Standard* reporter was attending a murder trial at Chelmsford Assizes. He telephoned an account to head office which was an inaccurate statement of the evidence given. The inaccuracy lay in the fact that evidence prejudicial to the accused (which had wrongly been allowed to be given by the examining magistrates) was prohibited by the judge at the assizes.[4] Presumably, the reporter thought that he had heard at the trial what in fact he had only previously heard before the magistrates. The untrue account which appeared in the *Evening Standard* (on sale in Chelmsford that evening) could have prejudiced the jury, who might very well have read the newspaper at home before returning to court the following day to continue their duties. The proprietors were fined £1,000 for contempt.

Another incident arose out of the trial of Dr Bodkin Adams in the 1950s. During his trial for murder *Newsweek* published matter highly prejudicial to the doctor which was not given in evidence at his trial. This publication was held to be contempt.[5]

Some Sunday newspapers have sought to increase their circulations by writing articles which purport to expose criminals who have not yet been brought to justice. In 1956 the *People* published an article, prepared by its crime reporter Duncan Webb, demanding that one Micallef be arrested and prosecuted for his brothel-keeping activities. The only object of the article was found to be to boost sales.[6] Micallef had been arrested the previous month for a crime of this type and had been committed for trial by a court operating within a mile or so of the *People*'s head office. No evidence of previous convictions is ordinarily allowed at a trial; while Micallef was awaiting his trial, however, not only had the *People* published a list, but the list apparently included many offences for which he had not been convicted; the prejudicial effect on any members of the jury who read the article is obvious. The editor, the proprietors, and Webb were all fined for contempt. It seems just that the court should have found the offence committed even though the accused's trial had not begun. The editor of the *Daily Mirror* was sent to prison in 1949 for publishing an article, when the murder trial of Haigh was pending, which might have suggested to readers that Haigh was involved in some other horrifying murders.[7]

It was thought at one time that newspapers were free to comment so long as no arrest had been made. In a Scottish case in 1959 the *Scottish Daily Mail* published prejudicial material before the accused was charged but when he was being questioned as a suspect:[8] this was held to be contempt, and a warning was given that if newspapers persisted in the independent interviewing of witnesses in a way that impeded the police it might be necessary to imprison those responsible.

In Scotland, however, there is no public investigation before magistrates, and it did not follow that the decision applied in England. Subsequently, the *Daily Express* and *Daily Mail* were fined in Northern Ireland for publishing information about a person whom the *Daily Express* described as the 'No. 1 suspect'[9] – he was later charged. Moreover, the Administration of Justice Act 1960 recognized that if proceedings were imminent, even though not pending, the crime could be committed. This extension to the period before anybody is charged may appear to place a newspaper in some difficulty. It would be wrong to muzzle a newspaper altogether before arrests are made : newspapers may be capable of uncovering criminal activities. In 1969 *The Times* published articles which alleged bribery and corruption by named Metropolitan detectives. Criticism that this was trial by newspaper seems misguided. If a newspaper can uncover crime and stir the authorities to investigate, it is serving the public interest, and will not go to the trouble unless it is free to publish. That activity is both commendable and lawful so long as it is not untrue, and therefore libellous, and proceedings are not imminent.

One can sympathize with the recent Australian decision that for contempt to be committed the criminal process must have been formally set in motion before the article is published.[10] In 1967 David Frost was concerned on behalf of thousands of car insurance policy holders about the affairs of the Fire, Auto and Marine Insurance Company and Dr Savundra's management of it. Savundra agreed to be interviewed on television by Frost. Seven days later he was arrested and later appealed against his conviction for conspiracy to defraud on the ground that Frost's trial by television had prejudiced his defence. The court dismissed the appeal (Savundra unsuccessfully appealed to the European Commission on Human Rights on the ground that the T.V. programme denied him a fair trial,[11]) but nevertheless added that the T.V. programme was intolerable and deplorable. It had previously been thought that 'imminent' meant that an arrest had taken place or was expected hourly. The court was here saying that if it was 'obvious to all' (unexplained) that an arrest was about to be made (we don't know whether at the time of the interview a decision to prosecute had been taken) the proceedings were 'imminent'.[12] Although Frost was not on trial (and had no chance to defend himself) these remarks by the court, with the uncertainty they caused, have understandably led to much protest by Press and television. This is unfortunate because the general attitude of the courts to contempt in the last few years has been much more satisfactory. The problem remains unsolved, and several recent attempts by M.P.s to secure the passing of an amending Act have failed in the absence of Government backing.

It is common for the Press to indulge in such euphemisms as 'the police wish to interview X who they believe will assist them in their inquiries', or 'X is detained by the police for questioning'. Everyone knows what these statements mean – they seem a clumsy and almost certainly ineffective way of avoiding possible proceedings for libel. X is a suspect, and it is there that the courts will draw the line for the purposes of contempt – the Press must not publish anything prejudicial to him. Above all, they must be careful not to publish matter of which the law forbids evidence to be given at the trial.

Photographs are a particular hazard for the Press. A flagrant case of contempt was that of the *Daily Record* in Scotland in 1959.[13] A well-known Scottish professional footballer was arrested : ignoring warnings from the police, the newspaper persisted in its inquiries and published a photograph of the accused. Obviously, whenever any issue of identification arises this is highly prejudicial. The newspaper was fined £7,500. It would of course be equally prejudicial to publish a photograph of a suspect before he is charged; this was one of the grounds on which the *Scottish Daily Mail* was convicted in the case cited earlier. Yet it might be countered that sometimes the Press and television organizations publish photographs at the request of the police. This in itself will not ensure immunity from conviction for contempt, but it does suggest that there are circumstances in which the publication of a photograph of a suspect is not contempt.

When the Administration of Justice Bill was before Parliament in 1960, the Opposition raised the question of defining contempt in the Bill, and in particular the relevance of the public interest which a publication might serve. The Government resisted these proposals on the ground that it was always clear whether a publication was prejudicial to the administration of justice and that the question of countervailing public interest could never arise. But is this so? Suppose the police ask a newspaper to publish the photograph of an escaped convict whom they believe to be committing, since his escape, a series of dangerous crimes. When the convict is ultimately captured and tried for these further crimes might he not be prejudiced by the photograph in the same way as any other accused standing trial? It is submitted that the law ought to be that the newspaper was not guilty of contempt, because the public interest in helping to capture a dangerous escaped convict outweighed the risk of prejudicial publication. One cannot, however, say with confidence that the defence of public interest is ever available, and it is to be regretted that the opportunity to clarify the point was missed when the Bill was in Parliament. Newspapers ought not to be put in the dilemma of either failing to protect citizens against dangerous men or exposing themselves to summary prosecution, and it is no answer that the court would probably only record a formal conviction without penalty, or that prosecutions for such acts are unlikely.

The discussion so far has avoided the question of whether the accused need have a guilty mind. In several of the cases already examined the court went out of its way to declare that a person was guilty, however innocent his conduct might have been. In the Micallef case against Odhams Press the accused pleaded that they did not know that Micallef had been charged. Lord Goddard held that the issue of intent was irrelevant. In fact his ruling was totally unnecessary; for the court found that the *People* had failed to take reasonable care to ascertain the facts, and it could therefore have held the accused guilty, not of innocent contempt, but of care-lessness. In the *Newsweek* case the distributors, W. H. Smith & Son Ltd, were found guilty, it being held that their defence that they were unaware of the criminal content of the maga-zine was irrelevant, and, as Lord Goddard observed, the gossipy nature of *Newsweek* and the well-known lack of restraint in American magazines when reporting crime might well have put the distributors on to inquire into the contents.

Why did the courts take this line? Not, it is submitted, because they were determined to be ruthless towards the Press. The evidence is all the other way. They have inflicted punishments reasonable in the circumstances and they have shown no tendency to punish the innocent or to interfere when the risk of prejudice was slight. Typical is the decision in 1960 that a newspaper report published between con-viction and appeal which, if published before trial, would have been prejudicial because of its likely impact on a jury was not a contempt because experienced judges of the Court of Criminal Appeal who would alone decide the appeal could be relied on to be completely uninfluenced by such a Press report.[14] (No doubt relying on this decision, the Press freely painted in the background of the Great Train Robbery and set out the criminal records of the prisoners at a time when they were awaiting the hearing of their appeals.) Simi-larly, the Speaker of the House of Commons ruled that the House would discuss the Wedgwood Benn case (an M.P., the eldest son of a peer who had died) although an election peti-tion had been presented to the Election Court, on the ground that the issues were purely legal, to be decided by judges who would not therefore be prejudiced by a Commons de-bate.[15] In a 1965 case,[16] the High Court ruled that the *Daily Telegraph* did not commit contempt by commenting on a case pending trial by a judge sitting alone, despite the allega-tion of the plaintiffs, who moved the contempt proceedings, that by pre-judging the case in a leading article the news-paper prevented witnesses from giving unprejudiced evi-dence; in order to constitute contempt it must be proved that the publication created a real risk that the fair trial of the action would be prejudiced. In their present mood the courts will not treat as contempt a discussion of the merits of any civil case which is awaiting trial by a judge sitting without a jury. Newspapers need not be silenced because the target of their criticism issues a writ; a courageous newspaper could expose the limitations of this gagging device, instead of meekly submitting to it, as is the present practice. The 1966 case involving Sir Oswald Mosley and the B.B.C. is the latest illustration of current judicial attitudes.[17] Mosley issued in 1962 a writ for libel against Paul Fox which arose indirectly out of a *Panorama* broadcast; the gist of the action was that it was defamatory of Mosley to say that he had in the past deliberately provoked violence with the aid of Blackshirts. The plaintiff had not brought his action to trial in 1965 when the B.B.C. in the *Radio Times* and on the Third Programme in connection with a series of programmes about Fascism in the 1930s made further reference to violence and Mosley. In 1966 Mosley issued a writ against the B.B.C. for contempt. The court dismissed Mosley's motion on the ground that if the trial eventually occurred no juror was likely to be influenced by these B.B.C. publications. In 1969 the will of a millionaire, Sir Oliver Duncan, by which a Miss Fay benefited, was challenged in the Probate Court. The *Evening Standard* gossip column said that she had been his mistress. Although that was a fact in dispute in the pending proceedings the judge ruled that there was no contempt – there was no valid risk of the proceedings being prejudiced by it.

In one's search for an explanation of judicial attitudes to contempt, one may seek an analogy outside the law of contempt altogether. Consider the outlook of top-ranking civil servants who cling to power at all costs and resist attempts to introduce into their decisions fair procedures with the force of law : a typical example is the attitude of the Secretary of State for the Environment to orders for compulsory purchase of land, as revealed in the evidence given before the Franks Committee on Administrative Tribunals and Inquiries. Both judges with respect to contempt and senior civil servants in the discharge of their duties to citizens intend to act fairly, but wish to keep the power in their own hands – justice is the judge's concern, and he wishes to have unrestricted power to decide when newspapers and others are guilty of contempt. Although the judges have exercised their wide powers with restraint, public opinion would not tolerate the wide powers which they arrogated to themselves in decisions like that of *Newsweek*. The reaction was rapid : the introduction of the Administration of Justice Bill. Senior judges were, however, closely consulted in the drafting of it.

Section 11 of this Act provided that a mere distributor was not guilty of contempt 'if at the time of distribution (having taken all reasonable care) he did not know that it contained any such matter as aforesaid and had no reason to suspect that it was likely to do so'. The *Newsweek* case had strongly suggested that importers and big distributors of foreign periodicals were likely always to be punished for contempts contained in any of them. The courts were apparently resolved that such contempts should not go unpunished. The distributors were the only targets, for these foreign publishers had no editorial units in Britain – the man in charge of *Newsweek* in London was found not guilty because he had no control over the content of the magazine – and, contempt of court not being an extraditable crime, there was no machinery for bringing the publishers from abroad to stand trial. Foreign publishers refused to indemnify Smiths against any fines imposed on them. If these decisions had stood there might well have been a great reduction in the number of foreign periodicals on sale to the British public. This provision therefore relieved firms like W. H. Smith & Son Ltd of much anxiety, although its scope must not be exaggerated. The distributor has the burden of satisfying the court that he could not, by taking reasonable care, have discovered the offending material. It is submitted that, if facts like those of the *Newsweek* case recurred, the courts could justifiably still convict.

The Act also provides that any person accused of contempt is not guilty if he proves that he did not know and had no reason to suspect that proceedings were pending or imminent. Although the Act reverses the law laid down in cases like Micallef's, its limits must be noted. On facts such as those, presumably the judge's decision would still be 'guilty', because a newspaper specializing in the reporting of sordid crime ought to know that a person has been committed for trial by a court in the immediate vicinity of its head office. It is easy to imagine the new provision putting newspapers in a dilemma. Nothing is more likely to restrain the Press than uncertainty about the legality of its proposed actions. There is no central register of summonses issued or committals for trial ordered throughout the country. What inquiries should a newspaper make before writing an article about a person? This question of fact remains solely for the judges. It may be assumed at least that once the police have issued their 'wanted to assist them in their investigations' notices, the Press and broadcasting companies publish at their peril. In the *Savundra* case, despite the court's criticisms, David Frost later wrote that he did not know that Savundra's trial was pending, although he had gone to some lengths to find out. The Attorney-General has recently said that he would not expect proceedings for contempt to be begun or successfully concluded save in cases in which the newspaper ought reasonably to have been aware of the likelihood of a very early arrest.

It has been widely assumed that under the Act publishers will not be guilty of contempt so long as they do not know the true facts. This is erroneous. The rule laid down by the judges that liability arises regardless of the publisher's state of mind remains untouched save on knowledge that proceedings were pending. It will be remembered that the contempt in the *Evening Standard* case lay in a misreporting of the trial at Chelmsford Assizes. Suppose that a court reporter cabled to head office his report of a trial, and, owing to the fault of the Post Office, there was an error in transmission, so that the report as published, which was a correct rendering of the report as received at the newspaper office, prejudiced a fair hearing. This would still be a punishable offence, and the Post Office would have no liability to the newspaper. For the new defence of 'innocence' specifically refers only to the fact that proceedings were pending or imminent.

This Chelmsford case raises another point. The *Evening Standard* pleaded that, even if its reporter was careless in sending an inaccurate report, it had done nothing criminal; it had merely published in good faith what had been telephoned to it. The court held that 'the principle of vicarious liability is well established in these cases and must be adhered to', which means that, once a servant of the newspaper proprietors acting in the course of his employment is guilty of contempt, the proprietors are themselves guilty. Under the Act, the principle of vicarious liability survives, it seems, in that if the editor knows that the proceedings are pending and none of the directors knows, the proprietors will be guilty, and likewise, even if the editor does not know but the managing director, although in his Bermudan retreat at the time of publication, does know, the proprietors will still be guilty. On the other hand, if the reporter knows and the editor is innocent, the reporter but not the editor will be guilty, for the reporter is not the editor's servant. Yet when this point of knowledge is not in issue an editor can be convicted, even though at the time of publication he was away from the office. In 1968 the *Sunday Times* was prosecuted in contempt proceedings for publishing an article about the background of a person awaiting trial under the Race Relations Act. Although the newspaper had an elaborate and reasonable system to avoid such happenings and the editor was not at fault – the mistake was by the barrister engaged as proof-reader – the newspaper was fined £5,000.

Before we leave this branch of contempt some side effects must be noted. First, a man may be denied a trial by a jury free from prejudice even though newspapers and others have not infringed this law of contempt. Take the case of Albert Jones who was first charged in 1960, not with the murder of Brenda Nash, whose death after sexual interference was prominently reported, but with the rape of another girl.

Shortly after his widely publicized conviction for this rape, he was charged with the murder of Brenda Nash. It is plain that the risk of the jury being prejudiced against Jones because of his preceding trial was much greater than was the risk in many of the convictions for contempt previously discussed. Yet the conduct of the police, the Press, and the broadcasting agencies did not infringe the law of contempt. Or take the later A6 'homicide case' in 1961-2. The police let it be known that a certain man was sought in order to help with their inquiries into a death in which foul play was suspected. When this man came forward he was charged with a quite separate offence of wounding another person on another occasion, and detained in custody. Then the police realized and stated that their suspicions of him in the context of the A6 death were unjustified. The sequel was that the prosecution stated at his trial for the wounding charge that they were now not offering any evidence, and he was forthwith discharged a free and innocent man. Had the police charged him with the A6 crime there would have been a risk of prejudice arising out of the publicity surrounding the other proceedings, and yet no contempt would have been committed.

The courts are astute to reinforce the law of contempt in other ways. For instance, a Mr Baker was found murdered. The Press discovered the photographer who had been employed to take photographs at his daughter's wedding and paid him £15 for them so that they could publish photographs of the murdered man. His son-in-law sued the photographer for breach of copyright. The Court of Appeal upheld an award of £400 exemplary damages. Such a high sum was justified because it might deter others from supplying 'to the Press information which they know is going to be used in a manner which will be so hurtful and distressing to the people involved'.[18]

Secondly, the legitimate principle that prejudicial comment on a pending case in an ordinary court of justice must not be allowed is being increasingly abused under the banner of *sub judice*. A peer who wished to raise in the House of

Lords matters arising out of the ministerial inquiry into the application for compulsory powers to work ironstone in Oxfordshire was told by Lord Kilmuir, the Lord Chancellor, in 1960 that his inquiry was out of order, because the matter was *sub judice*; although the inspector had completed his inquiry and his subsequent inspection of the site, the Minister had not announced his decision.[19] There is no legal warrant for that reply. The alleged reason was that the objective of the Government was 'to infuse into the operation of these inquiries a real sense of independent judging, with full responsibility, of the issues which are raised'. The guarded tone of this statement must be noted : the casual reader might think that the Lord Chancellor had advanced conclusive argument that these proceedings were judicial like those of a court, and therefore must be subject to the *sub judice* protection. But soon afterwards Lord Kilmuir was to defend in Parliament a decision reached by a Minister after an inquiry of this type, where the Minister reversed the recommendation of the inspector on new evidence which the aggrieved landowner was not even allowed to see : a course which would be inconceivable in judicial proceedings. Yet in this latter case Lord Kilmuir's stand was legally supportable : that only shows how wrong it would be to think that the ironstone inquiry was comparable to a trial. A careful reading of Lord Kilmuir's statement shows that he did not say so – he merely spoke of the object of infusing a sense of judging. In short, he wishes to have the best of both worlds, a logically indefensible position : to prevent comment on inquiries because they fall within the *sub judice* rule of trials; to allow evidence to be taken behind the back of parties (which is forbidden at trials) because they are not judicial in the sense in which trials are. And finally, the most absurd example, again from Lord Kilmuir a few weeks earlier, when he told Lord Teviot that he could not discuss the verdict the previous day in the *Lady Chatterley's Lover* prosecution, because the matter was *sub judice* pending a possible appeal. The fact is, of course, that no appeal was possible from the verdict of not guilty.[20] Yet the House of Commons discussed the George Blake treason case in 1961 when the time for his appeal against conviction had not expired, and when it did not know whether he had given notice of appeal.

The whole problem of parliamentary discussion in relation to *sub judice* needs re-examination. There is often a conflict between the desire not to prejudice a trial and the need for prompt parliamentary discussion of matters of public interest. In 1962 the Speaker of the House of Commons advised against debating the circumstances of dismissal of a charter aircraft pilot because a libel action was pending, and this despite the public interest in aircraft safety raised by the case. It would be deplorable if a man could avoid discussion of any matter in Parliament by the simple expedient of issuing a writ. It is submitted that the Speaker should himself weigh in the balance the conflicting interests involved before deciding whether to allow parliamentary discussion. The problem is quite distinct from the rule that parliamentary debates are not held on matters the subject of inquiry by royal commission or departmental committee – this is merely a convenient rule of parliamentary business.

A crude practice under the guise of *sub judice* seems to be developing with regard to proceedings before magistrates. During the preliminary proceedings before magistrates in the Great Train Robbery case a firm of solicitors engaged in the case circularized a statement, which purported to be approved by the magistrates, that if photographs of any of the accused were taken outside the court it would be reported to the court for appropriate contempt proceedings. Then at the same hearing counsel said in open court that if the Press published any of the evidence they would be reported to the Attorney-General with a view to bringing contempt proceedings. It is a common practice for lawyers to threaten on behalf of their clients proceedings which they know to have no chance of winning, but the matter becomes more serious when Press freedom is openly challenged. As the Press Council rightly said in castigating these statements, there was no authority whatever for suggesting that the newspapers would have committed contempt had they disregarded these lawyer's threats. Although the Bar Council and Law Society are not reported to have taken any action, it is to be hoped that the forthright stand taken by Lord Devlin who was then chairman of the Press Council will curb this undesirable intimidatory practice.

One problem arises from cheque-book journalism, despite the Press Council's attempt to quash the practice. Matters came to a head over the Moors murder trial when David Smith, the leading witness for the prosecution, stated that he was being paid by the *News of the World* in return for giving his story to the newspaper, and that he had already been paid something and that the size of his eventual payment depended on whether the accused were convicted. The newspaper did not deny the agreement to pay but denied that any payment was contingent on a verdict of guilty. The Attorney-General refused to prosecute the *News of the World*; he doubted whether a payment to witnesses during a trial, in return for exclusive information after it, was contempt. He promised to consider legislative reform. As we saw earlier, the Press Council sought to avoid legislation by formulating a Declaration of Principle in 1966.[21] Matters used to be much worse : the great advocates of the 1920s and 1930s, Marshall Hall, Patrick Hastings, Norman Birkett, often defended murderers for fees paid by newspapers who bought the exclusive story of the murderer for publication after trial.

In 1966 the B.B.C. cross-examined a witness of the Aberfan disaster on the dangers of uninspected coal tips the night before Parliament set up a tribunal of inquiry which the Prime Minister had already promised. An interdepartmental committee chaired by Lord Justice Salmon was constituted and reported in 1969 that the law of contempt should apply to tribunals of inquiry once they were appointed, and that interviews with witnesses which would affect the inquiry amounted to contempt.[22]

WHEN IT IS CONTEMPT TO CRITICIZE A JUDGE

The law of contempt imposes other restraints on freedom of comment in relation to the administration of justice, the justification for which demands careful consideration. In certain circumstances it is contempt to criticize a judge. If a judge's character is blackened he can sue for defamation in the same way as anybody else : there is no need for a special crime of contempt in order to protect his reputation. It is desirable that the performance of judges be subject to examination and comment; even more obviously the accuracy of the law laid down by them in their decisions should be the object of fearless scrutiny. Such freedom to criticize is essential if the high quality of judicial administration is to be maintained. It is a fact that English judges are criticized less openly and severely than those in many other common-law countries. This may be not because such criticism would necessarily be a crime, but because critics are unsure what the law of contempt is and especially how it will be applied by judges confronted with an alleged crime against one of their brethren. It will be recalled that contempts are summary offences tried by judges without a jury.

In 1900 Mr Justice Darling warned the Press before he heard a particular case that, if they published obscene matter given in evidence, he would make it his business to see that the law of obscenity was enforced against them. After the trial ended, an article was published in a local newspaper which stated :

> No newspaper can exist upon its merits, a condition from which the Bench, happily for Mr Justice Darling, is exempt. Mr Justice Darling would do well to master the duties of his own profession before undertaking the regulation of another.

The publisher was convicted of contempt because of this 'scurrilous personal abuse' of the judge.[23] In 1928 Dr Marie Stopes lost a libel action which arose out of the refusal of the *Daily Telegraph* to publish her advertisement advocating birth control. The *New Statesman* said of this trial that Mr

Justice Avory allowed prejudice against her views to influence his summing up and that 'an individual owning to such views as those of Dr Stopes cannot apparently hope for a fair hearing in a Court presided over by Mr Justice Avory'. The editor was found guilty of contempt.[24] These two cases establish that to abuse a judge or impute unfairness to him is the crime of contempt. Lord Hewart's reason for convicting the editor of the *New Statesman* was that 'the gravamen of the offence was that by lowering his authority it interfered with the performance of his judicial duties'. The court did not consider whether the attack was justified. It is thought that the law of contempt rightly condemns unjustified allegations of corruption or partiality. But why should it be a crime if the publisher can show that his comment was fair on the facts disclosed? In 1959 a Committee of 'Justice' under the chairmanship of Lord Shawcross held that such allegations, however true, should be punished as contempt[25] on the ground that complaints should be made only to the Lord Chancellor and members of Parliament, and that the Bar can be relied on to keep the judges within bounds. But the rules of parliamentary debate ordinarily prevent the casting of reflections on judges, and one has not encountered many recent examples of junior counsel successfully resisting domineering judges in the course of trials.

At the same time, the Committee of 'Justice' strongly recommended that fair criticism of a judge should not be discouraged; it had in mind commenting on his competence in the light of the law laid down by him. And it is the law that such criticisms may legitimately be made. The relevant case is one of many which show how fortunate it is that the Privy Council has had jurisdiction over appeals on contempts from overseas, for to that court we owe most of the wise restrictions and illuminating decisions appertaining to contempt. (English appellate courts in the past made no contribution because, as we have seen, no appeal to them used to lie against convictions for contempt.) When a newspaper editor in Trinidad who published a reasoned article on the human element in fixing the length of sentences was convicted of contempt by the local court, he exercised his right under the colonial law to appeal to the Judicial Committee of the Privy Council.[26] Lord Atkin, holding that the editor was the victim of a substantial miscarriage of justice, said.[27]

But whether the authority and position of an individual judge, or the due administration of justice, is concerned, no wrong is committed by any member of the public who exercises the ordinary right of criticizing, in good faith, in private or public, the public act done in the seat of justice. The path of criticism is a public way: the wrong-headed are permitted to err therein: provided that members of the public abstain from imputing improper motives to those taking part in the administration of justice, and are genuinely exercising a right of criticism, and not acting in malice or attempting to impair the administration of justice, they are immune. Justice is not a cloistered virtue: she must be allowed to suffer the scrutiny and respectful, even though outspoken, comments of ordinary men.

This judgment has been recognized as authoritative both in the courts and by the Lord Chancellor in the debate in the House of Lords on the Administration of Justice Bill, 1960. Such freedom is clearly necessary. The law cannot be improved if experts are not free to criticize it in the light of current decisions. Suppose that an appeal to the House of Lords is pending and yet legislation on the subject-matter of the case is being proposed. It is undesirable that newspapers should feel themselves constrained – as has happened – by fear of contempt proceedings from publishing letters on the subject. Suppose, too, that a newspaper feels that it can only usefully discuss the vexed and difficult problem of sentencing with reference to a case which is newsworthy at the time of the article : for instance it might wish to consider the crime of abortion in the light of a sentence of imprisonment just given.

On the discussion so far it might appear that there is a clear-cut distinction : an attack on the man is punished but criticism of his output in the shape of his judicial utterances is allowed. But look at the next case.[28] The magazine *Truth* said of Lord Justice Slesser, when he was trying a case against the Minister of Labour arising out of an Act of Parliament which he had steered through the House of Commons when Attorney-General in the previous Labour Government, that 'he can hardly be altogether unbiased about legislation of this type'. The editor was convicted and fined for contempt. Yet this was a reasoned observation. The court brought it within the rule that the judge's partiality was assailed, and so good faith and fair comment were irrelevant. In the context was there not force in the accused's contention that he was merely pointing out what is generally recognized : the dangers of *unconscious* bias in specific situations? The court's reasoning is obvious : this was an accusation of partiality and must be punished. It is submitted that the result is not just : a fair criticism of judicial competence is allowed, but a reasoned and reasonable speculation about a judge's unconscious bias is a crime. The evil results from the sharp distinction between allegations of corruption and partiality on the one hand, and of incompetence on the other. Ordinarily no harm will be done by treating as contempts wild and abusive allegations of judicial corruption. Such attacks should remain illegal : the defect of the present law is that judges can convict even though the accuracy or fairness of complaints of partiality is conclusively proved. In fairness to Lord Justice Slesser he has since recounted that the editor of *Truth* was deliberately committed for contempt behind his back because the powers that be rightly surmised that he would have stopped the contempt proceedings if possible : he could never find out who 'they' were who insisted that the public interest demanded the editor's committal.[29]

It is believed that the judges today would not follow the line taken in the *Slesser* case, and that honest criticism of judicial performance may be made with impunity provided that it does not amount to scurrilous abuse. In 1968 Mr Quintin Hogg made an inaccurate criticism in *Punch* of court decisions on gaming. The Court of Appeal held that he was not guilty of contempt, saying that 'no criticism of a judgment, however vigorous, can amount to contempt of court, providing it keeps within the limits of reasonable courtesy and good faith'.[30] Commenting in 1967 on a *Guardian* leader critical of the sentences imposed on Greek embassy demonstrators, Lord Chief Justice Parker said when dismissing their appeals that 'the Press is free to comment responsibly on verdicts and sentences, and that this freedom is a valuable safeguard and should not be curtailed'.[31]

In 1970 there was widespread severe criticism of the judgment of Mr Justice Melford Stevenson in the trial of the Cambridge University undergraduates with respect to the Garden House Hotel, but no contempt proceedings ensued.

A highly critical book on the judge's conduct of the *Stephen Ward* trial was published without contempt proceedings being brought. The public scandal of the conviction of Miss Sweet under the Dangerous Drugs Act 1965 (a teacher who owned but did not live in the house let off in flats and in which the police found tenants in possession of cannabis although the police agreed she did not know this) would not have been righted by the House of Lords in 1969 but for the campaign of *The Times* and other newspapers against the Divisional Court below.[32]

There have been suggestions that newspapers can commit criminal contempt even though they do not prejudice a fair trial or impute corruption or partiality to a judge : i.e. if they hinder the activities of the police. In the judgment against the *Scottish Daily Mail* Lord Clyde said that 'once a crime has been suspected and once the criminal authorities are investigating they and they alone have the duty to do the investigating'. The inference is that contempt is committed if the police are hindered while attempting the detection of crime. It would be unfortunate if this extension were accepted. It is not concerned with ensuring a fair trial ; it rests on the argument that the administration of justice extends beyond that which takes place in the courtroom to the crime-detecting activities of the police force. The objection is the greater when it is seen that such a contempt would be committed however innocent the newspaper, for it does not fall within those exemptions for innocent publications contained in the 1960 Act which we have previously examined. If the police showed that a consequence of the newspaper's investigation of a crime for which there was no known suspect was that they were impeded, that would be enough. Some of the language of Lord Hewart in the first case against the *Evening Standard* is rather similar. It is to be hoped that the English judges will not – though there is nothing to prevent them, unfortunately – extend the law of criminal contempt in this way. There is a separate crime of obstructing the police in the execution of their.duty; if a reporter has committed that crime let him stand trial in the ordinary way. Otherwise, the law of contempt should not interfere when there is no prejudice to any person whose arrest is known to be imminent. After all, newspapers occasionally rise above their usual level of ineffectiveness in this respect by actually uncovering some criminal scandal. This is a public service which, within proper limits, should not be discouraged by instituting criminal proceedings against them.

Until the passing of the Administration of Justice Act in 1960 English law had one unenviable distinction. It was the only legal system in Western Europe which ever denied a civilian sent to prison a right of appeal. The reference is, of course, to the law of criminal contempt. Despite some judicial opposition in the course of its passage through the House of Lords, the Bill now provides a right of appeal to those convicted of contempt. At the same time the Act introduces a right for the prosecution not found in criminal law generally; the applicant for committal for contempt has an equal right to appeal against a finding of not guilty. Why this one type of accused person should be prejudiced in this way is not clear. The Act leaves untouched all the other procedural aspects of contempt : trial remains summary without a jury, and punishments are without limit. The suggestion that no prosecution be made without the consent of either the Attorney-General or the Director of Public Prosecutions has not been implemented by legislation, although in practice the Attorney-General is now the usual originator of such proceedings. There seems no good reason why all these peculiarities of the law of contempt should remain; those who prejudice trials should be dealt with by the ordinary criminal law for the offence of interfering with the administration of justice.

RESTRICTIONS ON REPORTING OF CASES

We have seen that a person charged with an indictable offence first has his charge investigated by magistrates whose task is to decide whether to commit him for trial. Newspapers used to be free to report everything given in evidence at this hearing and did report sensational cases at great length. The prosecution of Dr Adams on a charge of murdering a patient raised in an acute form the much debated question of whether this freedom is consistent with that overriding need to ensure a fair trial which has been seen to explain much of the law of criminal contempt. Evidence was given before the magistrates that two other patients of the accused had died in peculiar circumstances while under his care. This evidence was not, and could not have been, given at the trial. Is it not clear that the jury might have been prejudiced by having read newspaper accounts of this evidence?

As a sequel to that case a Departmental Committee on Proceedings before Examining Justices was set up and in 1958 proposed extensive changes. Eventually their proposals were substantially embodied in the Criminal Justice Act 1967. By section 3 it is made generally unlawful to publish any report of committal proceedings, apart from the details of the court, names of the parties, a summary of the charges and the decision whether to commit. The evidence may not be published until the end of the committal proceedings if the accused is not committed, and not until the end of the trial if he is committed. If any of the accused asks for the reporting restrictions to be lifted the magistrates must allow full publicity for the entire proceedings. Of course none of these restrictions applies to the trial proper. At the same time the Act provides that the magistrates must sit in public unless they consider that the ends of justice would not be served as regards the whole or part of the committal proceedings. Although these changes have obviously curbed the powers of Press and broadcasting they strike a fair balance between the demands of justice and the freedom of Press and television.

Many judicial proceedings take place in chambers, i.e. in private in the rooms of the judge or some other judicial officer. These are often matters preliminary to trial itself, but not infrequently the final hearing of certain types of case. Judges have often held that newspapers could not report such matters, although the extent to which such reports amounted to contempt was disputed. For example, Mr Justice Paull suggested in the course of the protracted litigation between the Duke and the Duchess of Argyll in the early 1960s (which aroused so much Press attention) that it was essential for the administration of justice that hearings in chambers should not be reported, because they concerned only the parties. The Act of 1960 has clarified the law concerning reporting such proceedings by enacting that such reports shall not, subject to certain exceptions, in themselves constitute contempt, and has thereby rejected the views of Mr Justice Paull. The most important exceptions are proceedings relating to wardship or adoption or maintenance of children, matters relating to mentally disabled persons, matters of national security, or matters relating to a secret process which is in issue in the proceedings. In 1969 the High Court dismissed an application by foster-parents to prevent the B.B.C. putting in their *Cause for Concern* television series a programme entitled *The Case of the Spanish Parents*.

There are also important restrictions on the reporting of some other types of proceedings. Reporters may attend divorce trials but they are prohibited from publishing details of the evidence given. It must be remembered also that a vast number of legal disputes are settled behind closed doors by arbitration – one of the main reasons for the popularity of arbitration is its privacy. Judges, too, often request the Press not to report particular parts of a case – the Podola murder case was an example. The Press will comply, although it is not obliged to do so.

In 1965 the Press uncovered the fact that judges were sometimes sending persons to prison for contempt after holding a secret hearing in the absence of the Press and public. It took only a six weeks' campaign by the Press, despite judicial support for this practice of secrecy, to secure an amendment to the law, so that the details of any such case must in future be given in open court.

Contempt of Parliament

We meet here for the first time this separate branch of English law, the law and custom of Parliament. Although this law does not derive either from statutes or from cases by the courts, it is equally binding on members of Parliament and on ordinary citizens. It gives many privileges to members of Parliament both collectively and individually. There is an analogy with contempt of court in that a citizen who is in breach of such a parliamentary privilege commits a contempt. He may also commit a contempt even though his conduct does not involve any breach of privilege; if, for example, he casts aspersions on the dignity of the House of Commons. We shall see that the procedures for dealing with these contempts bear some resemblance to those for contempt of court. Again, only one particular class of contempts will here be dealt with : those which restrict the citizen's freedom of expression.

Both Houses have always maintained the right to prohibit the publication of debates or other proceedings in Parliament. In the eighteenth century John Wilkes, resentful of this aristocratic impatience with the pressure of public opinion, determined to challenge Parliament. The *London Evening Post* had started to print reports of parliamentary debates; in 1771 the House of Commons sent a messenger of the Serjeant-at-Arms to take the printer to the House. When the printer objected the messenger used force : Wilkes, as a city magistrate, convicted the messenger of assault. The House of Commons duly put Wilkes's fellow magistrates in the Tower for this, but Wilkes successfully defied its efforts to bring him to the House. The upshot was that this attempt to muzzle reporting failed, and Parliament no longer attempts to restrict fair reporting of its proceedings; but when its proceedings are reported in bad faith it has continued to hold the publishers liable to punishment, by virtue of the law of Parliament.

Parliament still, however, effectively curtails the activities of the Press in other ways by virtue of contempt powers, as a selection of examples will demonstrate. In 1956 the *Sunday Graphic* voiced its disapproval of the attitude to Egypt of Mr Lewis, M.P.: in an article it exhorted those who shared its disapproval to telephone him to that effect, and gave his private telephone number. In consequence Mr Lewis was inundated with calls which prevented him from having other important telephonic conversations on political matters. The House of Commons found the *Sunday Graphic* guilty of contempt of Parliament on the ground that it instigated others to molest an M.P. while in the execution of his duties. In 1960 Mr Pannell, M.P. for Leeds, asked a question in the House about Fascist propaganda leaflets left in telephone books in the Leeds area, and referred in his question to the possibility of instituting criminal proceedings against those responsible. He then received a letter signed with the name of Colin Jordan, organizer, British National Party, saying:

No doubt when you clamour for our prosecution you will be commended by the Jewish civilians of Leeds and their coloured allies for your zeal. You would do well to take into account the possibility that in the resurgent Britain of tomorrow you and your fellow renegades will face trial for complicity in the coloured invasion and Jewish control of our land.

The House of Commons referred this to its Committee of Privileges, which found the letter to be a breach of privilege in that it was an attempt by improper means to deter him from the performance of further parliamentary duties in relation to the leaflets. In 1968 the editor of the *Observer* was condemned for contempt because it published evidence about chemical warfare given in private to the House of

Commons Select Committee on Science and Technology which an M.P. had handed to it for publication with an assurance that no breach of parliamentary privilege was involved.

The House of Commons takes a serious view of any newspaper comments which reflect on the character of the House. The asserted justification is like that used for some contempts of court : that the respect due to the House is thereby diminished and consequently the performance of its functions interfered with. The *World's Press News* published in 1947 an article written by an M.P. on how newspapers could and did persuade M.P.s by buying them drinks to sell secret information acquired in party meetings. The publisher was reprimanded by the House of Commons for breach of privilege : his allegation of insobriety on the part of M.P.s was castigated as a gross breach of privilege. It further transpired that the M.P. who wrote the article was one of the M.P.s who was selling this information to the Press. The House expelled him.[33]

The introduction of petrol rationing after the Suez expedition of 1956 brought more cases. The *Sunday Express* published an article which suggested that politicians had allowed themselves to be unduly favoured over supplementary petrol. This was held by the House of Commons to be a grave contempt on the part of the editor.[34] The editor's contention that he merely wrote of *politicians*, not M.P.s, was rejected. The House found that the article was, *inter alia*, intended to hold it up to public obloquy as a result of its alleged failure to protest against unfair discrimination of which M.P.s were the beneficiaries. The London *Evening News* published a cartoon which stated that it was very thoughtful of M.P.s to look after their supplementary petrol allocations : this was also held to be a contempt. The editor of the *Romford Recorder* was found guilty for heading an article 'M.P.s Too Kind To Themselves'; he made an ineffectual protest to the Press Council that he was not even allowed to defend himself.[35] In a B.B.C. *Any Questions* programme Mrs Mary Stocks said that 'the only persons who are reasonably well off under the rationing scheme are M.P.s and potential M.P.s who are nursing constituencies and who apparently have as much petrol as they wish to drive round their constituency.' The Speaker ruled that it was a *prima facie* case of breach of privilege, but the Committee of Privileges in the House held otherwise : this criticism was neither intended to hold the House up to public obloquy nor calculated to diminish the respect due to it and so to lessen its authority.[36]

The severity of the parliamentary law of contempt becomes evident when its procedures are examined. A party may be found guilty without having a hearing, as happened in the case of the editor of the *Romford Recorder*, on the ground that where the breach of privilege is clear a hearing is a waste of time. The House can issue a warrant for the arrest of anybody whom it suspects to have committed a contempt and have him arrested without giving him any reason. They may so arrest him in order to require him to appear before the Committee of Privileges. There he may find himself cross-examined by several Queen's counsel, but he himself is not entitled to be represented by counsel, or by anyone else, and still less may he insist on cross-examining witnesses. When the House has found him guilty, it is its normal practice to summon him to the Bar of the House. He is expected, not to say invited, humbly to apologize : his punishment is likely to be the more severe if he does not. The powers of punishment are wide. There is a power to commit to prison. High Court judges, lawyers, sheriffs and magistrates have all found themselves imprisoned under this power. In 1955 two Australian journalists were imprisoned by the House of Representatives of the Australian Federal Parliament because of newspaper articles. In the opinion of the previous Clerk of the House of Commons, Sir Edward Fellowes, in 1956, the indispensability of this power to commit to prison has been amply demonstrated by experience :[37] this argument is difficult to accept in view of the rarity of the occasions in modern times when the House ever commits to prison. The House of Lords has frequently imposed fines, but the House of Commons has not done so for two centuries. Where the offence is not so grave as to warrant any of these punishments the offender is generally reprimanded or admonished by the Lord Chancellor or the Speaker; if he is not in attendance he may be ordered to be taken into the custody of the Serjeant and brought to the Bar of the House.

Is there any need for this crime of contempt of Parliament at all in so far as it bears on freedom of expression? If an M.P.'s character is attacked he has his remedy in an action for defamation. Serious attacks on institutions of government may be punishable as libel, either seditious [38] or defamatory.[39] The forbidding of reports of proceedings is an anachronism. Unlike contempt of court, contempt of Parliament does not, of course, prejudice litigants. What gap in civil and criminal law is there which needs to be filled by this crime? The case for it seems to stand or fall on a residue of instances where Parliament is hampered in the efficient discharge of its duties : the conviction of the editor of the *Sunday Graphic* for instigating the molestation of an M.P. is an example. The fact that such undesirable interferences with the due discharge of parliamentary functions do not fall foul of the criminal law indicates a small gap in judicial machinery, which ought to be filled. One disquieting tendency exemplified in the breaches of privilege alleged in the 1964–5 parliamentary session is for complaints to be of a partisan political nature and to be debated in the House of Commons in this way. The member who complained of the *Eastern Daily Press*'s saying that question time was being frittered away by infuriating supplementaries might well have looked at the ruling in 1948 in a case involving the *Daily Mail* [40] where the Committee on Privileges stressed that the law of parliamentary privilege should not be administered in a way which could discourage the free expression of opinion, however prejudiced or exaggerated the opinions.

Although there are gaps in the criminal law, it does not in the least follow that offenders should be tried according to the present procedures. No Englishman should be imprisoned without having had the right to defend himself, to be legally represented, to call and cross-examine witnesses, and to be tried by an impartial body, not by his accusers. The House of Commons ought not to treat trials of citizens as one of its functions : disciplining its members is one thing, punishing outsiders is another. It may well be difficult for the House of Commons to behave like a court : the solution then is for it to relinquish these powers of punishing citizens, by imprisonment or otherwise, just as it has surrendered its jurisdiction over disputed elections to the judges. The present arrangements have survived only because in recent times Parliament has exercised these powers of punishment with moderation. Let the ordinary courts decide when the freedom of the Press should be curtailed in the interests of the legislature and let the accused have his trial by jury in those courts of law.

In December 1967 the House of Commons Select Committee on Parliamentary Privilege recommended some modest improvements especially on procedure while proposing that the House retain, and indeed extend, its penal powers.[41] The Committee rejected the suggestion that the power to imprison or fine be transferred to the courts or other independent tribunal. No steps have been taken to implement these proposals, despite wide Press support for the procedural improvements recommended.

It may be wondered where the ordinary courts stand at present in relation to the powers of Parliament. These parliamentary powers, it has been seen, do not stem from statute, so that no doctrine of parliamentary sovereignty inhibits the courts. Each House asserts its right to be the judge of the extent of its own privileges, while admitting that it could not create new privileges. The courts treat the law and custom of Parliament as part of the ordinary law of the land. Consequently they reserve to themselves the right to declare the extent of parliamentary privileges and they reject the claim of Parliament to be the sole and exclusive judge of its privileges. At any given moment Parliament may claim that it has a certain privilege and the courts may deny it : there is no machinery for resolving any such dispute. Conflicts are avoided nowadays because the courts lean over backwards not to interfere in parliamentary affairs.

In the nineteenth century there was a head-on conflict. When one Stockdale had the temerity to bring and win an action for libel against Hansard for a defamatory statement contained in a parliamentary report, both he and his solicitor were put in prison.[42] Chief Justice Denman rejected Hansard's defence that there could be no libel because this was a matter of parliamentary privilege, over which the courts had no jurisdiction. The judge was, however, powerless to protect the prisoners, Stockdale and his solicitor, because the House, as it was perfectly entitled to, omitted to state the reasons for imprisonment on the face of the warrants – the courts cannot challenge a warrant of Parliament which is not illegal on its face; had the warrant set out the facts, the court would have been free to reach its independent decision on whether the imprisonment was a lawful exercise of parliamentary privilege.[43] The sheriffs of Middlesex were required by the court to levy execution for the £600 damages awarded against Hansard, but they sought to appease both court and Parliament by holding the cash which they duly obtained from Hansard. A court order compelled them to hand over the cash to Stockdale. For doing so the House of Commons imprisoned them. This lively story shows that Parliament has some effective weapons to use against those who rely on decisions of a court whose authority it will not accept. But the fact that Parliament might get its way is not equivalent to an authoritative declaration of law in its favour. Nothing has happened since the Hansard affair to resolve the kind of conflict which arose there.

CHAPTER 7

FREEDOM OF RELIGION

RELIGIOUS EXPRESSION

DURING the Middle Ages the Church, not the State, controlled the exercise of religious worship and expression of opinion on religious matters. The State recognized and obeyed the law of the Church, which, before the Reformation, was the papal canon law; the State merely helped the Church to enforce the Church's decrees. The link between Church and State remained very close even after the Reformation. The Tudor principle was that they had common objects : the Church should help the State to maintain its authority, and the State should help the Church to punish nonconformists and infidels. The king was the supreme head of both. The Church exercised its monopoly of control over matters of religious expression through its ecclesiastical courts. These courts had power to fine persons for not attending church, or for celebrating mass. They had exclusive jurisdiction over heresy, and as late as 1612, in the case of Legate, a heretic was burned in pursuance of a judgment of an ecclesiastical court.

Blasphemy and other Legal Restraints

The ordinary courts first interfered in 1618.[1] They claimed jurisdiction on that occasion by analogy with the offence of sedition : if the accused voiced his opinions on religion in such a way as to threaten a disturbance of the public peace, that was the concern of the ordinary courts. By the end of the seventeenth century the ordinary courts were exercising this jurisdiction regularly over blasphemous publications. Starting with Taylor's case in 1676,[2] they justified their jurisdiction by the claim that Christianity was part of the laws of

England and therefore any reproach of Christianity was an offence against the common law of the land. Prosecutions for blasphemy were quite frequent in the eighteenth century, too: the publishers of Thomas Paine's *The Age of Reason* were among the victims; later the publishers of Shelley's *Queen Mab* were convicted.

The last two hundred years or so have witnessed a complete undermining of the dominant position of the Church. It is true that there is still an established Church, with the sovereign as the head, but these two constitutional features are but meaningless survivals of the old political order. As we shall see, all sects are protected by the law, and the State exercises little coercive authority in religious matters. Parliament gave the lead by passing Acts which gradually removed the disabilities of other religions. A critical factor was the rapid growth of the spirit of toleration among educated classes in the eighteenth and nineteenth centuries. Publications such as Locke's *Letters Concerning Toleration* and Defoe's *The Shortest Way with the Dissenters* helped to create this new climate of opinion.

The reward of the Protestant nonconformists for their contribution to the cause of the Glorious Revolution was the enactment of the Toleration Act of 1689, which removed most of their disabilities and legalized their meetings for worship. In face of the opposition of George III, Burke and his followers were subsequently unable at the same time to sweep away the discriminatory laws against Roman Catholics: for some, Roman Catholicism was not a religious error but a political danger. In 1813 the Unitarians were given the same privileges as had been given to the other Protestant nonconformists in 1689. In 1829 Parliament, no doubt influenced by the fear of revolution in Ireland, passed the Roman Catholic Emancipation Act, whereby Roman Catholics were relieved of their disabilities, allowed to sit in Parliament and made eligible for most public offices. In 1846 Jews were relieved from the disabilities to which they had remained subject. Many of the disabilities had been imposed by requiring forms of oath which the members of particular

sects could not take. When the Test Acts were finally repealed in 1828 the taking of the sacrament ceased to be a
prerequisite for office. The campaign of Bradlaugh in the
courts and in the House of Commons in the 1880s resulted in
the removal of disabilities for atheists : the Oaths Act of 1888
permitted an atheist to become a member of Parliament
upon affirming his allegiance – an oath of allegiance ceased
to be insisted on. The same Act also permits witnesses in
court to affirm, instead of being sworn on oath, when they
are atheists or when to take an oath is contrary to their religious beliefs.

Parliament gave one other lead which was destined to
facilitate a change towards a correspondingly liberal attitude
on the part of the courts. In 1792 it passed the Libel Act,
whereby the whole matter in issue on an indictment for libel
was to be left to the jury; and libel included blasphemous
libel. In the nineteenth century judges and juries were increasingly reluctant to accept the logical implications for
the crime of blasphemy of the 'Christianity is part of the law
of England' formula. The judgment of Lord Chief Justice
Coleridge in 1883 was the watershed. He rejected the principle that Christianity was part of the law of England and
told the jury that 'if the decencies of controversy are observed, even the fundamentals of religion may be attacked
without the writer being guilty of blasphemy'.[3] Then in 1917
the House of Lords had to decide whether the objects of a
company were criminal because they necessarily denied the
truth of Christianity.[4] The House of Lords held that those
objects were not rendered criminal merely because they were
in conflict with Christian doctrine, and that the crime of
blasphemy was not committed by honestly denying the truth
of Christianity. The crux is the manner in which the
blasphemy is published, not its content. Lord Sumner said :[5]

Our courts of law ... do not ... punish irreligious words as
offences against God.... They dealt with such words for their
manner, their violence, or ribaldry, or more fully stated, for their
tendency to endanger the peace then and there, to deprave
public morality generally, to shake the fabric of society, and to be

a cause of civil strife. The words, as well as the acts, which tend to endanger society differ from time to time in proportion as society is stable or insecure in fact, or is believed by its reasonable members to be open to assault.... In the present day reasonable men do not apprehend the dissolution or the downfall of society because religion is publicly assailed by methods not scandalous.... The fact that opinion grounded on experience has moved one way does not in law preclude the possibility of its moving on fresh experience in the other; nor does it bind succeeding generations, when conditions have again changed. After all, the question whether a given opinion is a danger to society is a question of the times and is a question of fact.

There has been only one subsequent prosecution for blasphemy of the slightest importance. In 1921 one Gott was charged with selling pamphlets in a London thoroughfare entitled 'God and Gott' and 'Rib Ticklers, or Questions for Parsons'.[6] The Court of Criminal Appeal held that it was not enough that the selling of these tracts might provoke a man of strong religious feelings; the issue was whether they might provoke a breach of the peace by anybody sympathetic to Christian ideals, even though not a practising Christian.

This account of the development of the law of blasphemy furnishes an excellent illustration of the workings of the English judicial system. The theory is that the courts are bound by previous decisions, and that only Parliament can alter the law. Yet there is no doubt that what would have been blasphemy in the seventeenth and eighteenth centuries does not constitute that crime today, although Parliament has not altered the law of blasphemy. It will be noted how anxious Lord Sumner was to stress that the courts had not amended the law of blasphemy. We have seen how originally the courts were able to wrest control of blasphemy from the ecclesiastical courts by emphasizing their jurisdiction over matters affecting public order. Then the ordinary courts were soon to subscribe to the doctrine that any challenge to Christianity was blasphemous because Christianity was the law of the land. More recently, that view has become completely out of harmony with public opinion, whereupon the courts have rejected the contention that mere denial of Christianity is the crime of blasphemy. They purport to conceal this change in the law by turning the wheel full circle and saying that the essence of blasphemy is and always has been the publication of material in such a way as to shake the whole fabric of society and to provoke breaches of the peace. Liberty to attack Christian doctrine does not now endanger the safety of the state, so that those who voice the anti-Christian opinions do not commit the offence.

What of the future? The judges have left themselves free to take account of changes of public attitude by holding that if to express anti-Christian opinions in a certain way at a given time does in fact in the opinion of a jury shake the fabric of that society or provoke a reasonable element in it to breaches of the peace, this could still be punishable as blasphemy. This no doubt explains why Governments have from time to time refused to abolish the crime of blasphemy.[7] A more practical issue is whether the protection, however limited, which the law of blasphemy at present affords against attacks on the Church of England extends to other religious denominations, whether Christian or not. In 1838 Baron Alderson held that a scurrilous attack on a Roman Catholic nunnery could not be blasphemy.[8] He said that 'a person may, without being liable to prosecution for it, attack Judaism, or Mahomedanism, or even any sect of the Christian religion (save the established religion of the country)'.[9] But the reason for his decision was that the Church of England was the established religion and so part of the constitution of the country. We have seen that that idea is now exploded. Are we to say that an attack on any Christian doctrine, or indeed on any other religion, can be blasphemous provided that it is calculated to endanger the public peace? One can scarcely believe that protection of Christianity is now confined to the Church of England. Whether one could commit blasphemy by handing out ribald anti-Muslim tracts in the Arab district of an English seaport is a more debatable question.

Restraints outside the Law

The discussion so far has been of legal restraints on freedom of religious expression. In practice, though not by force of law, there are other restraints. Until recently the B.B.C. has rarely allowed the expression of rationalist views, and when it did the protest from the Churches used to be loud and long. We have seen that both the B.B.C. and the I.T.A. have religious advisory committees, and it would seem that they both strike a fair balance between the various Christian sects in their quite extensive religious programmes. As we have also seen, what is frowned on is the introduction of religious themes in other programmes – an I.T.V. play in which a bishop seduced an actress had to be cancelled at the last moment in 1971. Despite the large number of topical discussions now broadcast in such programmes as *Twenty-four Hours*, *Panorama*, *This Week*, and *Ten O'Clock*, it is remarkable how rarely controversial religious matters are the subject of discussion. The I.T.A. is not allowed to broadcast religious advertisements but in 1970 allowed a parson to preach a brief sermon in an advertisement for Blue Band margarine. Both the B.B.C. and the I.T.A. are restrained from interfering with attendance at religious services in that only adult programmes are permitted between 2 p.m. and 4 p.m. on Sundays, and that no broadcasts other than religious ones are permitted between 6.15 p.m. and 7.25 p.m. on Sundays. In 1964 the Government refused to introduce in Government contracts a condition that firms make no inquiry into the religion of applicants for employment 'because to do so would introduce questions of religious faith and conscience into commercial relations between Government departments and industry'.

RELIGIOUS DISABILITIES

We have seen that the restrictions formerly imposed on non-conformists, Roman Catholics, and Jews have successively been swept away. Nor will the Home Secretary in the exercise of his discretionary power to admit aliens apply religious tests, as he made clear in 1946 when a question was asked in the House of Commons about the entry into this country of members of the Oxford Group. A very few restrictions remain. The sovereign must be a member of the Church of England. A person who marries a Roman Catholic is excluded from succession to the Throne. A Roman Catholic probably cannot be Lord Chancellor. Clergy of the Church of England, Church of Scotland, and the Roman Catholic Church are disqualified from sitting and voting as members of the House of Commons — bishops of the Church of England have of course twenty-six seats in the House of Lords.

Although the law then does not generally discriminate against a person because of his religious beliefs, it often refuses to make special allowances for them. An accused's religious objection to the use of medicine will be ignored in deciding whether he is guilty of criminal neglect of somebody in his care.[10] Suppose the defendant has injured a Christian Scientist and contends that the plaintiff's recovery has been retarded through his failure to have surgical treatment : it is believed that the plaintiff (where he claims damages) would not be able to plead that it was reasonable for him as a Christian Scientist not to have such treatment if a reasonable non-Christian Scientist would have had it. Suppose, too, that where a doctor exercising reasonable skill would have advised a patient to have an abortion because the death of the patient is otherwise most likely to occur, and on moral grounds a Roman Catholic doctor neither performs this operation nor advises the patient to consult another doctor: the doctor's Roman Catholicism will not afford a defence either in an action of negligence, or, probably, in proceedings for manslaughter.

A certain intolerance towards non-Christian religions and customs persists in the law relating to divorce, which is really only equipped to deal with a Christian monogamous type of marriage. Consequently the courts will not dissolve a polygamous marriage : they will not recognize such a marriage as one in respect of which they are willing to exercise jurisdiction in divorce. A man and a woman domiciled in Nigeria married there according to a customary law which permitted polygamy, although neither of them, being Christian, intended to take another spouse. After settling in England they went through a marriage ceremony at a register office. The court held in subsequent divorce proceedings that it could dissolve the English marriage but not the Nigerian one. Presumably the parties remained married according to the law of their domicile.[11] The hardship of this rule is best illustrated by the fact that it prevents magistrates from entertaining proceedings for maintenance by a wife whose marriage was at least potentially polygamous.[12] A wife of a polygamous marriage whose husband has been killed may be severely handicapped if she wishes to claim damages under the Fatal Accidents Acts against those responsible for her husband's death. Claims for National Insurance benefits under social security legislation may also fail for the same reason.

Where a person wishes to create a trust, the objects must be consistent with the policy of the law – otherwise the trustee will be forbidden to carry out the trust at all. Before the passing of the Toleration Act trusts for noncomformist purposes were therefore void. It was not until the twentieth century that the House of Lords overruled earlier decisions and held that trusts for anti-Christian purposes[13] or for masses for the dead were valid.[14] A gift to the Royal College of Surgeons which excludes Roman Catholics from studentships is not contrary to public policy.[15] Even if a trust is consistent with public policy it may still be necessary to prove that its purpose is charitable in the eyes of the law. If there is an element of uncertainty in the objects of the trust the trust will fail, unless it is charitable, when its funds will be applied for charitable purposes which correspond as nearly as possible with what appear to the court to have been the testator's intentions. A trust cannot ordinarily be devoted to a particular purpose for ever where the effect would be to prevent alienation of the property – for this would infringe the rule against perpetuities – but gifts to charities are not subject to this rule. Moreover charities are exempt from income tax. The importance of a gift being held to be charitable is obvious. Trusts for the advancement of the Christian religion are charitable, and so is a trust for any shade of Christian object. A trust for non-Christian religious purposes would probably also be charitable although the law is not clear on this point. On the other hand, a gift for the establishment of a college for training spiritualistic mediums was held not charitable, and in the circumstances the gift therefore failed.[16] With present high rates of taxation, the effective worth of a valid, though not charitable, gift is greatly curtailed.

In 1969 the Court of Appeal held that the Home Secretary was entitled to refuse alien scientologists permission to stay in this country if he decided as a matter of policy that the practices of this religious sect were harmful to society.[17] Many hundreds of scientology delegates were banned by the Home Office from entering Britain to attend a congress, and Government employment exchanges were instructed not to refer unemployed persons on their register to vacancies notified by scientology groups. The scientologists unsuccessfully appealed to the European Commission on Human Rights.[18] In 1970 the Court of Appeal upheld the refusal of the Registrar-General to register a scientology chapel as a place of meeting for religious worship : the practice of scientology was not 'religious worship'.[19]

EDUCATION

Traditionally, organized education throughout the Western world was religious education. It could hardly be otherwise when the education of children meant chiefly study of the word of God. Even in Protestant countries like England, where the identification of Church and State had, as we have seen, become less close, the basis of education was largely the Bible. Even as late as the Reform Act of 1832 the State did not regard the furnishing of education as a public duty.

Elementary education was in the hands of two societies, the one desiring that religious teaching in the schools should be undenominational and the other seeking to teach the principles of the Church of England. Gradually the State started providing financial assistance, with increasing supervision, until by 1870 it was recognized that elementary education was a national responsibility.

Once the State supports schools out of public funds, controversy on the teaching of religion in them is inevitable. Some countries like the United States found the task of harmonizing multiform creeds impossible and prohibited religious teaching in schools altogether. Sharp though the conflict was between Anglican and Nonconformist, England was less heterogeneous religiously than countries like the United States, and a compromise was eventually worked out, which it was believed met with general satisfaction. The present arrangements, which are developed from the Education Act of 1870 and succeeding Acts, are founded in the Education Act of 1944, as amended. Schools are divided into two main groups, the county schools, established by local education authorities of every category, and the voluntary schools, which were originally erected by the voluntary efforts of persons usually associated with a particular religious sect, whether Church of England, Roman Catholic, or Nonconformist. The problem of welding the voluntary schools into the national system of education is complicated by the inability of the persons owning them to meet the increasing costs of education, for both capital improvement and maintenance, and by the existence of trusts governing the religious instruction to be given in them. Voluntary schools are of two main kinds. In 'aided schools' the managers or governors are responsible for the provision and equipment of the school buildings and for their repair, whereas the local education authority is responsible for running expenses and inside repairs. The Secretary of State for Education and Science makes a direct grant to aided schools of one half the cost of alterations and repairs. 'Controlled schools' are those where all the expense of maintenance, alteration, and repair is borne by the local education authority, the managers or governors having merely provided the premises.

The Act requires in the case of both county and voluntary schools that the school day shall begin with collective worship and that religious instruction be given. No county or voluntary school can impose a condition that the pupil shall attend or abstain from attending any Sunday school or other place of religious worship. A parent retains the right to withdraw his child from either collective worship or religious instruction. The Act then deals with the situation where the parent wishes his child to have some religious instruction which he has arranged for him instead of that from which he has been excused. If the local authority cannot conveniently move him to another school which provides that instruction, they will allow his withdrawal during the necessary periods so long as they are at either the beginning or the end of the school day. In county schools the collective worship must be undenominational and the religious instruction must not include any catechism and must conform to an agreed syllabus. A conference of representatives of religious denominations, teachers, and the local education authority is charged under the Act with the task of settling this syllabus. The Secretary of State for Education and Science has resisted recent pressure from some M.P.s to include courses in humanism as an alternative to religious instruction on the ground that he has no legal power to dictate the content of a school syllabus. It seems even less likely that the Government will heed the minority report of six members of the Plowden Council that religious education should cease to be an obligatory part of the curriculum in primary schools. The fact that the voluntary schools were built subject to trusts which regulated the religious instruction to be given naturally leads the Act to have different rules for them. Ordinarily religious instruction in controlled schools must still conform to the agreed syllabus, but, if the parents of any pupils so request, the managers are to arrange instruction in accordance with the trust deeds or previous practice. The rule is reversed in aided schools where, as a general rule, religious instruction should conform to the trust deed or former practice. For example, when a Roman Catholic school continues to meet out of its own funds one half the cost of repairs and alterations, in return it is recognized that religious instruction will be in Roman Catholicism. Yet, if parents in these aided schools so require, their children must be taught in accordance with an agreed syllabus, unless they can conveniently arrange for them to attend another school where that syllabus is in use.

The regulations concerning appointment of teachers reflect these arrangements. No teacher at a county school is disqualified by reason of his religious opinions, or of his attending or omitting to attend public worship, and no such teacher shall be required to give religious instruction, nor shall his pay or promotion be affected by any of the above factors. Up to one-fifth of teachers at controlled schools are to be 'reserved teachers', competent to give religious instruction in conformity with the trust deed or previous practice. Though these reserved teachers are also appointed and dismissed by the local authority, the managers or governors have the right of veto over their appointment and can require that the local education authority dismiss a reserved teacher who has not given religious instruction satisfactorily. Once again the 'voluntary' school which is not content to provide the premises but also helps to maintain them has the greater power in matters affecting religious teaching. The managers or governors of these aided schools have the power to appoint and dismiss on religious grounds, free from any control by the local education authority, those who provide religious instruction in accordance with the trust deed or former practice.

Section 76 of the Education Act of 1944 provides

In the exercise and performance of all powers and duties conferred and imposed on them by this Act the Minister and local education authorities shall have regard to the general principle that, so far as is compatible with the provision of efficient instruction and training and the avoidance of unreasonable public expenditure, pupils are to be educated in accordance with the wishes of their parents.

To what extent does this section give a parent a right to choose a school for his child? The matter was tested in *Watt* v. *Kesteven County Council* in 1955.[20] The plaintiff, a Roman Catholic, sent his two sons to a Roman Catholic boarding public school. There was no *local authority* grammar school in Stamford where the family lived, but the defendants, in accordance with their duties under the Act, had offered places for the boys at a suitable *independent* non-denominational grammar school in the town. The plaintiff sought to make the authority pay in full the tuition fees at the public school (which were in fact less than the fees at the Stamford school). The Court of Appeal held that the Act imposed no duty to provide free education at any independent school of the parent's choice. They held that Section 76

does not say that pupils must in all cases be educated in accordance with the wishes of their parents. It only lays down a general principle to which the county council must have regard. This leaves it open to the county council to have regard to other things as well, and also to make exceptions to the general principle if it thinks fit to do so. It cannot, therefore, be said that a county council is at fault simply because it does not see fit to comply with the parent's wishes.

There is no doubt that Section 76 was carefully drafted so as to prevent the authorities from being legally answerable should they fail to carry out the parent's wishes about his child's education, and that the court interpreted the statute correctly.

A decision in 1970 went further.[21] Birkenhead Corporation issued a circular to parents informing them that children at Catholic primary schools would be sent only to Catholic secondary schools. Parents who thought other schools more suitable to their children or who preferred a segregated education challenged the legality of the circular. The High Court held that the decision of the education authority was immune from judicial challenge even though it ignored parental views entirely, and even if the policy was unreasonable.

The Act contemplates that an aggrieved parent will forward his complaint to the Minister who will if he thinks it expedient issue an appropriate direction to the local education authority : this is the kind of administrative remedy normally provided where failure on the part of a local authority to perform its duties is in issue. But is it defensible that the aggrieved parent is not entitled to a hearing before the Secretary of State for Education and Science and has no means of knowing what evidence is before the Minister when he proceeds to make his decision?

SUNDAYS

Certain old Acts restricting activities on Sunday remain on the statute book. Of course these are no longer in harmony with contemporary attitudes, but they remain unrepealed because whatever party is in office it always believes that, by tampering with a religious issue, it stands to lose some votes and can hope to gain none. Best known of these Acts is the Sunday Observance Act 1780 which, as subsequently amended, makes it an offence to use a place for public entertainment or amusement on Sundays on admission for money, unless it is a licensed performance of films at a cinema or a musical entertainment falling within the scope of a music licence granted by a local authority or justices of the peace. Many of these licensing authorities have gone out of their way to widen the scope of the Act by attaching conditions to Sunday music licences that no properties or stage costumes or articles of a like nature shall be used. This has driven organizers to use ingenuity in bringing the entertainment within the terms of the licence : a singer may wear a kilt when singing 'Annie Laurie' if, and only if, he is a Scotsman who can claim that it is his normal dress. Still, with the abolition of the system of common informers rather less use of the Act has been made recently. Another curious survival is the Sunday Observance Act 1677 whereby contacts made by tradesmen and artificers on Sundays in the ordinary course of their business are unenforceable *by* them. The courts do not approve of the conduct of those who invoke the Act in order to avoid payment, and construe the Act very narrowly. For instance, in a recent case[22] it was held that the Act did not apply to a contract by a company, even though it was a one-man company. Such contracts are enforceable *against* the tradesman.

Much more modern and important restrictions, and yet also of an unusual character, are those on Sunday trading contained in the Shop Act 1950. Under this Act every shop must be closed throughout Sunday unless it falls within one of the exceptions set out. There are detailed rules about the circumstances in which Jewish shopkeepers may trade on Sunday, and provision for a tribunal constituted after consultation with the London Committee of Deputies of the British Jews to decide whether the shopkeeper is in fact a Jew. Shops are allowed to open for the sale of intoxicating liquors, meals (though fish and chip shops must not open), sweets, refreshments, flowers, fruit and fresh vegetables, fresh milk and cream, medicines, vehicle accessories, newspapers, periodicals, and tobacco. Post offices and undertakers may also be open. Local authorities may make orders allowing shops to open until not later than 10 a.m. for the sale of bread, fish, and groceries. Special orders may also be made allowing shops in holiday resorts to sell bathing, fishing, and photographic requisites, toys, souvenirs, books, stationery, postcards, and any article of food. No doubt these lists have been settled after consultation with the trade unions and employers' associations concerned, but they certainly strike the foreign visitor (and not a few Englishmen) as containing some oddities.

In 1964 a Departmental Committee on the Law of Sunday Observance[23] made some modest proposals for removing the most glaring of the anomalies, but the Government does not contemplate implementing its recommendations. In 1967, 1968, and 1969 private members' Bills dealing with Sunday entertainment made considerable parliamentary progress but, being without Government support, failed to reach the statute book.

CONSCIENTIOUS OBJECTORS

A chapter on religious freedom ought not to end without a reference to the English attitude to conscientious objection to military service. Both in war and in peace a person who 'conscientiously objects' to military service is entitled to appear before a local tribunal. If the tribunal is satisfied that he 'conscientiously objects' it may grant him unconditional exemption from military service, or exempt him on condition that he undertakes prescribed civilian work, or make him liable to call-up for non-combatant duties. The objector has an appeal to a central appellate tribunal, where once again he is entitled to appear personally and to be legally represented. With the abolition of compulsory military service, these tribunals have been wound up.

CHAPTER 8

FREEDOM AND SECURITY

PROBLEMS of national security have never been greater than they are today. The conflict between cherished individual freedoms and security of the state is sharp. We have to see now how, both in criminal law and in its administrative practice, the United Kingdom attempts to resolve this conflict.

SEDITION

In the eighteenth century the Government made great use of prosecutions for sedition in an attempt to restrict criticism of its conduct in the Press and elsewhere. It turned to this weapon especially, because with the lapse of the Licensing Acts in 1694 it no longer had powers of censorship.

John Wilkes's *Essay on Woman* and his article in the *North Briton* led to his prosecution for sedition in 1764. The most famous political commentator of the day, Junius, wrote in the *Public Advertiser* an open letter, which was also printed by one Miller in the *London Evening Post*, addressed to King George III which was very critical of the Government and its advice to the King. This is an extract : 'Sir, it is the misfortune of your life, and originally the cause of every reproach and distress which has attended your government, that you should never have been acquainted with the language of truth, until you heard it in the complaints of your subjects.' The Government could not identify Junius, and so it prosecuted the printer, Miller, for seditious libel. The judges of the day were determined not to let the jury acquit on the grounds that the writings were not seditious. Miller was tried by the leading judge of the day, Lord Mansfield, who told the jury that the writings were seditious, and that the jury had only to decide whether the paper was printed and published. The jury ignored what was virtually a direction to convict and promptly found Miller 'Not guilty', to the great joy of the crowds outside waiting in the hope of celebrating Miller's acquittal.[1] Junius followed up with scathing attacks on Mansfield, supported by that judicial champion of freedom whom we met in *Entick* v. *Carrington*, Lord Camden, and by a newcomer, Erskine, soon to become the most famous advocate of his day, if not of all time. Erskine successfully defended the Dean of St Asaph in a famous case of sedition in 1779. Later the Government proceeded against Thomas Paine for his *Rights of Man*. Despite much pressure from judges, statesmen, and his fellow lawyers, and even though the Government stripped him of a Crown appointment for doing so, Erskine insisted on his right to defend Paine, regardless of whether he sympathized with or abhorred his views, and thereby firmly established that vital principle of the English legal profession : that a barrister will accept a brief on behalf of any client in a court in which he holds himself out to practise. As Erskine said : 'From the moment that any advocate can be permitted to say that he will or will not stand between the Crown and the subject arraigned in the Court where he daily sits to practise, from that moment the liberties of England are at an end.' In 1791 Charles Fox proposed and Erskine seconded in the House of Commons a Bill establishing that it was the province of the jury, not the judge, finally to pronounce on whether a libel was seditious. Despite the opposition of the Lord Chancellor and other judges and their gloomy prediction of 'the confusion and destruction of the law of England', the Bill became the Libel Act of 1792.

The subsequent history of the law of sedition has merely confirmed how right the eighteenth-century juries were. No longer can Governments invoke this branch of the criminal law in order to secure the imprisonment of those who criticize their conduct. In 1886 John Burns, Hyndman, and other Socialists were prosecuted at the Old Bailey for their speeches at a meeting in Hyde Park.[2] The judge told the jury that 'a seditious intention is an intention to bring into hatred or contempt, or to excite disaffection against the person of Her Majesty, her heirs or successors, or the government and constitution of the United Kingdom, as by law established, or either House of Parliament, or the administration of justice, or to excite Her Majesty's subjects to attempt otherwise than by lawful means the alteration of any matter in Church or State by law established, or to raise discontent or disatisfaction amongs Her Majesty's subjects, or to promote feelings of ill-will and hostility between different classes of such subjects.' On the other hand, he told them : 'An intention to show that Her Majesty has been misled or mistaken in her measures, or to point out errors or defects in the government or constitution as by law established, with a view to their reformation, or to excite Her Majesty's subjects to attempt by lawful means the alteration of any matter in Church or State by law established, or to point out, in order to their removal [sic], matters which are producing, or have a tendency to produce, feelings of hatred and ill-will between classes of Her Majesty's subjects, is not a seditious intention.'[3] Turning more particularly to the case before them, the judge added : '... if you trace from the whole matter laid before you that they had a seditious intention to incite the people to violence, to create public disturbances and disorder, then undoubtedly you ought to find them guilty. ... On the other hand, if you come to the conclusion that they were actuated by an honest desire to alleviate the misery of the unemployed – if they had a real *bona fide* desire to bring the misery before the public by constitutional and legal means – you should not be too swift to mark any hasty or ill-considered expression which they might utter in the excitement of the moment.' The jury returned a verdict of 'Not guilty'.

Look next at the prosecution in 1947 of Caunt, the editor of the *Morecambe and Heysham Visitor*.[4] At the time when Palestinian Jews were attacking British soldiers in Palestine, the accused had written an article in his newspaper assailing the British Jews and complaining of their alleged black-market activities in strong terms. One paragraph stated :

If British Jewry is suffering from the righteous wrath of British citizens, then they have only themselves to blame for their passive inactivity. Violence may be the only way to bring them to the sense of their responsibility to the country in which they live.

He was tried at Liverpool Assizes by Mr Justice Birkett and a jury for publishing a seditious libel. Mr Justice Birkett told the jury that Caunt was guilty if he wrote the article with the intention of promoting violence by stirring up hostility and ill-will between Jews and non-Jews. It was not enough that hostility or ill-will was provoked; 'sedition has always had implicit in the word, public disorder, tumult, insurrections or matters of that kind'. He stressed that the prosecution had to prove that this was in fact Caunt's intention. If the natural consequence of his article was violence and ill-will between Jews and non-Jews, and no explanation or evidence was given by Caunt, then the jury could find him guilty of doing the act with the intent alleged; if, on the whole of the evidence, there was room for more than one view of the intent of the prisoner, and the jury were left in doubt, the prisoner was to be acquitted. He stressed also the great role which the jury had to play in protecting the freedom of the Press. Again, the jury acquitted.

In 1951 the Supreme Court of Canada had occasion to consider at length the common law of sedition.[5] They reached the conclusion that the crime requires an intention to incite to violence or to create public disturbance and disorder against the sovereign or the institutions of government and that proof of an intention to promote feelings of ill-will and hostility between different classes of subject does not alone establish a sufficient intention. There must be proof of an incitement to violence or retaliation or defiance for the purpose of disturbing constituted authority. This important case is in line with the progressive narrowing over the years of this offence and probably represents good English law.

The police must notify the Director of Public Prosecutions before they prosecute for sedition, and he always looks at the matter personally.[6] The crime of sedition is not, then, the means of oppression by Government which it used to be in the eighteenth century. Both judges and juries can be relied on to protect from conviction for sedition those who are devoting their energies to criticizing the Government and its policies, or advocating those changes which they are convinced are necessary.

In 1936 the printers and publishers of a newspaper which contained statements reflecting on the Jewish community as a whole were found not guilty of a seditious libel, but guilty of a public mischief.[7] The next edition of the leading text book on criminal law accordingly stated that the crime of public mischief compromises 'such acts as making scurrilous attacks, whether oral or in writing, on a class of the community, or disseminating rumours calculated to cause widespread alarm' and that the judge, not the jury, was to decide whether the statements were a public mischief.[8] In a book written in 1949 Mr Justice Denning (as he then was) criticized this case and the text-book view just quoted. The case has never been followed, the latest edition of the text book omits the quoted passage, and the prevailing attitude is that the offence of public mischief is to be restricted. In 1954 the Judicial Committee of the Privy Council heard an appeal from the Court of Appeal for the Windward Islands and Leeward Islands by a man who had been charged with both sedition and effecting a public mischief.[9] He had been found guilty on the public mischief charge only. Quashing this conviction, the Privy Council held that the judge wrongly told the jury that it was for him to decide whether the speech amounted to a public mischief : the Privy Council stated that it was for the jury to decide whether the facts, in the light of the law explained to them by the judge, amounted to public mischief. They also condemned the practice resorted to in this case of trying a prisoner both for sedition and for causing a public mischief by making the seditious speech, and left open the question whether there was any separate crime of effecting a public mischief, apart from cases of conspiracy. Perhaps, therefore, there is no serious risk of the police again invoking the crime of public mischief for statements like that in the case of 1936 just mentioned. At the same time, in view of the broad view of the crime of conspiracy formed by the House of Lords in the *Ladies Directory* case,[10] there is the danger of prosecutions for a conspiracy to create a public mischief arising out of publications of this kind; even so, it is believed that the last word on the essential element in the alleged crime would still be with the jury, and therein perhaps lies the greatest protection for the Press and other publishers.

INCITEMENT TO DISAFFECTION

In 1797 sailors of the Royal Navy mutinied at the Nore. Alarmed at the French Revolution which was in full spate across the Channel, Parliament resolved on legislation, and passed the Incitement to Mutiny Act 1797. Rather surprisingly, inciting troops to mutiny had not been a crime at common law. This Act provided that it was a felony maliciously and advisedly to seduce any serviceman from his duty and allegiance or to incite him to commit any act of mutiny. The Act was originally only a temporary measure and was allowed to lapse in 1805 when it was seen that there was no danger. Indeed, it is now clear that the Nore mutiny was not a politically motivated rising; the real grievance was inadequate messing and the withholding of pay. Yet the Act was revived in 1817 and remained in force substantially unchanged until the 1930s.

In 1934 the National Government announced in the King's Speech its intention to introduce a Bill concerning disaffection. It was widely expected that some wider powers for dealing with the Fascist Blackshirts were envisaged. The Bill itself, the Incitement to Disaffection Bill, was very different and created a major political storm. Moving its second reading, the Attorney-General, Sir Thomas Inskip, informed the House of Commons that subversive tracts had been circulated among members of the forces during the preceding few years, and that the object of the Bill was to facilitate the prosecution of those responsible. In fact, the

Bill proposed to extend the existing law so much that its opponents could not accept that this was its only object, especially as no adequate evidence of increased attempts to cause disaffection among troops was adduced. Sir William Holdsworth, a Conservative and the leading jurist of the day, described the Bill as 'the most daring encroachment upon the liberty of the subject which the executive Government has yet attempted at a time which is not a time of emergency'. The Society of Friends thought that the object of the Bill was to put in prison their members who possessed pamphlets advocating pacifism. Others held that the Admiralty, in a panic at the Invergordon uprising of the Navy, had insisted on the Bill. Another view was that the Government was determined to muzzle the expression of what seemed to it revolutionary principles recently voiced by Cripps, Trevelyan, Laski, and other Socialists. A more extreme version which gained currency in left-wing circles was that it was intended to prevent any criticism of the Government. Trade unionists discerned in it the determination of the Government to make troops fire on strikers.

Certainly, the National Government was disingenuous in presenting the Bill as a minor one making procedural changes. The Bill would have made several changes in the law. First, under the then existing legislation the prosecution had to prove, as is usually required in criminal law, that the accused had a guilty mind; for instance that he knew that the person to whom he was speaking was a soldier. Clause 1 of the Bill removed the words 'maliciously and advisedly' from the definition of the offence, so that a person could be found guilty even though the prosecution could not establish that he intended, say, to seduce a soldier from his allegiance. Secondly, not only did the Bill propose to create the new offence of being in possession of documents the dissemination of which would be a crime under Clause 1, but it provided that the mere possession of such documents was an offence unless the accused proved that he had lawful excuse for possessing them – and in practice it is often difficult for the accused to discharge this burden of proving his innocence. A pacifist might have some of his literature in a drawer at home : that would be enough for the prosecution to obtain a conviction unless he discharged the onus of showing lawful excuse. Thirdly, any magistrate, on the application of a policeman, could issue a warrant authorizing him to search the premises of the person named in the warrant and to seize any documents which the policeman reasonably believed to infringe the Bill. A policeman might seek out a magistrate who was a political opponent of the suspect, and without giving notice of hearing to the suspect, obtain the search warrant : the fears of pacifists, trade unionists, and other opponents of the Government were understandable. Fourthly, English law recognizes as of course that one who does not actually commit a crime may nonetheless be convicted of an *attempt* where he has done an act with intent to commit that offence, and where that act is a step towards the commission of that offence which is immediately connected with it. If, therefore, the Bill had been silent about attempts, they would still have constituted crimes as long as they fell within the definition in the previous sentence. But the Bill did not stop there. A person was to be guilty of an attempt if he did or attempted to do, or caused to be done or attempted, any act preparatory to the commission of an offence. The man who boarded a train to Portsmouth might find himself arrested on the train and he might be guilty of a crime under the Act unless he could prove that the object of his journey was innocent.

If all these provisions had passed into law, they would undoubtedly have curtailed civil liberties to a serious extent. In fact the Government bowed before the storm and none of these clauses survived. The words 'maliciously and advisedly' were put back into the Act so that a man would not be guilty unless he were shown to have a guilty mind. Possession of documents was to be no offence unless an intent to commit or help another to commit an offence under the Act were also proved. The power to issue search warrants was taken away from magistrates and was to be exercised by a High Court judge only, and the policeman applying for a warrant had to be at least of the rank of inspector. The clause which purported to extend the law of criminal attempts to merely preparatory acts was deleted altogether.

Nonetheless, in the form in which the Bill survived, there were some important extensions of the old law. The previous legislation restricted the offence to where the accused endeavoured to seduce a serviceman from his duty *and* allegiance; this Act replaced 'duty and allegiance' by 'duty *or* allegiance'. There can be no doubt that this is an important difference. Suppose that a wife persuaded her husband to take an illicit forty-eight-hour leave, or not to return to barracks until the day after his leave expired. Such conduct is certainly not an interference with allegiance, but it is an interference with his duty, so that the Act for the first time would make such conduct a crime. Or take a more serious example : suppose that a soldier could not reconcile it with his conscience to obey an order to fire on strikers, and that he was persuaded to disobey such an order by his father, an active trade unionist. The father's conduct was now made criminal, but it is extremely doubtful whether he would be seducing his son from allegiance – the soldier's loyalty to the sovereign could have remained unaffected.

The new offence of being in possession of documents remained (although the prosecution must now establish that the possessor intended to bring about an offence within the preceding paragraph). This section has the desirable purpose of enabling the police to prosecute the man behind the scenes, for instance, the printer who has the documents stored in his warehouse; previously the pawn who was handing out the documents was the only one likely to be apprehended. It is a possible objection that no act by the possessor need be proved – once the police establish possession and intention the man is guilty. The effectiveness of this provision is ensured by the wide powers of search and seizure conferred on the police by the section : under the warrant of the High Court judge they may enter premises by force, if necessary, and seize anything which they have reasonable grounds for suspecting to be evidence of the commission of an offence under the Act.

The Act made it possible either to charge offenders before magistrates for a summary offence, or to indict them and have them tried by jury at Assizes or Quarter Sessions. Previously it had not been possible to proceed before magistrates. The change was a good one, in that it enabled the unimportant mere distributor to receive the summary trial and limited punishment that his offence merited. The Opposition found another aspect of this new alternative sinister and objectionable. They were particularly worried about politically prejudiced magistrates trying such cases. Under the Bill as originally drafted, there was nothing to prevent the police from denying an accused the opportunity of trial by jury and insisting on trial by magistrates in a particular area. Suppose that the offence charged was that of dissuading soldiers from putting down a strike; there was a feeling that a bench of Conservative local employers would not give such a case a fair hearing. The Government responded to this pressure by altering the Bill so as to give the accused the choice of trial by jury. Another objection was not met by the Act. A prosecution under the Act cannot be tried by magistrates without the consent of the Director of Public Prosecutions. Although his post is a permanent non-political one, he is subject to the directions of the Attorney-General, a member of the Government of the day. The objection was that whenever the accused was likely to be tried by a bench sympathetic to him or even composed of persons of his own class the Government would insist on his being tried at Assizes instead, and that such practices would be discriminatory.

A leading text book on constitutional law has said that 'the Act goes a long way to arming the Executive with power to restrict the distribution of political propaganda and of pacifist literature'.[11] Was this a fair judgment on the Act in its final form? It must be remembered that there is no restriction on the distribution of any political propaganda unless intent to seduce servicemen from their allegiance or duty is proved. The Act does not restrict in any way the distribution of political propaganda to civilians – the one Act which does that is the Police Act 1964 which makes it a crime to do an act calculated to cause disaffection amongst the members of a police force. In practice, prosecutions under the Act have been very few, although it is true that the Act appeared to be used harshly on one occasion in the 1930s. A young student, son of a parson, engaged in casual conversation with an airman in a railway refreshment room. Learning that the airman was a pilot, he asked him why he did not fly to Spain and help the Republicans. The trial judge sentenced him to a year's imprisonment for breach of the Act.

The conclusion must be that although the original Bill conferred unreasonably wide powers on the Executive to interfere with the citizen, the Act, despite some objectionable features, is not now a serious threat to liberty. Indeed, this account of the passage of the Bill through Parliament furnishes an excellent example of the way in which Parliament can operate effectively as a watchdog for freedom.

GOVERNMENT SECURITY

In this section no attempt will be made to deal with the special problem of security in time of war. The scope of the crime of treason, which is particularly concerned with assistance to an enemy, and the emergency rules concerning the detention of enemy aliens will therefore not be examined. The emphasis will be on the safeguarding of such information in the possession of the Government as would, by its unauthorized disclosure, harm the interests of the country.

Official Secrets Acts

In 1878 a temporary writer in the Foreign Office, by the name of Marvin, found himself dissatisfied with his employment : he particularly resented the short working day of his superiors. In August 1878 he had to copy in the course of his duties a secret treaty negotiated between England and

Russia. At the end of his day's work he walked down to the office of the *Globe* newspaper and gave them particulars of the secret treaty. To the astonishment of the Government, these were published next day in the *Globe*. The leak was traced to Marvin and the decision made to prosecute him. But for what offence? The Government had the mortification of unsuccessfully prosecuting him for removing a State document.[12] The criminal law was not equipped for conduct like his, so long as no document was stolen. An attempt was made to fill the gap by passing the Official Secrets Act of 1889. This Act made it a crime (among other matters) for a person wrongfully to communicate information which he had obtained owing to his position as a civil servant. The Act could fairly be regarded as an orthodox enactment of criminal law : the burden of proving guilt was on the prosecution, the offences were defined with adequate particularity.

As tension between Britain and Germany developed in the early twentieth century the Government concluded that the Act of 1889 was not effective to stop German spying. In 1909 a German Secret Service officer came to London, for the purpose, as he announced, of interviewing 'suitable candidates' for a new and greatly enlarged espionage system to cover all England. Scotland Yard advised the Government that there was no offence for which they could arrest him. When the police prosecuted those who were using field glasses in the vicinity of harbour installations and the like, they had difficulty in securing convictions because they could not disprove the accuseds' assertions that they were merely bird-watching.

The upshot was the passing of the Official Secrets Act, 1911. Despite its innocuous title, 'An Act to re-enact the Official Secrets Act 1889 with Amendments', this Act was a very different kettle of fish from its predecessors. In it were many provisions weighted strongly against the accused, and of a kind most rare in English criminal law, especially at that time. Yet the astounding fact is that this extremely important Bill was given its second reading in late August in the House of Commons, the Attorney-General giving no proper explanation of its provisions and resisting successfully any discussion, and that in less than twenty-four hours from its introduction it passed through all its stages in the House. This Act made it a felony if any person for any purpose prejudicial to the safety or interests of the State approached any military or naval installation or other prohibited place, or obtained or communicated to others information which would help an enemy, or if he made a sketch or note which might help an enemy. The important new features were as follows. The onus was no longer on the prosecution to prove that the accused had a purpose prejudicial to the State. Moreover, if the accused denied that he had such a purpose, the prosecution was free to lead evidence of his bad character, including previous convictions, a course which is ordinarily prohibited in criminal cases. Section 2 of the Act also made it a misdemeanour for a person who has any information of the kind mentioned above, or information which has been entrusted in confidence to him by an officer of the Crown or which he obtained as a Crown servant or while employed in connection with contracts with the Crown, to communicate that information to an unauthorized person or to retain a sketch or other document without any right to do so. Anyone receiving such a document or information who knew or had reasonable ground to believe that the communication contravened the Act was also guilty unless he proved that the communication to him was contrary to his desire.

In 1920 the Coalition Government, fearing civil war in Ireland, announced its intention to strengthen the Official Secrets Act in the light of war-time experience. Introducing the Bill, Hewart, the Attorney-General, was at pains to allay the fears of those who thought the new Bill an attack on the freedom of the Press. This Act, the Official Secrets Act 1920, made communication with foreign agents a felony under the Act of 1911. It also introduced an offence of a kind not previously found in the criminal law. Ordinarily, before a person may be convicted of an attempted crime he must have taken a step towards the commission of that crime which is immediately connected with it. This Act made it a felony to do any act preparatory to the commission of a felony under the Official Secrets Act.

Do these Acts strike a fair balance between the security of the State and individual freedom? It may be argued that where the safety of the country is involved it is proper for the criminal law to be much harsher than usual. What must be realized, however, is that the Official Secrets Acts are deliberately framed in terms so wide as to go far beyond the protection of national safety and to cover all kinds of official information unrelated to security : in that extended area such extraordinary rules have no place. It may be retorted that even if the Acts are so extensive it is merely the usual technique of British Governments to assume wider powers than necessary on their reliable assurance that these will not be used except for the important and restricted purpose. What is more sinister is that the Acts are used to threaten citizens with prosecutions for matters unconnected with espionage. There have been more prosecutions in the last few years. For example in 1965 a journalist revealed that some of the Queen's telephone calls were being intercepted : he was threatened with a prosecution under the Official Secrets Act because he allegedly had asked G.P.O. telephone operators whether they ever intercepted telephone messages.

A few random illustrations will show that the Acts have been used for matters unconnected with national security. The *Empire News* had to drop its advertised plan of serializing the memoirs of Pierrepoint, the hangman, under threat of prosecution under the Official Secrets Acts – there would have been communication of information which Pierrepoint had obtained as an officer of the Crown.

Major Clayton Hutton invented, designed, and produced many of the escape devices used during the Second World War : buttons containing compasses, silk maps of every country in Western Europe, flying boots with tops that could be ripped off to make a waistcoat leaving a non-military pair of shoes. What follows is his published version of his experiences after the Second World War.[13] He believed that he would get permission to write a book about his war-time adventures but was eventually told that he would be prosecuted under the Acts if he carried out his plan. He heard this news while on an American lecture tour on the same subject, which the War Office had permitted him to make. On his return home he was met by two soldiers who required him to surrender all the documents borrowed from contractors in support of his claim for inventor's rewards from the Royal Commission on Awards, and all lecture notes relating to his service in the Forces. He did not comply and was charged under the Official Secrets Acts with failure to obey the directive and with unlawfully obtaining certain sketches, models, and documents. Hutton then produced letters from a senior officer at the War Office sending him in 1946 sets of various inventions and a receipt from King George VI's secretary for a similar set of articles and asked whether he too was to be prosecuted. The police took a statement the next day but objected to including the reference to King George VI. Hutton stated that he would inform the court that the police 'prevailed' on him to exclude these matters from his statement. Air Marshal Sir Basil Embry, despite warnings from the Air Ministry, intimated that he would give evidence for Hutton, whereupon the police asked that he should not appear in uniform. At the hearing the Crown offered no evidence and obtained permission to withdraw the charges.

In 1938 the *Daily Dispatch* published a statement that X was wanted by Southport police on some comparatively minor charge of false pretences. A Southport police officer went to the home of the reporter responsible for this news item and demanded to know from whom he had got his information. The reporter refused to tell him. He was thereupon prosecuted under the Official Secrets Acts for failure to give information to a police inspector, and his conviction was upheld by the High Court.[14] This conviction led to a parliamentary debate. Obviously, no issue of State security was raised, but there was an official secret, the 'wanted notice' which Southport police had put out to other police authorities but had not handed to the Press. Parliament refused to be content with the Government's assurance that similar prosecutions would not recur. The Official Secrets Act 1939 consequently amended the Acts, but only by requiring the police to obtain the Home Secretary's permission before exercising their powers under the Act : a journalist who refused a similar request today would still commit an offence under the Acts provided that the police officer had the Home Secretary's backing. Nothing has been done to confine 'official secrets' to matters affecting State security.

In 1962 the House of Lords ruled that members of the Committee of 100 who conspired to incite others to enter a R.A.F. station thereby committed the crimes of conspiring to commit and to incite a breach of the Act. The House held that the accused could give no evidence that their purpose was the peaceable one of protesting against nuclear weapons. Their conduct was for a purpose prejudicial to the safety or interests of the State if it interfered with dispositions of the armed forces. The Court would not listen to evidence that the purposes of the community would be benefited, not prejudiced, by the nuclear disarmament campaign.[15] The Court upheld the dangerous doctrine that whatever is Crown policy is necessarily in the interests of the State. A charge of conspiracy to violate the Official Secrets Act also evades the need for the Attorney-General's consent to prosecution.

There is increasing disquiet in the Press (who are always more concerned with their own liberties than anyone else's) about these Acts. Prosecution or the threat of it is used by the Government to muzzle criticism or restrain the passage of information. The Acts, and especially section 2 of the 1911 Act, are so widely drawn that Ministers, civil servants and the Press are committing offences all the time. In 1965 'Justice' in its *The Law and the Press* recommended that it should be a valid defence to show that the national interest or legitimate private interests confided to the State were not likely to be harmed and that the information was passed and received in good faith and in the public interest. In 1969 a private member's Bill was introduced along these lines. The Government opposed it and, in a White Paper, *Information and the Public Interest*,[16] declined to limit the scope of the Acts. A similar Bill failed in 1970. The Government refuses to let the courts interpret public interest and claims that such questions are exclusively for the Executive. All is well (it maintains) because the Attorney-General will not prosecute unless he is satisfied that national security or major public interest is involved. The present law is unfair to the Press, and 'Justice's' proposals should be implemented. In other areas, for instance claims for Crown privilege in the disclosure of documents which departments wish to keep secret, the courts have taken away from the Executive the decision whether public interest demands secrecy. Parliament should restrain the Government's powers here, too. There have been important developments in 1971. The editor of the *Sunday Telegraph* and others were acquitted on charges under section 2 of communicating a Government report on the Nigerian war to unauthorized persons. Mr Justice Caulfield told the jury that the section should be 'pensioned off' because it allowed a claim of public interest not involving any issue of national security to interfere with necessary Press freedom. He directed the jury that the accused were innocent unless the Crown proved their guilty knowledge and the confidentiality of the documents. The summing up and jury's verdict were enthusiastically received, and the Government has felt constrained to undertake a review of the Acts. The United States Supreme Court did its best to protect the right of the *New York Times* to publish the Pentagon Papers, even though the Government's wishes to the contrary were very clear.

'D' Notices

It might be wondered how the intolerable restrictions on freedom in areas totally unconnected with national security which are implicit in this legislation have survived Press opposition. Obviously, if a statute so widely drawn were rigorously applied, the Press would continually be under the threat of prosecution for matters of no importance to security and would be afforded no defence. As is commonly the case, the explanation lies in unpublicized unofficial arrangements behind the scenes. It is not surprising that the Radcliffe Committee on Security Procedures in the Public Service (1962) found that

the Official Secrets Acts are not an effective instrument for controlling Press publication of that kind of 'military' information of some though perhaps no great individual importance, which it is nevertheless most desirable to keep from hostile intelligence ... [and that] it must often be impossible at the critical moment of publication for the editor himself to say whether he is within or without the provisions of the Acts.[17]

At the same time the Committee misinterpreted the Act in believing that it was confined to information about prohibited places and information obtained through a wrongful communication by an official; the Committee wrongly inferred that an editor who published information falling outside these categories did not commit an offence under the Acts. Almost as soon as the Act of 1911 reached the statute book the Government had to seek ways and means of clarifying and alleviating the position of the Press. Their solution was to set up in 1912 a Committee whose object was to let the Press know unofficially when they could commit an offence without risk of prosecution. This system has survived in essentials to the present day. The 'D' notice system was obviously important during the Second World War, when the Home Secretary had power by Defence Regulation 2 B (1940) to forbid the publication of any newspaper if he were satisfied that it was systematically publishing matter calculated in his opinion to foment opposition to the prosecution of the war to a successful issue (it will be noticed that the Home Secretary was given in law uncontrolled power to decide when a newspaper must cease publication). The existence of this Committee first came to the public notice in 1961 in connection with the conviction under the Official Secrets Acts of George Blake. To judge from the comments of members of the Royal Commission on the Press in 1948 when questioning witnesses such as Mr Michael Foot, M.P., they too were unaware of the peace-time operation of the Committee.

The Services, Press and Broadcasting Committee consists of sixteen members. There are eleven representatives of the Press and broadcasting, and the Permanent Secretaries of the Admiralty, the War Office, the Air Ministry, the Ministry of Defence, and the Ministry of Aviation. Its Secretary is Vice-Admiral Sir Norman Denning: as with other unofficial organs of censorship which we have considered, the Secretary is that man who has really counted in the working of the censorship. The Committee has no legal basis whatever. The aim of the arrangements is to make clear to the Press what the Government is willing that it should publish on security matters and what it does not wish it to publish. The Press and broadcasting bodies have the unofficial assurance that they will not be prosecuted under the Official Secrets Acts on those security matters so long as they comply; the Government expects to prevent the disclosure of technical and strategic information – one may contrast the publication in American newspapers of missile sites under construction. The lists of permitted and forbidden matters are circulated in 'D' notices to the publications likely to be concerned : during the Second World War 'D' notices circulated by the Press Censorship Division of the Ministry of Information contained lists of subjects which were considered detrimental to national security. In addition, 'D' notices were issued from time to time with special prohibitions : this explains, for instance, why, if one wanted to know during the war what was stated in propaganda leaflets dropped on Germany, one had to read American newspapers.

The Minister concerned with the particular subject-matter initiates a 'D' notice (which must relate to 'naval, military, and air matters the publication of which would be prejudicial to the national interest') the contents of which are approved by such members of the Committee as are available in London. In recent years only two new ones have been introduced, both revisions of previous notices. The Committee meets only when there is an objection on a new issue of principle. It has, from time to time, sought modification or rejection of a Minister's proposed 'D' notice, although there would be nothing then to prevent the Minister from ignoring the Committee and circularizing the Press directly with a request not to publish certain material. In an emergency the Secretary may issue a 'D' notice on his own responsibility with the concurrence of only two Press members. Individual newspapers are under no obligation to conform to a 'D' notice which the Committee has approved. For instance, in 1967 the *Daily Express* published the names of the head of M.I.5 and M.I.6 despite a 'D' notice. Lord Denning's report on the *Profumo Affair* disclosed that when Mr Profumo realized that the publication of Christine Keeler's memoirs in the *Sunday Pictorial* was imminent he at once sent for the Head of the Security Service, who was apparently invited by Mr Profumo to stop publication by a 'D' notice. Although a Minister has been held by the Prime Minister (Mr Macmillan) to be politically responsible for issuing a 'D' notice, this notion of ministerial responsibility has that mythical content which it so often has when national security is involved. Just as Sir Anthony Eden would not answer questions about underwater activities when Commander Crabb disappeared, so also Mr Macmillan stated that the House of Commons cannot require a Minister to justify his decision to issue a 'D' notice.

In the case of Blake, after a preliminary hearing *in camera*, he was committed for trial on 24 April 1961. On 1 May the Services, Press and Broadcasting Committee issued a letter requesting newspapers not to publish certain facts, and pointed out that the lives of certain persons were in danger. On 3 May Blake was convicted after a trial partly *in camera*. On 4 May newspapers were asked not to reproduce stories from foreign newspapers; this ban was lifted on 8 May. The ban aroused much protest since these reports only contained two facts : that Blake was an agent for both the British and the Russians, and that he had given away other agents in Berlin. It was not obvious how the reproduction of these facts from foreign newspapers would have affected national security, and the Prime Minister in the House of Commons did not clarify the matter.

The most important recent 'D' notice incident occurred in 1967. Chapman Pincher reported in the *Daily Express* that security bodies collected and read telegrams and cables sent out of the country, a practice authorized by section 4 of the Official Secrets Act 1920. The Government announced that this was a grave breach of two 'D' notices and set up a committee of Privy Councillors to investigate. The committee found that the *Daily Express* was not in breach of any 'D' notice but criticized the *Spectator* for publishing the texts of the 'D' notices.[18] It also revealed that sixteen 'D' notices were in force. The Government promptly rejected the committee's findings in a White Paper which also proposed reforms of the system.[19] This 'D' notice affair led to the resignation of the Secretary to the committee.

Baldwin used other unofficial machinery in 1936 to persuade the British newspapers not to follow the American example of reporting the doings of Mrs Simpson and Edward VIII. Compare too the successful request from the Palace in 1946 to the newspapers not to publish Prince Philip's application for British nationality. Sometimes the Secretary of the Committee puts pressure on the Press not to publish material outside 'D' notices. For example, the *Daily Express* was prevailed upon by him not to reveal negligence in constructing parts of the Windscale nuclear reactors.

Service Clearance for Books

The Government imposes other unofficial brakes on freedom in the interests of security. Each service Ministry has recognized machinery for clearing books which touch on service matters. In January 1946 all publishers received a circular from the Services, Press and Broadcasting Committee asking them to refrain from publishing certain information about escapes by prisoners of war. Mr Selwyn Lloyd has explained in the House of Commons that service departments work to certain rules of scrutiny when deciding whether to 'clear' books submitted to them – in part these consist of a secret list of prohibited items. Copies of these rules are not available to the public, and they have no legal effect. Presumably these rules must be general in so far as they are not merely a secret list. When clearance is refused reasons will be given. But the author is given no opportunity to argue his case before those who decide; indeed their identity is concealed from him. This is yet another example of a matter which can closely affect a person's livelihood being decided by unknown civil servants according to undisclosed rules without the citizen having any opportunity to present argument or test the reasons on which his application is about to be refused. The usual Government apologia, ministerial responsibility for a collective departmental decision, accountability to Parliament, necessary anonymity of civil servants, decisions of policy, matters of security, are as unconvincing in this instance as they usually are in decisions of this kind.

The Government expects all books affecting security to be submitted to it, and has issued a 'D' notice to this effect about 'escape' books. Ordinarily, it has no legal means of securing compliance, other than the ever-present threat of prosecution for contravention of the Official Secrets Acts. It will be recalled from the Hutton case discussed earlier that the Air Ministry there issued a directive to him that he surrender immediately all the documents in his possession relating to his service in H.M. Forces and, upon his failure to comply, prosecuted him under the Acts for retaining information and documents contrary to his duty. It uses other methods to secure compliance. For example any employee or consultant of the United Kingdom Atomic Energy Authority is required to sign a declaration that he understands that any note made or acquired by him during the tenure of his appointment must be surrendered unless he has written sanction to retain it, and that he is liable to be prosecuted for retaining it without that sanction. Yet the Official Secrets Acts merely make it an offence to retain a note 'which relates to or is used in a prohibited place ... when he has no right to retain it'. Plainly, the Act is much narrower than the terms of the declaration which the employees and consultants are given to sign, although the form gives the misleading impression that the signatory is merely declaring his understanding of the consequences of his violating the Act. At the same time the declaration gives the false idea that whether the consultant commits an offence by retaining a document depends on whether he has first obtained permission of the Authority to do so.

Civil servants (even retired ones) had to have books written by them about Government cleared before publication by the civil service head of their department. Disquiet at the publication of Sir George Mallaby's intimate account of the Cabinet Office in his *From My Level* (he was formerly First Civil Service Commissioner) caused the rules to be tightened even more in 1965 : no civil servant, serving or retired, established or unestablished, may now even enter into a contract to write a book without prior official approval of his manuscript. This neither prevented Mr Macmillan from publishing his autobiography nor restricts the flow of war generals' memoirs.

The publication by Lieutenant-Commander Lithgow of a book, *Mach One*, which contained information about military aircraft, revealed one legal control sometimes available to the Government. Mr Lithgow had obtained this information in his capacity as an employee of Vickers-Armstrongs, and had not submitted the manuscript of his book for security clearance because he was under the mistaken impression that his employers had done so. In 1954 Mr Selwyn Lloyd, in reply to a parliamentary question, explained that all manufacturers of aircraft and other security weapons are under a contractual obligation to obtain security clearance for books published by them. The legal sanction behind that arrangement is obvious. What is far from clear is Mr Lloyd's further statement that the firms concerned were also made responsible for their employees. How can a contract between a Ministry and a firm impose liability on the firm if somebody who was an employee publishes a book without security clearance? Only if the firm were required to include in its contracts of employment with each employee a clause that the employee was not to publish a book without prior Service clearance. It is not the practice to have such terms in contracts of employment. Presumably the sanction is of an indirect kind only; there is no means of reaching the employee unless he is prosecuted under the Official Secrets Acts – he is not in contractual relation with the Ministry – but the Ministry could in future contracts prevent the firm (or any other firm) from employing in connection with the work a person who had ignored the security clearance arrangements.

Those who have disclosed to foreign powers secrets about atomic energy obtained in the course of State employment, such as May and Fuchs, have been convicted under the Official Secrets Acts. The Government has decided, as a matter of policy, to conduct research into atomic energy, even for peaceful purposes, through its own agencies, especially the Atomic Energy Commission, rather than in universities. One consequence is that such work, and the knowledge acquired from it, is a State secret, so that those employed are subject to the Official Secrets Acts. Had such work been carried on in universities without any contractual relation between Government and university, even though with Government finance, university staff who mentioned to their scientific colleagues the results of their researches would not for that reason have been guilty of offences under the Acts.

When the impending publication of the Casement diaries by a crime reporter was announced in 1926 the editor was promptly summoned to the Home Office, and informed by the Home Secretary and his chief legal adviser that he would be prosecuted under the Official Secrets Acts if he proceeded. The editor has related how, in consequence, he had to abandon publication of the book.

Cabinet Secrets

A particularly important body of secret information is that derived from Cabinet meetings. Control over Cabinet secrets is effected first by the all-pervasive Official Secrets Acts. Any member of the Cabinet who reveals to others, however long after the event, any information obtained at a Cabinet meeting is guilty of a criminal offence. In 1943, the son of Mr George Lansbury was convicted under the Official Secrets Acts for publishing verbatim in a biography of his father a memorandum prepared by his father for the Labour Cabinet of 1929–31 of which his father was a member. One upshot of this case was a change in practice which made the offence less easy to commit – for the first time Cabinet members were prevented from retaining Cabinet papers.

Cabinet members are subject to another more subtle form of control. They are always made Privy Councillors, all of whom are required to swear an ancient form of oath to keep the Queen's counsel secret. The disclosure of any information obtained as a member of the Cabinet would violate this oath. There is a recognized procedure when a present or former Cabinet Minister wishes to act contrary to his oath. He applies to the Prime Minister of the day, who refers the matter to the Secretary to the Cabinet. The Secretary advises the Prime Minister whether publication would be detrimental to the public interest, and the Prime Minister advises the Queen accordingly. Thus, Sir Winston Churchill was permitted, under the Attlee administration, to include Cabinet material in his war memoirs, and Sir Anthony Eden included Cabinet secrets in his book on Suez with the approval of Mr Macmillan. There is a misconception, especially in the House of Commons, that there are many exceptions to this rule : Mr Bevan believed that he needed no permission to explain to the House why he had resigned from the Attlee administration. It is widely believed that the procedure applies only to publishing Cabinet papers, and does not prevent a Cabinet member from explaining his part in some decision of policy arrived at by a Cabinet of which he was a member. In fact, there are no exceptions to the requirement. What often happens in practice is that the Government turns a blind eye when former members (especially Prime Ministers) disclose Cabinet secrets in violation of their oath of secrecy. In 1967 Anthony Nutting published *No End of a Lesson*, his book about the Suez crisis, at which time he was a Minister. He did not submit the manuscrpit to the Cabinet office but agreed at page-proof stage to the suggestion of the Secretary to the Cabinet that names of civil servants be deleted. Although an ex-Minister might in this book have communicated information to unauthorized people (the general public) the Attorney-General refused to prosecute under the Official Secrets Act. Every Minister is precluded from writing books or articles on current political affairs while still in office, and Mr Jeremy Bray had to resign his post as Parliamentary Secretary in 1969 in order to publish a book called *Decision in Government*.

Government Papers

What of the disclosure of Governmental information by permitting scholars and others to have access to it for research purposes? The normal practice of the Government by virtue of the Public Records Act 1967 is to transfer to the Public Record Office, and thereby to make available to public inspection, documents thirty years old. Even then documents in certain classes, together with any other documents named by the Government of the day, are excluded. A typical expression of discontent with this rule was afforded by the repeated demand for access to the diaries of Sir Roger Casement. The rule is one typical facet of British public life. A British student of government will often learn more from a short period in Washington about the American administrative process than he can learn about his own from a lifetime in England. The Government and the senior members of the Opposition are agreed on one thing : that the less the public knows about the process of decision making the better. Whether this is an understandable confusion of what is politically and administratively convenient with what is in the public interest may well be asked. One consequence of this, among many, is that the British citizen has less protection when decisions affecting his private rights are made than in many Western countries. Whether he be an author being refused permission to publish a book or a householder being refused a telephone, he has no legal right to a hearing, or to know the reasons for refusal. Those who seek improvement of these procedures are met by a solid wall of resistance from the Government of the day, whatever its complexion. Civil servants themselves are usually helpful in discussions with outside experts and often appreciate exchange of views with them about their work, but when the time comes for permission to publish, they have to refer the decision to the top, where the answer is only too likely to be 'No'. And American visiting scholars, coming from a country without 'D' notices or Official Secrets Acts, to whom it never occurs to seek permission, are not popular with the British Treasury and other departments when they inform the British public for the first time of the processes by which they are governed. Threats of prosecution under the Official Secrets Acts are used in order to reinforce a cardinal principle of Civil Service administration – that government must be carried on in secret. Another form of bluff is to inveigle persons into signing an 'Official Secrets Acts declaration'. This practice has no legal sanction and no legal consequences, yet, for example, repeated pressure was put on Mr George Woodcock in 1965 to sign in his capacity as member of the National Economic Development Council, until he finally agreed after four months. It is the flexibility of the Official Secrets Acts, coupled with the fact that the Attorney-General alone decides whether to prosecute, which makes the system so easily workable in Britain. What is particularly irritating is that top people in the Government have appeared quite willing to violate even the Official Secrets Acts in disclosing information to the appropriate other 'top people', like the editor of *The Times* – one has only to read memoirs and biographies of the thirties for proof of this. The 'leak' is no new Transatlantic phenomenon of the 1960s. As Lord Devlin has put it : 'The danger of the system is that it installs as the judges of what ought to be revealed men whose interest it is to conceal.'

Security Tests on Employees

Although the Official Secrets Acts constitute a strong penal sanction against disclosure, they operate only to close the stable door after the horse has bolted. The British Government has also rightly concluded that the imposition of loyalty oaths on the American pattern would be ineffective. No doubt the test oath is of value against a Jesuit, a Presbyterian, or a Quaker, but to invoke it against those who accept lying as a legitimate political weapon is peculiarly naïve. For these reasons, it is accepted that the State as an employer is entitled to keep bad security risks out of employment involving security considerations. At the same time, as the Radcliffe Committee on Security Procedures in the Public Service pointed out in 1962,[20] when criticizing the Report of the Conference of Privy Councillors of 1956, the real threat to security is not from declared Communists who might have access to State documents, but from the Russian Intelligence Service.

In March 1948 the defections of scientists like May and the course of the cold war caused the Government to introduce special measures for the first time while we were at peace. Where a particular post involved some security risk, a special investigation was to be conducted to ascertain whether the civil servant selected to hold the position had any Communist or Fascist associations (the 'positive vetting' procedure). A civil servant whom his Minister found to be unreliable was allowed to have his case reviewed by three Advisers, specially appointed for such purposes. Sir Hartley Shawcross stated that by the end of 1953 these security measures had been applied to about 17,000 out of over a million civil servants because the posts they occupied might involve some degree of security risk. As a result, 148 were suspended. Of those, 28 were reinstated after inquiry had shown that they were loyal and reliable; 69 were transferred to non-secret work; 19 resigned; and 9 were on special leave pending decisions in their cases; only 23 were dismissed, and these because their qualifications were such that they could be employed only in secret work. In the following two years three were transferred, one resigned and none was dismissed.

The escape to Russia of Burgess and Maclean, senior civil servants in the Foreign Office who had access to vital information, caused the Government to set up in November 1955 a Conference of Privy Councillors to examine the security procedures applied in the public service and to consider whether any further precautions were called for and should be taken. The members were the Lord President of the Council, the Lord Chancellor, the Home Secretary, Lord Jowitt, Mr Herbert Morrison, and the Permanent Secretary to the Treasury. The Conference reported to the Government in 1956, but the Government stated that in the public interest neither the report nor the recommendations could be published in full. All that was issued was the substance of the report, so far as the Government thought that it could be made public, and some of the recommendations.[21] This document pointed out that the chief risks were not professional agents for foreign powers but Communists and their sympathizers, whose loyalty to their country was undermined by their political beliefs. It took the view that a serious character defect, such as drunkenness, homosexuality, or drug addiction, might well be the determining factor in deciding whether to dismiss or transfer a civil servant.

The Government accepted the recommendations in principle and in 1957 announced revised procedures for dealing with security risks (the purge procedure). A civil servant employed on work vital to the security of the State was to be regarded as in doubt on security grounds if he were, or had recently been, a member of the British Communist or Fascist parties, or, in such a way as to raise reasonable doubts about his reliability, was or had recently been sympathetic to Communism or Fascism, associated with Communists or Fascists or their sympathizers, or was susceptible to Communist or Fascist pressure. No further clarification of 'sympathy' or 'association' could be afforded : each case would be decided on its own merits.

The Minister first rules whether there is a *prima facie*

case. There is perhaps an analogy with the ruling of magistrates whether to commit an accused for trial. The outstanding difference is that whereas the accused in the latter case is given notice of the charge, confronts the witnesses for the prosecution, and may cross-examine them and be legally represented and give evidence himself, here the first the civil servant learns of it is after the Minister has decided that there is a *prima facie* case against him. When he is told of his *prima facie* guilt, he will not be given any particulars which might involve the disclosure of the sources of the evidence against him. The Minister will reconsider his *prima facie* ruling in the light of any written representations sent to him by the civil servant. If he adheres to his ruling the civil servant may ask the Minister to refer the case to the three Advisers. None of these is a lawyer, and in 1948 the Prime Minister, Mr Attlee, said in reply to a parliamentary question that there was no need for them to be legally trained.

The terms of reference of the Advisers were also revised. Mr Attlee had stated in 1948 that details of the charges would be available to the civil servant. This is no longer allowed in so far as the disclosure of sources of evidence might result. He is not allowed to be represented, whether by a lawyer or otherwise, except that in September 1962 the Prime Minister acceded to a request of the staff side of the Civil Service National Whitley Council that a friend, who might be a staff association official, could accompany him in presenting his opening statement, but would be prohibited from being present at the rest of the proceedings. He is not entitled to know of the evidence against him, and he is denied any opportunity to cross-examine witnesses. He is not allowed to bring witnesses to contradict whatever he might guess the evidence against him to be, except that he may ask third parties to testify as to his record, reliability, and character. He has no facilities by way of subpoena for ensuring the presence of witnesses. There is no machinery for having the evidence against him given on oath. No members of the public are allowed to be present.

The Advisers then advise the Minister whether his *prima*

facie ruling has been substantiated. If they disagree or have no firm opinion they are to assess the evidence in detail. The civil servant knows nothing of the advice tendered. The Minister can still adhere to his original opinion even though the Advisers dissent. Between 1962 and 1964 one person was dismissed and one barred from secret work because they were adjudged security risks.

The Government interferes not only with civil servants but also with employees of private firms engaged on secret work. It does so by always including in a contract for such work a provision for defining the secret matters on that contract. The Minister is empowered by the contract to call for a list of employees who will have access to these secrets in the course of the work, and to direct the contractor that particular named persons on the list shall not have access. In short, the Government exercises a contractual right to bar named employees of contractors from access to secrets as defined in the contract. Upon breach by the contractor, the Government is empowered to terminate the contract. Up to 1956 this power had been formally exercised nine times, although there is no doubt that many more employees had been dismissed or transferred on Governmental suggestion, even though the firm had not resisted to the point of the Government having to issue a formal direction. An employee of a private firm was not entitled even to those minimal protections accorded to civil servants, nor could he have the case heard by the three Advisers.

In 1956 Imperial Chemical Industries had to dismiss their assistant solicitor, Mr Lang, because the Government announced that a condition of placing any further secret contracts with the firm was that he should have no access to the secrets. In fact, he could no longer be employed as assistant solicitor in view of this requirement. There was a debate in the House of Lords and the matter was raised at question time in the House of Commons. The Government refused to inform Lang of the charges against him or to state after the event why he was to be denied access to secrets. The Government refused to allow him to bring his case either before the three Advisers or a panel of independent legal advisers : he had previously been given the choice of being interviewed by the Second Permanent Secretary to the Ministry of Supply or of waiting to see whether eventually the Advisers would be empowered to deal with cases like his. He saw the civil servant, and came away with the impression that the reason for the action against him was that before marriage his wife had been a Communist. Although Lang was denied an appearance before the Advisers, the Government announced at the end of the debate on his case that in future employees of private firms would be allowed to go before them. These employees are denied representation at the proceedings.

Are these procedures fair? The Government's attitude is only understandable in the light of the policy declared by the Conference of Privy Councillors and accepted by the Government :

It is right to continue the practice of tilting the balance in favour of offering greater protection to the security of the State rather than in the direction of safeguarding the rights of the individual.

The procedures afford the maximum protection to State security and leave the citizen stripped of any rights which might, even remotely, militate against security.

Above all, the citizen has no legal rights whatever under these procedures. It is the consistent policy of British Governments to avoid putting themselves under judicial controls whenever possible. If a person is not accorded the protection, such as it is, allowed him by the arrangements already described, there is no court to which he can complain. This defect is particularly important where one is dealing with vague words like 'security'. 'Security' is an abstraction, and the citizen is at the mercy of the administrators who will define it as they please. To tilt the scales against liberty in favour of security is serious enough – when security is undefined the threat to the citizen is manifest. Contrast a case in the United States, where a civil servant was liable to dismissal 'in the interest of the national security of the United

States' : he was able to take his case to the Supreme Court of the United States, which reversed the Administration's dismissal of him on the ground that there had been no proper determination that 'national security' was affected.[22] Or take the decision in 1959 of the United States Supreme Court that the right to follow a chosen profession free from Governmental interference is so important that in the absence of Congressional authorization it was unconstitutional to deny a worker access to classified materials essential to his job by proceedings in which he was denied the safeguard of confronting adverse witnesses.[23] The justification in the innumerable cases of Englishmen being denied access to the courts in situations where judicial scrutiny is standard practice in the rest of the Western world is always the same : ministerial responsibility. In the words of Lord Kilmuir, then Lord Chancellor, the balance 'must be struck by a Minister who is responsible to Parliament; whose decision it is; who can be questioned in Parliament; ... and who is there to be shot at.'[24] The value of this protection can be measured by looking at the proceedings of the House of Commons ten days previously. The Minister of Supply was asked on what grounds he had denied access on the part of Lang to secrets : he refused to answer, and no doubt was within his constitutional rights in so refusing. What is the point of stressing the right to ask a question on matters of security when the Minister can be relied on never to answer? The political accountability of a Minister is a completely inadequate substitute for the right to take one's case before the courts.

Forgetting for the moment that the citizen, then, has no legal 'rights', we must now appraise the effectiveness of the unofficial safeguards afforded to him under the existing procedures. It is obviously of the first importance that the employee should have full details of the charges against him : it is not enough that vague statements like association with Communists be used; he should have the names and dates. The rules laid down by the Government in 1957 make no such specific references. There is no means of knowing whether such details are given; one can only say that the rules do not appear to envisage their being given. If the employee does not know when and where he is supposed to have been associating with Communists, how can he refute the charge, or perhaps show that security officers are in error? One's guess is that such details are not given, lest the source of the evidence be revealed.

We have seen that the employee cannot be represented by anybody throughout the hearing before the Advisers. To deny him legal representation is absolutely inexcusable. When the Society of Civil Servants protested at this the Prime Minister told them that the Advisers were the employee's friend, and that the presence of yet another friend might lead to the Advisers having to abandon or severely curtail their attempts to give the individual the maximum chance to clear himself. In short, the argument is : we have decided to appoint the judges as your advocate; if you have your own advocate the judges will cease to be your advocate. This argument is unconvincing and the objection remains in substance after the limited concession of September 1962 already referred to. Even if the Advisers really fear that a representative would glean intelligence from their questions which an unaided civil servant would not, why not put a security check on the representatives? Why not let the employee decide what will serve his interests best? The hearing itself bears no resemblance to a court proceeding. None of the witnesses for the Government is there to be cross-examined. Why not? Because it would disclose their identity. But the evidence may be that of a neighbour, or a fellow-employee. Departments were requested by the Report of the Privy Councillors to inform on employees. The interests of security may demand that the identity of security agents be concealed. But why should a man whose whole livelihood is menaced be prevented from confronting his workmates or neighbours who have spied on him? The answer that they will be discouraged from informing in the future is inadequate, but it shows the consequences of the 'tilting' to which the Government is committed. When a man is charged with a specific offence, as in the George Blake case, none of these rights is withdrawn. The solution there is to hold the trial *in camera*. Why should a person charged with treason be allowed to confront his accusers, and yet a person about to be dismissed because he is likely to commit treason be denied these minimum judicial rights?

The task of the Advisers is a curious one. They do not see witnesses; they cannot elicit information beyond that supplied by the Minister. They are at one and the same time to help the employee and to evaluate the cogency of each strand of evidence. This seems a job for the most experienced judges in the land. But when the system was introduced in 1948 Mr Attlee announced that it would be better not to employ any lawyers : the task was given to a couple of superannuated civil servants and an octogenarian retired trade union official. And yet even at the height of the war, when large numbers of enemy aliens were being detained under the defence regulations, they were entitled to have their cases heard by a distinguished lawyer before the Home Secretary decided upon internment.

The position of the Minister is even more curious. He first of all decides whether the employee is *prima facie* guilty without ever seeing the employee, but presumably having seen the other witnesses. He then takes advice from three men who do not see the witnesses he has interviewed, but who can see any witnesses, whom he has not interviewed, called by the employee. Upon receiving advice from the three men he decides whether to adhere to his original view. After the Minister has decided to uphold his decision he gives the employee a further opportunity to make representations. What about? The employee gets no transcript of the record before the Advisers; he is shown nothing of the advice given by the Advisers to the Minister. The Minister's decision is final.

These procedures are a travesty of justice as Englishmen are accustomed to it. They are what is to be expected in an area where Government is in the saddle, and the senior Opposition politicians soon hope to be. That civil servants and privately employed citizens should have their careers ruined by procedures like this is inexcusable. One wonders whether the British Government is aware of how badly its procedures compare with those followed in other parts of the Western world, where it would be unthinkable, for instance, to deny a man a lawyer. It may be said : look how few dismissals and transfers there are. But does the Government publish regular lists of the cases heard by the Advisers? And the Institution of Professional Civil Servants sees something more sinister in this rarity of instances – transfers and denials of promotion for security reasons without the victims being told and without their being able to invoke such protections as there are. It is a further weakness of the arrangements described that the civil servant has no legal redress if he is by-passed completely. The Radcliffe Committee found that, rather than refer a case to the three Advisers where it was doubtful whether Communist associations could be proved, the establishment officer would be astute in seeing an opportunity to remove the suspect to a less sensitive post; the Committee found this to be a not altogether satisfactory state of affairs.

There is another big gap in the procedural arrangements. The Government has publicly stated that character defects, as distinct from Communist sympathies, might prejudicially affect promotion or posting, and might result in exclusion from a sensitive post. Such cases are outside the jurisdiction of the three Advisers. The Radcliffe Report stated that 'Departments appear to follow no consistent practice as regards intimating to him [the suspect] any formal finding or decision adverse to him or providing him with a right of appeal to the Head of the Department under normal departmental procedures.'[25] Failure to obtain clearance on 'positive vetting' must often prejudice a career; to deny a victim even the minimal protections of the purge procedure in this class of case seems quite wrong.

Soldiers, too, are liable to be dismissed on security grounds: twenty-seven were dismissed in the five years to July 1956. Those engaged on secret work are also screened. Other countries recognize that their cases should be heard by procedures similar to those for civilians. Not so Britain. The soldier is challenged, given no information which would compromise the source from which it is obtained, and invited to make representations. He is given no opportunity of going before the three Advisers or any similar body. The War Office correctly points out that the Crown may lawfully discharge a man at any time in his own interests or to meet the requirements of the Service, and maintains that it would be contrary to the policy of the Department to disclose reasons for its decisions in this matter.

Screening also takes place of persons seeking secret employment. The Ministry of Supply has expected university teachers to answer detailed questions about both their students and colleagues who seek employment on secret work. Information as to their political affiliations is particularly sought. Schoolmasters are expected to notify M.I.5 officials, upon request, of the political affiliations of their pupils, a practice which has had the support of the Ministry of Education.

In 1964 the Government set up a Security Commission. This is a panel of public figures from the judiciary, the armed forces and the civil service, which investigates at the request of the Prime Minister in consultation with the chairman breaches of security in the public service, and advises on any changes in security arrangements. It has a quorum of three, and Lord Justice Winn is chairman. Some disquiet has been voiced at the fact that the Commission, which is nominally an unofficial body and meets in private, should in its very first report castigate named officials who were not allowed to be legally represented before it.

Some may be deluded into thinking that the citizen's rights have been increased in this security area by the establishment of the Parliamentary Commissioner under an Act of 1967. This is not so. The exceptions to his jurisdiction are great and include any action taken for the purpose of protecting the security of the State.

CHAPTER 9

FREEDOM TO WORK

ONE of man's most cherished freedoms is the right to earn his living. 'Freedom to work' is a slogan less familiar to the Englishman than say 'freedom of property'. Consequently, its legal basis is less secure. Yet one would conjecture that it is a freedom which is going to become more important and obtain more legal protection. Britain has lagged behind in its industrial charter; in its devising of solutions to problems of redundancy, movement of labour, automation, provisions for adequate notice. In the last few years there have been signs that Parliament will gradually create a much greater legal protection for the worker. In 1964 the Contracts of Employment Act 1963 came into force, whereby employers were required to give a minimum period of notice of dismissal : four weeks for employees of five years' standing, and two weeks for those of two years' standing. In 1965 the Redundancy Payments Act was passed. This gives to redundant workers certain rights to payments by their employers out of a Government-administered Redundancy Fund, and it sets up industrial tribunals to determine disputes about claims to redundancy payments

The most important breakthrough of all is in the Industrial Relations Act 1971. It extends the protection given by the Contracts of Employment Act so that, for instance, employees with ten and fifteen years' service are entitled to six and eight weeks' notice respectively. But more than that it gives an employee for the first time a right not to be unfairly dismissed, the criteria for which are set out in the Act. If he is unfairly dismissed, even though it was not in breach of his contract of employment, he can claim damages before an industrial tribunal.

We shall not deal again with restraints on that right imposed in the interests of security. Our concern here is with the protection afforded by the law to the worker against his employer and against his trade union, and with the obstacles in the way of his earning a living in the way he chooses.

CONTRACT OF EMPLOYMENT

If an employer dismisses his employee in breach of contract, the employee cannot ordinarily compel the employer to keep him in the job – the courts will order the specific performance of many types of contract, contracts for sale of land, for instance, but they will not require an employer to carry out a promise to employ a man for a certain period. In exceptional cases like the one we shall now describe, however, the courts will treat a relationship as creating a status going beyond that of employee. All the dockers of the United Kingdom are employed by the National Dock Labour Board, which is responsible for allocating them to available work on the docks. In 1955 Vine, a docker, was summoned to appear before the disciplinary committee of the Southampton Dock Labour Board for an alleged refusal to obey an order to work for a particular stevedore. After inquiry, the committee struck him off the register of dockers. Vine was thrown out of work : once he was removed from the register he was unemployed as a docker. Vine took an action against the Board all the way to the House of Lords. The House of Lords found that the disciplinary committee acted illegally in removing him. The Board had no power to entrust to the disciplinary committee the power to remove for breaches of discipline : that was the responsibility of the Board alone. The House of Lords had no difficulty in deciding to award damages to Vine for wages lost between the removal and the trial. But Vine wanted more than that : he wanted his name to be put back on to the register of dockers and a declaration by the court to that effect. The House of Lords declared him to be reinstated, so that it was as if he had never been off the register, distinguishing his case from the ordinary case of unlawful dismissal on the ground that Vine had more than an employment : he had the status of a docker, and this key to his employability had to be protected as such.[1]

Cases like that of Vine are exceptional. In the ordinary case no harm is done provided that the unlawfully dismissed man is fully compensated in damages, for he can seek elsewhere alternative employment in his trade. If, say, a man has a contract which has three years to run, the courts will estimate how much earnings he has lost through the employer's breach. This does not mean that he will recover three years' loss of salary – from this figure there will be deducted everything that he will earn in some other job in the same period, or that he could reasonably earn if he took diligent steps to obtain other work. If, however, he is dismissible on a week's notice, his damages will not exceed the loss of a week's earnings. Frequently, a man may be dismissed in a totally unreasonable manner and in circumstances which expose him to public humiliation. The dismissal may even be made in such a way that it will be very difficult for him to obtain fresh employment. It is a serious defect in English law that the employee gets no compensation whatever on account of losses of that kind. He cannot recover any more than he would have earned during the period which he was legally entitled to stay in the employment – the law of contract gives no compensation for humiliation, distress, the reprehensible behaviour of the employer, or the harm to reputation and character which is suffered by the dismissed employee.[2] English law falls behind that of other Western countries in this matter.

An employer often requires an employee to agree that after leaving his present employment he will not compete against his employer, either by setting up in business on his own account or by entering the service of a rival trader. The law, however, does not allow the employer to impose such restrictions as he thinks fit on the employee. The employee is entitled to use his skill once he has left that employment, even if he acquired it there. Two matters only may the employer guard himself against : the use of trade secrets learned by the employee, and the risk of his customers being exploited. If the employment is such that customers will rely on this employee's skills or deal with him directly to the exclusion of the employer with the result that he may gain their business if he sets up on his own account, then the employer can protect himself by covenant. Even so, the agreement must be reasonable with respect to the interests of the parties, both in respect of area and duration. A contract by a junior reporter on a Sheffield newspaper not to be connected with any other newspaper business carried on within twenty miles of Sheffield was held to be void,[3] a lifetime's restraint imposed on a pathologist's assistant was also void.[4] In short, the courts recognize that it would be contrary to public policy to allow a servant to deprive himself or the State of his labour, skill, or talent.

THE TRADE UNIONS AND THE WORKMAN

An important right, in both political and industrial spheres, is the freedom to associate with others in a common enterprise. Englishmen are great 'joiners', and they have been aided by the law in this. English law gives citizens remarkable freedom to join together in political associations. The trade union movement also benefits from this liberty. The Trade Disputes Act 1906 put on a firm basis the unions' freedom of organization. The only category of employees to be denied this freedom of organization are the members of the police force, although civil servants were similarly restricted between 1927 and 1946. The trade unions have of course utilized this freedom to create the conditions in which a man is able to work for a fair wage in proper conditions. But along with this unrestricted freedom for trade unionism are attendant risks of abuse of power. In particular, there is a clash between freedom of union organization and the right to work.

It is a commonplace that in many factories there is now a closed shop : a man cannot be employed in a particular trade unless he is a member of a particular union. There is no law which lays this down – it is the practical expression of the power of the union – and, conversely, English law does not make 'closed shops' illegal. How and in what circumstances will the courts aid a workman who is prejudiced by the 'closed shop' system?

The common case is of the man who has been expelled from the union, and is thereby effectively prevented from following his trade. Mr Spring, along with 10,000 other dockers, left the Transport and General Workers Union and joined the National Amalgamated Stevedores and Dockers Society. The Trade Union Congress had a Bridlington Agreement designed to prevent unions from poaching each other's members. Because they thought Spring had been poached, the Trade Union Congress ordered the National Amalgamated Stevedores and Dockers Society to expel him. Spring had never agreed to this condition about poaching, so that to exclude him on that account was illegal. He therefore obtained a declaration from the court stating that his expulsion was void and an injunction restraining the union from denying his status as a member.[5] As other trade unionists have found out, the sting in an injunction is that those who ignore it are liable to be imprisoned for contempt of court. A decision of the House of Lords extends the protection.[6] Mr Bonsor was expelled from the Musicians' Union : he could not obtain employment as a musician in consequence, and was driven to accept a job scraping rust off Brighton Pier. When he sued the union, the court declared that the branch secretary acted in breach of the rules of the union in removing him. So far the case is simple : it merely confirms that the court will not allow a union to disregard its own rules in punishing a member. But Mr Bonsor was not content to seek reinstatement – what he (and later his widow) sought was damages for loss of livelihood. The House of Lords laid down the important rule that when a union expels a member in breach of contract – the union rules form the contract – the member is entitled to damages for breach of contract, as well as reinstatement. Whatever reason the union may have for exclusion (or lesser deprivation such as denying him office in the union) –

to take some actual incidents, the man may fall in with his employer's requests to work overtime, he may refuse to join in an illegal strike, he may work too hard and upset the union's plans for piece work rates – the courts will give him a remedy if the union violates its rules. Moreover, whatever the rules may say, he is entitled to notice of the complaint against him, to be heard by the union before he is punished, and to have a fair hearing not marred by the grosser forms of bias : these rights of natural justice the courts will insist on. In 1970 Mr Edwards, a coloured Guyanese member of the Society of Graphical and Allied Trades (SOGAT), complained of his union's treatment of him. SOGAT wrongfully expelled him from the union. Because of the closed shop, all he could then obtain was employment with a non-union firm, which dismissed him for refusing labouring work. He then became unemployed again. He sued the union for their unlawful expulsion which he said because of their closed shop system had made him virtually unemployable at his skilled trade of printer. The High Court awarded him £6,760 damages against the union.[7] The Court of Appeal confirmed that a union was liable for arbitrarily or capriciously controlling his livelihood. On the union's undertaking to the Court of Appeal to issue a full membership card the damages were reduced to £3,500 and interest at 6 per cent.

We turn next to the case of Mr Huntley.[8] His offence was to refuse to join in a one-day strike at a Hartlepool shipyard. He was summoned to appear before a branch meeting of the Amalgamated Engineering Union, then told that the matter was one for the district committee, although nobody mentioned what action against him was contemplated. When he left the room the meeting decided to recommend his expulsion. The district committee was informed of this recommendation, but not that it had been done behind his back. Huntley was summoned to the district committee, where, despite his objections, the chairman allowed a charge to be investigated which was totally different from the one intimated to him in the notice. This district committee also recommended expulsion. In consequence Huntley

243

found difficulty in getting work. Meanwhile the general executive council of the union refused to carry out the recommendation to expel, although the district secretary sent a letter to them containing false reasons for the recommendation. The secretary did not tell Huntley of the executive council's decision : instead his committee purported to expel him behind his back. When Huntley eventually got work at a Tees-side power station, the Hartlepool district committee put pressure on Tees-side to have him sacked, pressure which succeeded with the aid of false accounts of what had happened at Hartlepool. Huntley sought to recover damages for what he had suffered through these actions. He was unable to prove breaches of contract, and so fell back on a civil action in tort. The union movement had exacted from the Liberal Government of 1906 an immunity from liability in tort which survived until its repeal by the Industrial Relations Act 1971. Instead of suing the union Hartley sued the various officials concerned for the tort of conspiracy. If two or more persons combine together with the object of harming another and not for some legitimate object, they are liable for conspiracy. The court held that Huntley had established such a conspiracy against the various unionists and awarded him £500 damages.

Matters were straightforward for Huntley because he could prove a conspiracy. The next question is whether the trade unionist victim of industrial pressure can succeed even though he cannot prove a conspiracy.

Draughtsmen at London Airport had agreed with their employers, B.O.A.C., to settle disputes by arbitration and not to resort to strike action. Barnard and Fistal, branch chairman and shop steward respectively of the Association of Engineering and Shipbuilding Draughtsmen, resented the refusal of Rookes, a draughtsman there, to join their union. Under threat by Barnard and Fistal of strike action, B.O.A.C. had to dismiss Rookes, after giving him the notice to which he was entitled. Rookes sued Barnard and Fistal. The House of Lords upheld the trial judge's verdict in Rookes's favour, but found the award of £7,500 damages to be too high;[9] the damages were settled out of court later at £4,000. The House held that if an individual illegally causes economic loss he is liable to damages, and that the threat of an illegal strike in breach of contract was such an illegality. The Government then introduced the Trade Disputes Act 1965 which reversed for the future the effect of *Rookes* v. *Barnard* and has been amended by the Industrial Relations Act 1971. It is no longer actionable for a person in contemplation or furtherance of an industrial dispute to threaten breach of contract or to threaten to induce a breach of contract by another. This tort of intimidation survives except that, if an unfair industrial practice is involved, a claim for damages lies to an industrial tribunal under the Industrial Relations Act 1971. The difference between conspiracy and this other wrong, often called intimidation, is this. Conspirators are liable, even though there is no separate illegal act, provided their object is to harm; the individual is liable for intimidation only if his conduct is illegal – the illegality may be use of physical force or threat of it, or conduct which violates a statute, or libel, but illegality there must be. The courts will not listen to vague words like coercion or industrial pressure, unless the plaintiff points to some specific act of an unlawful character : thus the House of Lords held that a union official who maliciously induced an employer not to engage employees from a rival union did not commit a tort against persons thereby deprived of a job.[10] Even if conspiracy is proved the defendant may still have a statutory defence. If the defendant proves that his act was done in contemplation or furtherance of an industrial dispute, the plaintiff must then prove some wrong independent of the conspiracy; e.g. that violence or fraud was resorted to.

The courts do give some protection to the employee against the excesses of his union and its officials. The employee cannot be expelled except after a fair hearing in conformity with the union rules. He can obtain damages from the union if he proves a breach of contract. He can sue officials who either conspire to harm him or individually use illegal means (other than threatening breaches of contract) in doing so. An official who has recourse to illegal threats of the kind described above has no statutory defence. The courts have been vigilant to keep within reasonable bounds the extraordinary concessions to trade unionism made by the Liberal Government of 1906. The Industrial Relations Act 1971 reinforces this judicial protection by abolishing the immunity from suit of trade unions and by recognizing that unions, like everyone else, may be accountable for the wrongs of those who work for them.

TRADES REGULATED BY STATUTE

Many professions, such as medicine and dentistry, are closely regulated by Act of Parliament. If a member of such a profession maintains that he has been removed from the register of qualified persons by proceedings which violate the Act or otherwise violate the rules of natural justice, he can take steps to have his name restored to the register by the courts. Probably he will be able to sue for damages in tort – the question of breach of contract could not arise.

Many other occupations are controlled, not by Parliament, but by informal arrangements. For instance, Mr Lee was a showman and a member of the Showmen's Guild, which had an elaborate set of rules. He was allocated a site at Bradford Moor Fair by Bradford Corporation. Another showman, Mr Shaw, also claimed this site, and maintained that he was entitled to it according to the rules of the Showmen's Guild. Lee insisted on using the site despite Shaw's protest. Shaw complained to the guild, which expelled Lee. Lee then sued the guild on the ground that he had not violated the following rule on which the guild had relied in expelling him : 'No member of the guild shall indulge in unfair competition with regard to the renting, taking, or letting of ground or position.' [11] The court felt free to decide for itself whether Lee was guilty of 'unfair competition' within the rule, and, finding that he was not, issued a declaration that he was still a member and an injunction restraining the guild from interfering with his membership rights. The task of obtaining damages as well in such cases is harder. If the plaintiff can prove breach of contract, he will succeed. He will succeed if he can show intimidation. Whether he will recover damages by merely proving expulsion in breach of these 'non-legal rules' is doubtful. In principle, the answer should be 'Yes', but in an imperfectly argued case in 1952 the Court of Appeal issued a rather peremptory 'No'.[12] In practice nobody can be a corn-porter in the Port of London unless he is on a register kept by a committee, which has no rules or constitution of any kind. Abbott was removed from this highly lucrative occupation register by the committee. When Abbott sued, the court held that the committee had exceeded its powers in removing him for having committed an assault on a trade union official in the street, but refused to hold that there was a tort for which damages could be awarded.

Even more indirectly powerful are those bodies which control professional sport. No law authorizes the Football League to suspend players, the Jockey Club to ban racehorse trainers, the British Board of Boxing Control to license boxers and their managers. These bodies do not extend membership to those sportsmen but none the less they exercise great powers over them. Their powers are probably less than those concerned believe; it was a pity, for instance, that the threatened proceedings by Sunderland footballers, who had been suspended with consequential loss of pay, were settled before trial on terms whereby the Football Association officials submitted to an order giving the players all the damages which they could claim, for the courts might well have exposed the flimsy basis of much of the control now exercised. The case in 1963 of *Eastham* v. *Newcastle United F.C.*[13] is significant. Eastham was prevented by the retain and transfer rules of the Football Association from leaving Newcastle United. He sued the club, the Football Association and the Football League, and got a declaration in the court against all of them that the restrictions imposed by the rules were void because they unjustifiably restrained freedom of employment. Proceedings have also been taken against the

Jockey Club and the National Hunt Committee. The courts have maintained that these self-appointed and self-perpetuating bodies, even if they have given no contractual rights to those whom they have deprived of their livelihood, must observe the rules of natural justice, and also the rules of their own organizations. Any attempt to contract out of the obligation to give a fair hearing will be probably void as being contrary to public policy. If there is a breach of contract the deprived sportsman will obtain damages as well as an injunction. In 1966 the court dismissed the plea of the Jockey Club that a judge could not interfere with their refusal to grant training licences to women.[14] In the absence of contract, at the most he can recover damages in tort. The doubts about the availability of this remedy are the same as those expressed in the preceding paragraph. Judicial pressure is gradually compelling these sporting bodies to introduce elements of fairness into their procedures.

LICENCES

Britain, like the rest of medieval Europe, had the guild system, whereby persons could practise particular trades only if they were members of the guild. As these guilds became more powerful, they became more openly monopolistic, restricting entry into the crafts, and imposing long apprenticeships. The decay of this guild system was heralded as a triumph for free enterprise and freedom of competition. The guild system of occupational control disappeared. Today, however, in its place we have many varied forms of occupational licensing which impose restraints of a not dissimilar kind.

Many professions have long possessed the power to regulate the entry into their ranks, and, subject only to appeal to the courts, the power to remove from the register. Leading examples are medical practitioners and solicitors. More and more professions take the initiative in seeking this statutory self-regulation : dentists, architects, and opticians are twentieth-century examples. No doubt the object is said to be the public interest, but what of prestige and the financial benefit from a closed shop? In the United States hundreds of occupations, egg-graders, yacht salesmen, well-diggers, tile-layers, for example, have all obtained legislative protection. In the United Kingdom hairdressers repeatedly sought a statutory system of registration under their own control and finally succeeded in 1964. Veterinary surgeons complain that the People's Dispensaries for Sick Animals are allowed to function as they do. The effect of such self-controlled professions is, of course, to restrict the freedom of those outside to make their living as they choose.

Occupational licensing extends far beyond self-regulating professions. Local authorities have had wide powers conferred on them by general statutes. Pedlars, hawkers, street traders, pawnbrokers, taxi-drivers, animal trainers, nursery and child-minders, bookmakers, theatrical employers and agencies, game dealers, riding-stable proprietors, pleasure-boatmen, marine-store dealers : these are examples at random of trades which cannot be carried on unless the local authority in the area permits. In Scotland, a Governmental commission reported that many trades were licensed unnecessarily : golf caddies and newsvendors, for instance. Local authorities are continually pressing for further powers to be given to them in Private Acts. Licences to take photographs on the highway, to sell goods on the promenade, to be a masseur or provide heat or sun-ray treatment, to run a shop in which meat, fruit, or vegetables are stored ; these are typical examples of powers which several local authorities have obtained for themselves from Parliament. And once one local authority has obtained a particular licensing power, other local authorities will request Parliament for the same power, pointing to the first granting of it as a precedent. It is easy to see that in many cases the interests of public safety, public health, and the like justify this interference. Yet it is difficult to understand the need for local variations in occupational control, and, whenever licensing of some occupation is introduced for the first time, the onus ought to be firmly on the Administration of proving that there are some considerations of public benefit which outweigh the right of a man to pursue his employment.

Licensing is not merely at the level of local government. Pilots, airline operators, master mariners, public-service vehicle operators, aliens seeking any employment whatever, are examples of persons who are subject to forms of central licensing. Add to the above catalogue the restrictions of the apprenticeship system, the activities of unions, the unofficial bodies previously described, and the result is very considerable restraint on freedom of work. So diffuse is this licensing that the general public fails to realize its scope and impact. We should be vigilant to see that mere sectional interests, whether a central or local bureaucratic urge for tidiness and power, or a profession's desire to up-grade its status and to protect its financial interest, do not masquerade as the public interest and needlessly restrict man's freedom to work.

CHAPTER 10

PROTECTION AGAINST PRIVATE POWER

OUR concern so far has been mainly with the legal content of liberty. We must also look at something else if we are to have a balanced view of the state of freedom as a whole in the country. We must round off the story by ascertaining what in fact is done within the law to put a different gloss on the practical scope of freedoms.

THE PRESS

We have seen already that English law endorses the proposition that the Press is free. But does English law enable the Press to abuse this freedom in an unwarrantable way? By 'freedom of the Press' the law means freedom to publish, no more, no less. Cynically and deliberately, the Press distorts the maxim in order to justify freedom in collecting news. The British Press gate-crashes into private parties of Royalty, spies on them in their holiday retreats, and uses concealed cameras to photograph them while undressing for a bathe, cruises round in boats, cameras clicking, if a royal parent wishes to instruct his son in sailing, and so on. It regards itself as free to burst into hospital wards in order to photograph those lying there seriously ill, and to press them for interviews. Intruding on the grief of a murdered person's relatives is justified by the Press because they have 'a story'. To incite relatives to stop a wedding dramatically at the last moment in order to have a photograph of the scene at the altar is conduct which a newspaper will indulge in and defend against criticism. Freedom of competition being what it is, the packs of rival newspapers will hunt in droves for the same story. Photographs of the dead, however lurid, are permissible if they feed the sacred cow of circulation.

Suppose that a newspaper reporter stumbles across an ex-convict who is struggling to adjust himself to society, and also is happily married to, employed by, and lives among persons unaware of his past. What a good story to republish the account of the sensational crime of twenty years ago, to reveal what the criminal is now doing! What does it matter that it will cost him his marriage and his job if it titillates the Englishman in bed on Sunday morning? The Press may publish the story secure in the knowledge that the courts will afford no remedy against it to the ruined victim. It is only doing its duty of publishing the truth, which of course cannot be libellous.

What is more sinister is that the privacy of certain persons only is invaded : we are told nothing of the private lives of newspaper proprietors; a Minister may have, to the general knowledge of Fleet Street, a mistress, but on this there will be silence. But let Mrs Gilliatt expose the methods of the leading gossip columnists in an article in *Queen*, and she will be hounded by squads of reporters from the *Daily Telegraph* and other national dailies who will report her minute-by-minute movements in the company of playwright John Osborne.

Why are such practices allowed to go on? Simply because English law does not make them unlawful and because the Press Council, even if it wishes, is powerless to control the offending newspapers. Once again the United Kingdom, mother of the common law, lags behind other countries which have developed that same common law to accord with changed circumstances.

Take the United States, for example. Under the lead of jurists writing articles in academic legal journals, and virtually unaided by legislatures, American courts have moulded the common law so that it protects the victims of behaviour of the kind described. The aim of their courts is to award damages whenever a person's interest in seclusion, or in his personal dignity and self-respect, or in being free from emotional upset, is interfered with by conduct which they regard as intolerably anti-social. They have therefore awarded damages in the following situations : installing tape-recorders secretly in hospital wards in order to have the account given by the victim of an accident to her relatives; tapping another's telephone call; publishing lurid photographs of the victim of a car accident; publishing X-ray photographs of the deformed pelvis of a woman celebrity; photographing the body of the plaintiff's dead husband; photographing a plaintiff mother's Siamese twins and publishing the picture. In none of these cases would the English courts afford any remedy to the victim; the freedom of the British Press is intact.

Both courts and Government share the blame for this gap in English law, a gap which is the more serious when new electronic devices make eavesdropping so easy. The courts are as free as the American ones to develop a law of privacy. But there is no spirit of adventure or progress, either in judges or counsel, in England today. Today's English judges are not the innovators that some of their distinguished predecessors were; in the hands of modern judges the common law has lost its capacity to expand. They have not been helped by counsel. Cases are argued and tried by a narrow circle of men who seldom look beyond the decided cases for guidance. The entire development of the American law of privacy can be traced to an article in a law periodical published by Harvard Law School. It is inconceivable that the views of an academic journal would exercise similar influence in Britain. This inward- and backward-looking attitude of the English Bar serves only to increase the likelihood that the courts will fail to make the law fit the needs of the time.

A Government committee sat for many years in order to consider reform of the law of libel. Its attention was directed to this problem of invasion of privacy by the Press. Characteristically, it found this problem to be outside its terms of reference and reported in 1948 that it had no proposals on it to make. In 1970 'Justice' produced a detailed Report which recommended a statute protecting the right of privacy. Despite Press opposition, the Government, in the face of public pressure, was compelled to set up a departmental committee under the chairmanship of Lord Younger to consider the matter. The Committee has not yet reported. Meanwhile there is increasing disquiet about privacy. A typical 1971 instance is the revelation by the *Guardian* that income tax offices, banks, the post office and others give confidential information to 'private eyes' : tax returns, bank balances, ex-directory telephone numbers, everything.

English law affords no protection against commercially exploiting another's personality. In each of the following cases the newspaper or advertiser has no legal obligation to pay for the use of the other person's name. A newspaper may freely say that Sir Blank Blank reads and enjoys it; an advertiser may promote the sale of his football boots by saying that Bobby Moore wears them; he may reproduce another's photograph for instance to lend tone to an advertisement, or on postcards offered for sale, or on cigarette cards. Untrue statements may be made. Statements may be made without permission, they may deprive the affected party of the opportunity to exploit for his own profit a valuable asset of his : none of these considerations counts with our courts, which leave him remediless. In contrast, in States like New York there is a cause of action for damages against those who so misappropriate without permission the name or likeness of another; for instance a model whose picture was used for an advertisement without permission recovered damages, whereas in England she would have no remedy.

The influence of the Press may be discerned in other ways. As a casual reading of many newspapers shows, and as complaints to the Press Council have confirmed, many newspapers review only those entertainments which are advertised in their columns. Or, as a typical example, take the *Sunday Times* and *Observer* of 16 September 1962. The *Observer* contained one advertisement for investment in a unit trust and the paper's investment adviser recommended investment in that unit trust and mentioned no other. The *Sunday Times* contained an advertisement for another unit trust; the adjoining investment editorial column mentioned that other trust and no others. One may contrast, too, the readiness with which the sins of the B.B.C. are commented on, with the reluctance with which organs of the Press are criticized in newspapers. Newspapers do not publish accounts about industrial unrest in their industry; hence in 1970 the *Observer* promptly withdrew a letter and an article by its industrial correspondent on the subject because its printers threatened industrial action. Later that year the London *Evening Standard*'s staff stopped the presses because they objected to an industrial cartoon in the newspaper. More unhelpful still to the reader is the attitude of the Press to consumer durables. Descriptions of goods which purport to aid the shopper are regular features in newspapers, the Press Council's predictable protests notwithstanding. Damaging criticism and invidious comparison with competing products have almost never been found, presumably out of deference to advertisers or potential advertisers. The intelligent shopper, of course, is not taken in by the fulsome praise of products which is habitually in the Press, but he is denied the advice which he needs. As we have seen, the excuse that the Press is scared of having to pay damages for libel if it subjects products to honest and well-grounded criticism is without legal foundation. These deficiencies of the Press have made possible the success of *Which?*, a periodical which is devoted to objective analyses and comparisons of consumer products and services.

The Press may discriminate in exercise of their power to refuse advertisements. They may refuse advertisements for temperance because their important advertisers from the brewing industry would object. Some will refuse advertisements because they conflict with their moral views – advertisements on birth control or for football pools, for instance. Most national newspapers refused to publish advertisements for *Which?*'s book on contraception (no doubt in fear of their Catholic readership), but it did not prevent them from writing about the book in a sensational manner.

Private power may detract from freedom of expression in less obvious ways. The Hulton Press was unable in 1965 to launch a new newspaper, the *Sunday Star*, because the Newsagents' Federation refused to handle it on the same discount terms as other Sunday newspapers, and the Newspaper Proprietors' Association refused to allow it to use the special newspaper trains and distribution facilities controlled by the association if the Hulton Press gave better terms. On another occasion Mr Randolph Churchill published a pamphlet critical of the British Press. W. H. Smith & Son Ltd refused to distribute it as wholesalers or to sell it from its own bookstalls. Mr Churchill complained to the Press Council about what seemed to him to be a hindrance on free expression designed to insulate the Press from criticism. The Press Council refused to interfere, and thought that W. H. Smith & Son Ltd had no moral obligation to accept the pamphlet. Subsequently the same distributors refused to handle *Private Eye*. The firm admits that it refuses to stock (or sometimes even to handle) many books and periodicals but claims the right to make its own decisions on these matters even though it is the largest retailer in the country— Elizabeth Bowen's *Eva Trout* was a 1970 victim. It refuses to give its blacklist even to its shareholders. A comparable example is the refusal of shipping companies to include in the libraries of ships on the South Africa run books favouring the rights of African Negroes. In 1969 the Royal Court Theatre withdrew a press card from the *Spectator*'s theatre critic because they disliked her attitude to their productions. We have previously mentioned the B.B.C.'s practice of dispensing with the services of those like the Muggeridges and Altrinchams who elsewhere criticize untouchable topics like the monarchy. (In 1964 the Garrick Club, of which Muggeridge was a member, sought the script of an American broadcast by him on the monarchy in order to decide his suitability to remain a member.) More subtle but no less restrictive is the play-safe approach – the avoidance of adult controversial films by the cinema industry, or the rootless mid-Atlantic film of television which sacrifices artistic standards in the interests of a double market.

ECONOMIC POWER

One evil against which the public has to contend is the commercial practice of foisting on to them contracts in fine type full of conditions unfair to the buyer and calculated to exempt the manufacturer as much as possible from liability for his defective goods. Under the guise of a 'guarantee' the buyer of a motor car is lured into buying a car with fewer rights, in the event of its being defective, than if he had bought it without the benefit of any express contractual terms. The courts have strained the existing law to the utmost in an attempt to protect the innocent buyer from this kind of dealing, and the consumer organizations have done what the Press has failed to do hitherto, namely, draw attention to the liability-evading character of the 'guarantees' of particular firms. It would be rash, however, to expect the average unsophisticated buyer to guard against these pitfalls. There are enough votes in 'consumer protection' to make it likely that these unfair trade practices, or at least the most heinous of them, will be outlawed by Parliament sooner or later.

Our system of credit is also closely affected by private financial powers. Decisions by banks about the purposes for which they lend money are legally unregulated. Finance houses are free from controls (other than on the size of deposits) in their hire-purchase dealings. The whole structure of hire-purchase law calls for further overhaul, and it is to be hoped that the sweeping changes proposed in the 1970 Report of the Crowther Committee on Consumer Credit will be made by Parliament. It has suited the finance house to take up the legal status of seller-hirer instead of the dealer – a fact of which the hire-purchaser is usually unaware – and yet the finance house strives by its one-sided forms of never-to-be-altered printed contracts to opt out of the responsibilities for the condition and quality of the goods which the law would ordinarily impose on the seller and to assume the limited responsibilities of banker instead. It has been found convenient for the finance house to save the expense of working a credit-rating system as in countries like the U.S.A. and Canada, and then to justify its own contracting out of liability and imposition of harsh terms on the hire-purchaser on the ground that otherwise the house would suffer losses from disreputable dealers foisting expensive (often worthless) cars at grossly inflated prices on persons of limited and un-investigated financial resources. The country cannot endure indefinitely a system in which the finance house demands for itself the privileges of a seller but insists on casting off the liabilities which the law impliedly attaches to a seller. Even when modest credit rating systems are in use the law fails to protect the innocent. A man may be posted without his knowledge as a defaulter because he would not pay for a defective article or an unsolicited magazine and will never know why thereafter he cannot get credit. Insurance companies are free to fix insurance rates on arbitrary grounds, or arbitrarily to deny insurance altogether to particular groups, even when insurance is compulsory. Not for Britain the laws of other countries which set up special commissions to protect the citizen against abuse of power by insurance companies.

SOCIAL POWER

Ordinarily, manipulation of social power will be seen as less important. Perhaps it is of no great moment that certain golf clubs will not allow Jews to be members, and that Coventry public houses used not to allow Indians in certain public rooms, a practice with which Coventry licensing magistrates refused to interfere. When one passes to the educational sphere, the problem becomes more serious. There is the educational institution which requires a photograph from each applicant because (it is thought) it restricts its intake of

Jews and Negroes. If there is any substance in the often-voiced complaint that some Oxford and Cambridge colleges will more readily admit the product of a leading public school than the similarly qualified candidate from a State grammar school, this would be a serious grievance – the more so as such institutions are dependent in practice on the State's financial support for their survival in their present form. In the 1960s Lord Mancroft was called upon to resign from the board of the Norwich Union Insurance Societies because their Arab customers objected to a Jew being on the board. Property developers can decide the terms on which citizens will be allowed to live in particular neighbourhoods.

CONTRACT

A contract enables a dominant party to it to exercise power. No law prohibits employers from denying union membership to employees. Yet no Government department will hand out a Government contract unless the firm accepts the Fair Wages Resolution of the House of Commons – a resolution without legal effect. One of the clauses in this Resolution is that the employer must recognize the freedom of all his work-people to be members of trade unions. We have seen, too, how the Government uses the contract device as a means of ensuring that firms do not employ security risks on defence contracts. This was the weapon which it threatened to use in the case of Lang and the Imperial Chemical Industries, Ltd.

The attempts made by the royal family to maintain privacy furnish another example. Large sums are offered by the Press to the Queen's nannies and other servants in the hope that they will reveal the intimacies of the royal family. Appeals to the sense of loyalty of such employees not having succeeded in stopping the flow, contract had to be resorted to. Now all royal servants, upon entering their employment, must accept the following clause in their contracts :

Communications to the press. You are not permitted to publish any incident or conversation which may be within your knowledge by reason of your employment in the royal service, nor may you give to any person, either verbally or in writing, any information regarding her Majesty or any member of the Royal Family, which might be communicated to the press.

None the less, several royal employees have not been deterred from publishing, whereupon the Treasury Solicitor has applied to the courts in the ordinary way for an injunction restraining this breach of contract. To disobey the injunction is a contempt of court, punishable by imprisonment. Henceforth, royal servants will be lucky if they manage to publish more than one instalment of their intimate revelations before the Palace and the courts catch up with them – witness the fate of the Snowdons' chef in 1966 : injunction and costs against him. On the other hand, the Palace remains powerless, to cite one actual instance, to prevent advertisements showing a photograph of the Queen going down a mine in overalls, safety boots, and helmet : the indirect advertisement value to the manufacturer of the equipment is obvious, but the dislike of the royal family for such practices is equally understandable.

PRESSURE GROUPS

Many members of Parliament on both sides of the House are paid by outside organizations to look after the interests of these organizations when matters affecting them come up for parliamentary discussion. Likewise, organizations employ other persons as 'contact men' with Government departments. These pressure groups (as well as the more familiar lobby groups like the C.B.I., the T.U.C., and the Lord's Day Observance Society) are a commonplace of public life. One well-known example is the pressure group of members of Parliament with large financial interests in advertising, entertainment, and television which was able to convince an unenthusiastic Prime Minister of the country's need for commercial television. English law is lax on these matters in contrast to that of many other countries. Members of Parliament are not bound to publish details of the organizations which they are paid to represent. The Government turned down again in 1969 proposals for a public register of those M.P.s paid by outside bodies – the increasing number of M.P.s who act as paid P.R.O.s for business can continue undetected. Other contact men are not bound to register themselves. Members of Parliament, Ministers even, are legally free to retain large shareholdings in companies which enjoy lucrative Government contracts. The only *legal* restriction is contained in an Act of 1792 denying a vote to a member with an interest in a Government contract, but the provision is useless today because 'interest' does not cover shareholdings, however large, in companies. There is, however, a parliamentary *practice* whereby a member who has a financial interest, direct or indirect, in the matter on which he is speaking in the House discloses the fact in his speech : enforcement of the practice is spotty because of the vagueness in defining what is an 'interest' in the issue being debated. By parliamentary practice, too, Ministers must resign from all lucrative employment other than that connected with family estates or philanthropic undertakings. They must dispose of their controlling interest in any company and divest themselves of all shares in companies concerned with the business of their Department. Accordingly, when Mr Marples became Minister of Transport in 1960, he sold his controlling interest in a public works company, Marples Ridgway and Partners. There is a corresponding absence of law, and vagueness of practice about the financial interests, post-service employment, and gift receiving, within the civil service.

All this is in contrast, not only with the comparative precision of United States law on all these matters, but, more surprisingly, also with our local government law. Legislation requires local government officers and members to declare all pecuniary interests, direct or indirect, and prohibits voting on matters in which there is such an interest. The courts interpret this local government legislation in such a way as effectively to maintain high standards of integrity in this part of local government.

The freedom to associate, which English law allows, also serves to facilitate pressure groups. In the typical statute, when the Minister is required to consult before he promulgates delegated legislation, it is obvious that he will consult the trade association more fully than the general public. Decisions of the courts have aided this process. The restrictions on the sums spent on advertising at a parliamentary election do not prevent a company from spending money to advertise one political party.[1] A sugar company which launched a big advertising campaign against the plans of the Socialists to nationalize the sugar industry was entitled to set off for income tax purposes the expenses of this campaign against its profits.[2] In 1967 the Court of Appeal struck down a rule whereby the Pharmaceutical Society sought to prevent chemists' shops from selling vacuum flasks, handbags and all goods outside the traditional range of pharmacists' shops – the court held that the restriction would be against the public interest.[3]

There is no space here to evaluate pressure groups in British politics. Suffice it to say that their ramifications are deeper and more extensive than many recognize, that they are virtually free from legal control, and that in consequence they are able to function concealed from the public gaze.

LOCAL AUTHORITIES

English law allows local authorities to take many decisions affecting individuals without giving them a hearing. Local authorities have also resisted pressures for legislation making it compulsory for meetings of the authority and committees always to be held in the presence of the public and the Press. This absence of publicity makes it easier for members of local authorities to wield private power. Take the controversial matter of allocating local authority houses to tenants : a local authority is under no compulsion to allow an applicant to put his case before its committee, it need give no reasons why that applicant has not been given a house, it need not disclose the principles, if any, by which it, its committee, or its staff, decides upon individual allocation.

Local authorities take many decisions which impinge upon freedom. One may decide to ban a procession, another, as the Middlesex County Council used to do, may refuse to employ Communists as head teachers (compare the dilemma of Coventry Education Committee over Jordan, the National Socialist leader and Coventry teacher), another, like Flintshire Education Committee formerly, may insist on children being educated at a school where Welsh is the medium of instruction for half the subjects in the curriculum, in face of the parents' desire to send their children to another English school also run by that education authority in the same town. Or take Caithness library sub-committee, whose librarian was willing to let his own children read Bruce Marshall's novel of the Spanish civil war, *A Fair Bride*. In 1954 the committee banned the book after the member introducing the motion to do so had said : 'The book is foul, filthy, and obscene. But are you surprised when the heroine is a harlot and the hero a renegade Catholic priest? And are you surprised that it should be admitted to a Protestant Caithness library? There is an insidious sneaking Roman Catholic propaganda in it which I detest. I move that this book is not fit to be taken into the family circle and should not be allowed to lie on the shelves of a Protestant Caithness library.' One may compare the practice of the British Museum. It keeps thousands of books on several themes (including the most comprehensive collection of erotica in the world) in a Private Case and omits them from the Catalogue available to readers, and it has a further set of books which it suppresses because it regards them as confidential or libellous, or because a Government department has so requested on security grounds, and to which it denies access altogether by the public. Exposure of these practices has led to a promise that in due course the Museum will mend its ways. We have seen that many local authorities have unofficial approved lists of comic postcards which will not be the subject of prosecutions for obscenity. In 1964 Rhyl U.D.C. refused to exhibit on the promenade posters advertising a new repertory company's plays, on the ground that they conflicted with the interest of the existing theatres; none of the others presented plays, and Arthur Askey was appearing at the U.D.C.'s own theatre.

LEGAL AID

However extensive the freedoms conferred by the law, they are of little value unless the citizen may have free access to the courts in order to have them defended there. One of the great triumphs of post-war English judicial administration has been its development of legal aid, for which both Governments and the legal profession take credit. A committee of lawyers investigates the merits of litigants who are contemplating civil proceedings and decides whether the cause has merit before issuing a legal aid certificate. A means test is applied in a precise manner to determine the amount of legal aid. The system works well, and has greatly increased the accessibility of justice. It is particularly necessary that Britain should have a generous legal aid system in civil cases because of the peculiar rules about costs of legal proceedings. In many countries, each litigant pays his own costs regardless of the outcome of the suit. In the United States, the poor litigant who is, say, the victim of a car accident will usually employ a lawyer on the terms that he pays nothing if the action fails, and that he hands to the lawyer an agreed percentage of the damages (say a third) if the action succeeds. In Britain the loser pays the winner's costs as well as his own. Suppose that a suitor wins at the trial, the other party unsuccessfully appeals to the Court of Appeal but then by a majority of three to two secures a reversal in the House of Lords. In short, six of the nine judges who have tried the case have found for the loser, yet he has to pay all his own legal costs and those of his opponent also, an amount which might well total £10,000. Without legal aid, the private person in this kind of legal system is unfavourably placed when his opponent is, say, a public body or commercial organization. He would often be deterred from embarking on litigation at all. Some gaps in civil legal aid remain and need to be filled as soon as financially feasible. A few actions like libel are not covered, and no proceedings before administrative tribunals, which transact an increasingly large slice of judicial business affecting the citizen, are legally aided. Perhaps, too, the financial ceiling for those seeking aid ought to be raised. There is also provision for obtaining legal advice under the legal aid scheme. Further, nobody accused of serious criminal offences will be denied legal assistance in presenting his case owing to lack of financial resources.

CHAPTER 11

FREEDOM OF MOVEMENT AND RACIAL DISCRIMINATION

OUR first concern here is with the freedom with which people can enter and leave Britain. Until now it has been very difficult to state the law, because it has been contained in a tangled mass of legislation, decided cases, statutory instruments, departmental rules, and the practice of the Executive. The Government has now piloted a new Immigration Bill through Parliament, which embodies the law in a single Act of Parliament with rules and regulations made under it. This tidying up of the jungle of existing law is welcome. At the same time, the new Act, as we shall see, besides being controversial, introduces new complications into the substance of the law.

Until 1962 there was a sharp distinction between British subjects and aliens. British subjects were free to enter and leave the country as they pleased, whereas aliens were subject to tight controls which were applied in an arbitrary way. A rapid rise in the influx of British subjects from the West Indies, India and Pakistan led to the Commonwealth Immigrants Act 1962. That Act restricted the freedom to migrate to the United Kingdom of all Commonwealth citizens other than those born in the United Kingdom or holding United Kingdom passports. Commonwealth citizens were subject to fairer procedures under the 1962 Act than aliens.

Until 1968 citizens of the United Kingdom and Colonies holding a U.K. passport had an unrestricted right to enter Britain. Against a storm of protest the Commonwealth Immigrants Act 1968 took away that right from some in the following circumstances. The Kenya Independence Act 1963 allowed those Kenya residents who did not become Kenya citizens to retain United Kingdom citizenship and of course to be given U.K. passports. No doubt the Conservative Government of the time had in mind European farmers, but the Act also protected over 100,000 Asians in Kenya. When, years later, large numbers of Asians began to exercise their right of settling in England the 1968 Act was rushed through Parliament in a few days. It took away the automatic right of entry from a U.K. citizen not born in the U.K. unless he, or at least one of his parents or grandparents, was born or naturalized in the U.K., or became a citizen by adoption or registration in the U.K. The effect of these rules was much greater on coloured than on white persons – most whites would qualify, whereas few coloureds would. About 300,000 were affected. These Acts also gave powers to deport Commonwealth citizens in certain circumstances.

The new controls over Commonwealth citizens were never so strict as those over aliens. The former did not have to register with the police, they had greater rights to stay, and a lesser liability to deportation, and their families had greater freedom of entry. Nevertheless, the Government felt compelled to respond to pressure by setting up a committee in 1965 to review the procedures. This committee produced in 1967 a widely acclaimed report (the Wilson Report) which recommended a statutory system of immigration and deportation appeals for both aliens and Commonwealth citizens. Most of this system was accepted by the Government and incorporated in the Immigration Appeals Act 1969.

The 1969 Act set up special appellate bodies outside the ordinary courts to hear appeals from decisions of immigration officers. Appeals were normally heard by an adjudicator appointed by the Home Secretary, and a further appeal lay to an Immigration Appeal Tribunal, whose members the Lord Chancellor appointed. Restrictions were imposed, contrary to the Wilson Report, in cases involving national security. The Home Secretary might direct the appeal to go straight to a special panel of the Tribunal, whose decision he was free to ignore, and any matter which he certified would be contrary to the interests of national security to disclose to the appellant was to be presented to the Tribunal and with-held from the appellant. These last provisions excited controversy in the case of Rudi Dutschke. He appealed against a decision of the Home Secretary that he should not be allowed to remain in this country as a student. The Home Secretary appointed a special panel, which heard some evidence in secret; neither Dutschke nor his counsel was allowed to be present during the hearing of evidence on certain security matters in secret on the order of the Home Secretary. His appeal failed on the ground that he might become a security risk in future; *The Times*, the *Guardian*, the *Observer* and the *Sunday Times* alike were highly critical of these unfair procedures and the way in which the special tribunal discharged them.

The Immigration Act 1971 repeals most of the legislation just described. The Act, and the rules made under it, will make immigration controls over incoming Commonwealth citizens the same as the strict ones for aliens, and will contain future immigration within close limits.

The United Kingdom, the Channel Isles, the Isle of Man and the Irish Republic collectively form a common travel area. Passengers are examined for the purposes of immigration control at the point at which they enter the area, and are then free to enter any other part of it without further examination.

Controls on and after entry to the common travel area apply to all except three categories.

1. Citizens of the U.K. and Colonies who have acquired their citizenship in the U.K., the Channel Isles or the Isle of Man or who are the children or grandchildren of such persons.
2. Citizens of the U.K. and Colonies who have at any time been settled in the British Islands for at least 5 years continuously.
3. Commonwealth citizens who are children of U.K. and Colonies' citizens who were born in the British Islands.

Those in these three exempted categories are said to have a right of abode and are called 'patrials'; citizens of the

Republic of Ireland are also within this exemption. Those in the second and third categories require a certificate of patriality. The criticism is made that, although there is nothing in these provisions which overtly amounts to racial or colour prejudice, in practice the dividing line will be racial, because the majority of white European Commonwealth citizens will alone be able to bring themselves within the exempted categories.

All non-patrials require leave to enter the United Kingdom. Control of entry lies with immigration officers. Treaties making visas unnecessary have been concluded with over fifty countries, including the U.S.A. and all Western Europe, but they are still required for nationals from most foreign countries in Eastern Europe, including the U.S.S.R., and from most Asian countries. Commonwealth citizens are expected to apply in advance to the appropriate British representative in their country for the issue of an entry certificate. There are tight rules about the admission of members of the family of someone already resident here; the resident must always be able to maintain them (a new requirement which could cause hardship if, say, the resident were temporarily unemployed at the time); but in addition they must have a visa, or entry certificate, or, if a non-visa foreign national, a Home Office letter of consent.

Visitors will ordinarily be given leave to stay for six months if the immigration officer is satisfied that they are genuine visitors able to support themselves and meet the cost of their return journey. Rigid limits are set to the definition of those entitled to enter as students, and in any event permission will be only for twelve months in the first instance. The course must be a full-time day one (not a correspondence course) suited to the educational qualifications of the passenger.

Doctors, dentists and nurses may enter for the purpose of working in this country for a year, on production of an entry-clearance. Almost all other categories require a work permit before they are allowed to enter for employment. Permits are issued by the Department of Employment and

Productivity in respect of a specific post with a specific employer.

Even if the obstacles set out above are surmounted, there is a further discretionary power to refuse leave for any of the following reasons : All except returning residents and their families may be refused leave on medical grounds, or for failure to submit to a medical examination. So also those convicted of extradition crimes, which we shall define later in this chapter. There is an overriding power to exclude those other than residents and their families on the ground that exclusion is 'conducive to the public good', an expression which is nowhere defined.

When a non-patrial (other than a visitor for no more than six months) is given leave to enter for a limited period, he will normally be required to register with the police. This new requirement for British subjects has been strongly opposed on the ground that the already precarious police/coloured relationship will be gravely disturbed. If registration is necessary, need it be with the police, critics ask ? Rules are laid down which regulate the variation or removal of conditions on which entry has been permitted. Substantially increased terms of imprisonment and fines are prescribed for the various crimes under the Act : illegal entry, failure to leave, breach of landing condition, assisting illegal entry or harbouring illegal entrants. There is a case for those, but a new power for any policeman to arrest without warrant 'anyone who has, or whom he, with reasonable cause, suspects to have, committed or attempted to commit an offence' has given rise to understandable anxiety about its possible effects on relations between the police and coloured citizens. Coloured people may well feel at risk unless they always carry with them their certificate of patriality or their passport; this would be invidious when the carrying of identity cards is not required of the community as a whole.

The Act extends the power of the Home Secretary to deport a non-patrial. He can deport for breach of entry conditions or remaining beyond the permitted period, and more significantly on the ground that his deportation is conducive to the public good. The wife and children under eighteen of a deported person have also to leave. If a person over seventeen is convicted of an offence for which he is punishable with imprisonment and the court recommends deportation, the Home Secretary can deport him. Even though the court decided not to recommend deportation, the Home Secretary can still deport for the public good. Deportation will normally be to the country of which he is a national, or that which last provided him with a travel document, but in exercising his discretion to which country to direct his removal the Home Secretary may also consider the expense that falls on public funds. A Commonwealth citizen or citizen of the Irish Republic who was ordinarily resident in the U.K. on 31 July 1971 is not liable to deportation if at the material time he has been settled in the British Islands for the last five years.

The Act retains the appellate bodies (the adjudicators and the Immigration Appeal Tribunal) set up under the 1969 Act, but the grounds of appeal are more restricted. Appeals will lie to the adjudicator against refusal of leave to enter, or the refusal to grant a certificate of patriality or an entry clearance, or any variation of the leave (whether about duration or conditions) or against any refusal to vary it. A person may appeal against deportation orders, or refusal to vary deportation orders, against the validity of directions to remove an allegedly illegal entrant, and against being sent back to a particular destination. When notice of appeal is given, a summary of the facts of the case is sent to the appellant. Either party to the appeal may appeal from the adjudicator to the Immigration Appeal Tribunal.

The exceptions and limitations to these rights of appeal are very important. There is no appeal against a refusal of leave to enter or a refusal of an entry clearance if the Home Secretary certifies that the direction has been given by him personally on the ground that exclusion is conducive to the public good. If a person has had his leave cut down or his request for more refused or his request to revoke a deportation order refused there is no appeal if the Home Secretary certifies that departure is for the public good, or if he personally made the decision now questioned. There is no appeal against the making of a deportation order on a court's recommendation. Where a family are included in a deportation order a relative can appeal only on the ground that the order was beyond the legal power of the Home Secretary, and a person who entered the country as a member of the family is now precluded from denying it. Members of the family are to be given the opportunity to leave voluntarily and if they decline are to be allowed to appeal against deportation direct to the Appeal Tribunal.

Those whom the Home Secretary intends to deport on grounds of national security or other reasons of a political nature lose their present right to an appeal to a statutory tribunal. Instead they are to be allowed a right to make representations to 'three wise men', according to procedures similar to those discussed earlier for Civil Service security cases : the Home Secretary will still decide, and no legal representation before the advisers will be permitted. In other cases when he deports because he deems it conducive to the public good there will be a right of appeal to the Tribunal.

It will be noticed that the vital matter of granting work permits is a matter solely for the Department of Employment and Productivity. Thousands of applicants each year will no doubt continue to be refused without a hearing, without being given reasons, and without the rules to which no doubt the departmental officials work being published. And it is not only refusal; it will be recalled that the permit controls the place and duration of the employment. It is entirely in the Government's discretion how many work permits are issued. In another matter which greatly affects freedom under the laws discussed in this chapter the discretionary powers of the Home Secretary are increased. Previously, Commonwealth citizens could acquire citizenship of the United Kingdom and Colonies by registration after five years' ordinary residence; the Act now provides that even if the citizen satisfies the five-year and other rules laid down registration is in the Home Secretary's discretion – and no appeal is provided.

Before the 1969 Act aggrieved immigrants often sought redress from the courts. The cases showed that the courts' powers were few, but, such as they are, they remain untouched by the 1971 Act. In 1969 the Court of Appeal held that American scientologists had no 'right' to enter or stay in the U.K., and so it could not ensure them fair treatment or consider whether it was for the public good to deport them.[1] Commonwealth citizens have been given limited rights by the courts to be treated fairly.[2] In practice the courts' rule is now less important; the immigrant's main hope of judicial aid now lies with the appellate machinery of the 1971 Act. But the courts may still insist that an unappealable decision must be arrived at fairly and that the claimant should have the opportunity of making representations to the Home Secretary before the final decision is made.

It is not surprising that the Immigration Act has met with strong criticism. What it does above all is to take away from British subjects rights which they have had for centuries, and to group millions of them with aliens, who have always received scant protection from English law. The emotive effect is the greater because a high proportion of the British subjects so deprived are coloured. Equally disturbing is the way in which the Act turns its back on the judicial process. No more Dutschkes for the Government. Leave as much as possible to administrative discretion uncontrolled by statutory bodies which would apply published rules. Let the Home Secretary have the final word on 'conducive to the public good', and the Department of Employment and Productivity operate secret rules without appeal on work permits. One also asks whether it is wise to confer new arbitrary powers on the police.

The Government of the day is entitled to determine its own policy on immigration, and to have the electorate have the last word on that, but can it ever be justified in applying its policy with procedures which deny the basic principles of natural justice?

POLITICAL ASYLUM

An associated topic is political asylum. When an alien's life or liberty is in danger or he has a well-founded fear of persecution of such a kind as to render life insupportable (e.g. denying him ration or employment cards) on account of his race, religion, nationality, or political opinion, it has been the practice of the British Government to allow him to stay in Britain. He may have no visa, he may not fall within the usual categories of admitted aliens, but nonetheless he may be allowed to stay. Obvious examples are the sailors from behind the Iron Curtain who from time to time desert their ships in British ports and seek refuge here. The same now applies to all non-patrials. The U.K. – and other states do the same – will allow such persons to stay. The Home Office makes the decisions and will first interview the non-patrial, who will not be allowed to retain residence here under the guise of a claim for sanctuary. The Home Office keeps no statistics about the numbers granted asylum. The principles are adequately summarized in the *Draft Immigration Rules: Control on Entry*,[3] which state that they are applying criteria in accordance with the international Convention relating to the Status of Refugees :[4]

A passenger who does not otherwise qualify for admission should not be sent away if the result would be his going to a country to which he is unwilling to go owing to well-founded fear of being persecuted for reasons of race, religion, nationality/ membership of a particular social group of political opinion nor will he be deported.[5]

The case of Dr Cort in 1954 illustrates the limits of this practice. Dr Cort, an American citizen, was a qualified doctor of medicine employed by Birmingham University. Before leaving the United States he had been rejected for military service because of a tubercular condition. He was approached in England by the American authorities with a view to his reporting for a medical examination in connection with military service. Dr Cort was convinced that the object of the American Government was to make him give evidence before the McCarthy Committee of the Senate on Government Operations in Washington – he had at one time been a Communist, and his former associates had been subpoenaed before the Committee and had their reputations besmirched by the Committee. Accordingly, he refused the American request. Britain then informed him that it would not renew his alien permit and that he would have to leave the country. The Government was pressed in the House of Commons on several occasions to grant Cort political asylum, but the Government refused on the ground that the facts fell outside the scope of asylum. The Government maintained (erroneously [6]) that Cort's refusal, which amounted to evasion of military service, was a ground, according to American law, for depriving Cort of his citizenship, and that it was not the practice, except in 'asylum' cases, to allow an alien to remain in England when there was no country which would be required to accept him as its national when he finally left Britain. There was, in the Government's view, no evidence that the United States would threaten his life or liberty for his political opinions – Cort's apprehensions were not supported by the known facts. Cort left England, and, fearing to return to the United States, emigrated to Czechoslovakia.

If an American national-serviceman deserts to England, under the Visiting Forces Act 1952 a U.S. military policeman can seize him without seeking extradition. In practice he has no protection under English law, and even though his reason is conscientious objection to the Vietnam War, the British Government has not invoked the right of asylum in any of these cases.

EXTRADITION

Closely linked with asylum is the law of extradition. The United Kingdom has entered into many treaties with other states agreeing to hand over any person who has committed a crime in one of these countries, on the condition that the other country will hand over to the United Kingdom criminals wanted by it. Extradition to such states is then governed by the Extradition Act 1870. The most publicized recent case was the extradition of an American in 1968 on the charge of murdering Martin Luther King. These treaties apply to nationals as well as to aliens, but not to political crimes. The Bow Street magistrate decides whether there is sufficient evidence that the person whose extradition is sought has committed an extraditable crime – there is an appeal to the Divisional Court of the Queen's Bench Division from the magistrate's extradition order. Extradition for a political crime is forbidden. Thus, in 1954, the members of a Polish trawler took charge of the ship, imprisoned the captain, and steered her into Whitby because they feared that they would be punished for their political opinions if they returned to Poland. Their purpose was to escape from political tyranny. Poland applied for an extradition order : although the court found that there was a *prima facie* case of revolt on the high seas and of unlawful wounding, the extradition order was refused and the men set free because the offences were of a political character.[7] The House of Lords has held that the idea behind 'political offences' is that the fugitive is at odds with the state that has applied for his extradition on some issue connected with the political control or government of the country.[8]

Extradition with Commonwealth countries has been governed by separate legislation, until recently the Fugitive Offenders Act 1881. This Act did not except political offenders from its scope. Dissatisfaction with its working came to a head in 1963 when the Home Secretary allowed Chief Enahara to be sent to Nigeria to stand trial there for alleged political offences.[9] This followed swiftly on a decision by the House of Lords that it could not prevent the making of an extradition order relating to two Cypriots who had helped the British authorities in riots in Cyprus and who maintained that their lives would be in danger on that account should they be handed over.[10] In consequence the Commonwealth members agreed in 1966 to new extradition arrangements which would exclude political crimes, and the Fugitive Offenders Act 1967 was passed. The Home Secretary decides whether to issue a warrant for the return of the accused, but no person shall now be returned to a Commonwealth country if it appears to him that the offence is of a political character, or that the purpose is to punish him on account of his race, religion, nationality or political opinions, or that he might be prejudiced at his trial or be punished or detained by reason of his race, religion, nationality or political opinions. The Act removes the defects of the former law.

The case of Dr Soblen in 1962 illustrates the interrelationship of extradition, deportation, and the right of asylum. Dr Soblen was found guilty in the U.S.A. of delivering defence information to aid the Soviet Union and was sentenced to life imprisonment. He was released on bail pending appeal. As soon as he learned that his appeal had failed he flew to Israel on his brother's passport. He was forcibly removed from Israel and put under American escort on an El Al airline plane bound for the U.S.A. via London. While on the plane he inflicted such severe wounds on himself that at London he was removed unconscious from the plane to hospital. A notice of refusal to land could not be served on him until two days later; the following day he was served with a notice detaining him as a person refused leave to land, pending the giving of directions on the means by which he was to leave. By *habeas corpus* Soblen challenged the validity of the detention order : both the trial judge and the Court of Appeal ruled that the circumstances of his arrival in England amounted to a refusal by the immigration authorities of leave to land, and that his subsequent detention was valid.[11] Thereupon the Home Office directed El Al airlines to remove Soblen: this they failed to do by the specified time.

The Government maintained that the facts fell outside the scope of political asylum because political offences for that purpose were restricted to situations where two or more political parties within the State were engaged in a contest in which they were seeking to impose the government of their choice on the State. The ideological struggle between East and West was not a political issue in the U.S.A. for this purpose. The Government therefore refused an application for political asylum.

The Home Secretary then issued a deportation order, under the Aliens Order on the ground that he deemed his deportation to be conducive to the public good, which Soblen again challenged by *habeas corpus*. On appeal to the Court of Appeal against the trial judge's refusal to grant him his freedom Soblen made two main points.[12] He alleged that the Home Secretary had refused to let him give evidence or to argue through counsel before the Home Secretary that his deportation was not conducive to the public good, and that this failure to give him a hearing was a breach of the rules of natural justice which invalidated the deportation order. The Court of Appeal ruled that in the interests of security an alien was not entitled to any hearing before he was deported. Secondly, he argued that the Home Secretary was abusing his power to deport, that under the guise of deportation he was really surrendering a fugitive criminal to the United States at the request of the American authorities. He was doing this because extradition was impossible here; the offence was espionage, for which extradition is not allowed. The Court of Appeal found that the offence was one for which extradition was not available, and that the United States had asked the British Government to return Soblen. The Court further held that the power to deport under the Aliens Order included a power to place him on a particular ship or aircraft making for his own country. The Court found no evidence that the deportation order was a sham; on the contrary there was evidence that the Home Secretary had made up his mind to deport Soblen by an aircraft bound for the United States before the United States Government intervened. Had there been evidence that the Home Secretary made the order in order to achieve the same result as an extradition order, and at the request of the United States, the Court would have required the Home Secretary to give an explanation; had he then refused to do so, or claimed (as he would be entitled) privilege for the communications from the United States Government so that neither Soblen nor the Court would be allowed to see them, the Court of Appeal would have set Soblen free.

FREEDOM OF TRAVEL

In early common law a British citizen was prohibited from leaving the realm without leave of the Crown, since to do so would deprive the king of the subject's military or other feudal services. Magna Carta subsequently gave every free man the right to leave the realm at his pleasure in time of peace. Writing in the eighteenth century, the great English legal author Blackstone said that the Englishman had a common-law right to leave the realm, subject to the prerogative right of the Crown to restrain him by writ of *ne exeat regno*. Originally that prerogative writ was issued to assure the carrying out of the military obligation to defend the king and the realm; later it became limited to preventing the evasion of legal liabilities. Now it is obsolete.

Before we go on to conclude that the subject must then be free to leave the realm at his will, we must consider the passport. It was not until the nineteenth century that the passport emerged in its modern form as a personal document to be carried on foreign travels. In essence a passport is a document which identifies the holder and provides evidence of his nationality. Whatever rights of protection the British citizen has abroad, he does not enjoy them because he has a British passport; he enjoys them because he is a British citizen. The passport is merely *prima facie* evidence of his nationality.

May a British citizen enter and leave the country at will without a passport? There is a restriction, surprisingly enough, in the Aliens Order 1953 as amended : that is not an Act of Parliament, but an item of delegated legislation which will have the force of law so long as it is within the powers conferred by its parent Act, the Aliens Restrictions

279

Act 1914 as amended. Article 7(1) of this Order provides that 'every person of or over the age of 16 years who lands or embarks in the United Kingdom shall, if so required by the immigration officer, produce either a valid passport with photograph or some other document satisfactorily establishing his identity and nationality or citizenship'. This does not apply to journeys between the United Kingdom and the Isle of Man, Ireland, or the Channel Isles. Where it does apply, the immigration officer may examine the traveller 'for the purpose of determining whether he is a patrial and it shall be the duty of every such person to furnish to an immigration officer such information as that officer may require for the purpose of his functions under the legislation.'

It is clear then that under the Bill a British subject can still leave and enter the country without a passport, so long as he produces alternative evidence of identity and nationality. But suppose that he does not produce satisfactory evidence, although he is in fact a British subject. It has been maintained in this book since it first appeared in 1963 that, despite the Aliens Order, the subject remains free to leave. In 1968, Ian Colvin, a *Daily Telegraph* journalist, attempted to leave Heathrow airport for Portugal without a passport, but with documentary evidence of his identity and nationality. The Chief Immigration Officer prevented him from leaving. When the matter was raised in Parliament the Home Office admitted that a citizen could not be refused permission to leave merely because he has no passport. The case showed that in practice immigration officials did refuse in such circumstances. The Home Office sought to justify the refusal on the ground that the officer had himself to be satisfied beyond question of the person's nationality. This view cannot be accepted; the Order did (and the Bill does not) say 'if the immigration officer is satisfied . . .' and so it would be for the court not the officer to decide whether the evidence was satisfactory if proceedings were brought against the officer for an allegedly unlawful refusal. Unfortunately Colvin did not have this point established in the courts by suing the Chief Immigration Officer. Under the Aliens Order an immigration officer had no power to detain a British subject and if he mistakenly did so he acted at his peril. Under the Bill he is empowered to detain everybody pending his decision. He may perhaps still be answerable in the courts for detention after he wrongly determines that the detainee is non-patrial. It is, of course, proper for an airline or shipping company to insert in the contract of carriage a requirement that he shall possess a passport, for they might otherwise have the expense of transporting him whence he came.

So far we have concluded that a citizen of the United Kingdom is free to leave and enter his country without a passport. It is when we consider his freedom to enter other countries that the passport becomes significant. Each country is free to demand such documents as it pleases of foreigners wishing to enter. If it will not admit without a passport, then a British subject has no legal right to enter that country without one. What has in fact happened is that, when visa requirements were widely abolished after the war, the United Kingdom secured this abolition by a series of treaties on a reciprocal basis with the various other countries. It is standard form in these treaties to stipulate that the countries party to them will admit British citizens without visa on production of a British passport. The legal consequence is that a British citizen without a passport cannot enter foreign countries.

At this point, it is of the first importance to consider whether a British citizen is entitled to a passport. The answer is that no British citizen is so entitled, even though his British nationality is beyond doubt – he may even have obtained a declaration of the High Court that he is a British national. Granting a passport is entirely a matter of royal prerogative which is exercised on behalf of the Queen by the Foreign Office. The subject has no legal right to a passport, the Crown can refuse him one without giving any reasons, he is not entitled to a hearing in order to argue his case for the grant of one, there is no court to which he can appeal if he is refused one, and he is not entitled to compensation for any loss suffered because of the refusal.

The freedom to travel is of course an important freedom, as the European Convention on Human Rights recognizes : men want to travel abroad on business, for family visits, to consult with experts in their profession, for educational and recreational purposes. It is startling that the citizen should seem so rightless. Contrast the United States where, when the Government refused a passport to a physicist on the ground that they believed him to have Communist associations, the Supreme Court held that the Secretary of State had acted without authority in withholding a passport because of a person's beliefs or associations.[13] As one might have expected, it is not by some carefully thought-out decision that the present rules operate. The Crown has had prerogatives in foreign affairs and retains those which Parliament has not taken away. Passports are treated as falling within that prerogative domain of foreign affairs, and have been left untouched. This is, moreover, a real problem, as from time to time British citizens are denied passports; for example, scientists who have wished to attend conferences in Russia have been refused passports.

Nor do the Crown's arbitrary powers stop there. In other parts of the Commonwealth it has been held that a Minister was not entitled to insist on a subject's handing back his passport. The passport issued in Britain is worded so that it remains the property of the Crown, who can demand its return at any time for any reason. Its withdrawal may be insisted upon whenever it suits the whim of the Crown – for instance, to restrain the movements of a former member of the royal household who may wish to enjoy in the United States the fruits of his articles in American newspapers on the doings of the royal family.

In 1968 Sir Frederick Crawford had his passport withdrawn because of his activities in connection with the Smith regime in Rhodesia. He was sufficiently influential to have the matter debated in Parliament, but without effect. One optimistic M.P. thought that the Parliamentary Commissioner would be entitled to review the Commonwealth Secretary's act under the Parliamentary Commissioner Act 1967.

Both Conservative and Labour Governments in the 1960s insisted that no reasons for withdrawal of passports would be given, because the power is a prerogative one. Predictably, the Commonwealth Secretary promptly certified that the passport withdrawal affected relations between Governments and so was no business of the Commissioner. Despite the unanimous protest of the Press, the grant and withdrawal of passports remains totally free from review by courts or Commissioner. The opportunity provided by the Immigration Bill 1971 to rectify this defect was deliberately not taken. About $2\frac{1}{2}$ thousand passports a year are seized, but only about one a year on political grounds such as in the Crawford case. The largest group is that of stranded holiday-makers repatriated on Government loan.

Racial Discrimination

Britain has no laws which discriminate against persons on account of their race and colour. A Jew, a Chinese, a Negro, for example, all enjoy the same voting rights : they must merely comply with the same rules about nationality and residence as everybody else. They are equally entitled to the facilities for education and to the benefit of the social services. The law does not order segregation in public transport or anywhere else. We have already discussed the circumstances in which incitement to racial prejudice is an offence. In these respects Britain is free from the legal restraints which have agitated the United States so much. In this sense, there is equality before the law.

An equally important practical question is the effectiveness with which the law takes positive steps to ensure that persons are not discriminated against on account of race or colour. To say that the law does not discriminate is one thing, but does the law compel persons not to discriminate, or otherwise protect those who are liable to be discriminated against?

It was to deal with this question that Parliament for the first time in the Race Relations Act 1965 introduced legislative controls. That Act had limited application and was based on inadequate research, but experience of its operation was helpful in preparing the much more comprehensive Race Relations Act 1968 which has replaced it.

RACE RELATIONS ACT 1968

The 1968 Act makes it unlawful to discriminate on the ground of colour, race or ethnic or national origins by treating someone less favourably than other persons would be treated. Segregation is less favourable treatment. It applies to discrimination in those areas where racial discrimination is an important social problem. The first area specified is the provision of any goods, facilities or services. These wide expressions cover places of public access or entertainment or refreshment like dance halls, public houses, theatres, cinemas, cafés and public libraries. It covers hotels, boarding houses, trains, buses and air services. Businesses and professions which provide services are included : doctors, and estate agents for instance; and so are public bodies which provide services. There must be no discrimination in educational facilities or in banking or insurance facilities. Let us look at typical examples under the Act. A car-hire firm could not refuse a car to a Trinidadian on the ground that their insurance cover did not extend to those born outside the U.K. : Lloyds had to bring about changes in car insurance policies. Nor could a Lloyds underwriter refuse owner-driver discounts to someone because he was born in India. In 1971 it was stated that the Race Relations Board had made motor insurers stop charging higher premiums to those born abroad. Mecca could not refuse coloured youths admission to its Locarno Ballroom, Streatham, merely on the ground that to admit any coloured might result in disturbances. A Lancashire estate agent who offered mortgage facilities to house buyers could not refuse to put up to the building society for whom he acted as agent an application by a Pakistani.

The Act prohibits an employer from discrimination by refusing a coloured applicant employment, by giving him different terms of employment or opportunities for training or promotion or by dismissing him. Here and elsewhere the Act applies to the Crown; the Government has gone further by stating that it will withhold contracts from firms practising racial discrimination in employment. The supermarket could not refuse to employ part-time a coloured schoolboy because its customers might object; a firm which does employ coloured workers has had to abandon a policy of never upgrading them to skilled positions.

It is unlawful for trade unions or employers' organizations to discriminate by denying membership or refusing benefits. A textile plant had a closed shop and wished to bring some Pakistanis into it; the union therefore denied them membership. Because of the Act the Pakistanis were offered membership and the next available vacancies in the plant.

The Act applies to discrimination in housing, either by refusing to dispose of it to the applicant (whether sale or lease) or by treating him differently when he is in the accommodation. There is an exception where the landlord lives there, shares accommodation with others and has accommodation for fewer than seven persons other than those in his household. Discrimination with respect to passengers' cabins on ships is also not unlawful. Municipal housing is covered, so that local authorities cannot have rules for allocating council houses which discriminate against coloureds or foreigners; successful complaints under this part of the Act have been made against Ealing and Wolverhampton, for example. A property owner could not refuse accommodation to a Kenyan on the ground that he did not mix white and coloured tenants; an Indian doctor was discriminated against when he was told on the telephone that a house on a new estate was available but when he called at the builder's office in person was informed that all the houses were sold. In housing, employment and elsewhere discriminatory advertisements are also prohibited.

The machinery for enforcing the law is exceptional in Britain; the criminal law is not invoked. The Act is enforced by a Race Relations Board of twelve members; in practice its employment functions are discharged by its Employment

Committee, and other complaints within its powers are handled by its General Committee. The Board has appointed nine regional conciliation committees whose members are unpaid; three in London, one each for West Midlands, East Midlands, Yorkshire and the North-east, North-west, Scotland, and Wales and the South-west.

The aim of the Act is to settle cases by conciliation. Complaints affecting the Crown, and so far those concerning insurance, local authority housing and education, are handled by the Board; the remainder (except for the special case of employment) are handled by the appropriate regional conciliation committee. The complaint is investigated and an opinion formed whether an unlawful act has been performed. If it is not thought unlawful that is the end of the matter. If thought unlawful every effort is made to settle the difference, and where appropriate to secure a written assurance against any repetition.

There is the same emphasis on conciliation in employment cases, but it has been thought desirable to have special machinery whereby the industry concerned has the opportunity to participate. Employment complaints must be referred to the Department of Employment and Productivity. If the particular industry has set up machinery for handling complaints the Department refers the complaint to it. If there is no such machinery the case is dealt with by the Board in the same way as other complaints. Many areas of industry have not instituted special machinery, so that fewer than 25 per cent of employment complaints are dealt with by industrial machinery. Anybody aggrieved by such a decision may notify the Board, which is then empowered to make its own investigation. Twenty-eight complained to the Board against the findings of industrial machinery from 1 April 1970 to 31 March 1971.

The Board may investigate even though no complaint has been made where in consequence of an allegation of discrimination it has reason to suspect discrimination. It has made extensive use of this power in employment. In one case the Board suspected that a manager of a section of a multiplant company was pursuing a policy of not employing coloured permanent staff. Its suspicions proved to be well-founded, and the company agreed to change its policy at the plant. Where the Board fails to obtain a settlement or satisfactory assurance of a matter which in its opinion constitutes unlawful discrimination, it decides whether to institute legal proceedings before a county court judge sitting with two assessors with special knowledge and experience of problems connected with race and community relations. Several remedies may be sought in the county court. If the court is satisfied that the defendant has previously engaged in similar unlawful conduct and is likely to do so again in the future, it may grant an injunction restraining him, breach of which would be contempt of court ultimately punishable by imprisonment. The court may grant special damages for expenses caused by the discrimination and further damages for loss of benefit which the complainant might have had but for the Act. In the first case which reached the county court a Huddersfield builder was found to have discriminated by refusing to sell a house on his estate to an Indian. In the second, damages were awarded against a Wolverhampton working men's club for refusing admission to a Jamaican telephone exchange girl at a G.P.O. party for which the club had been hired. The High Court has held that Ealing Borough Council was infringing the Act when it confined its waiting list for council houses to British subjects.[14]

The Act is a well-drafted one which has been subjected to unfair criticism. For example, it has been said that its 'racial balance' clause drove a coach and horses through the employment provisions. This criticism is unfounded; discrimination for the purpose of securing a balance of different racial groups is permitted, and the Board has been able to ensure that this is fairly applied. Opponents of the Act seize every opportunity to ridicule it by bringing frivolous complaints. All lawyers know that England is a country of frivolous would-be litigants, and race relations is no exception. Advertisements illustrate the point. For good reason the Act covers discriminatory advertisements; the Board has thereby been

able to stop 'no coloured' advertisements about flats. Someone, not of course anybody connected with the Board, com-
plains about an advertisement for a Scotswoman able to do
plain cooking. Needless to say, the Board takes no action
against the advertiser, yet the Press seeks to ridicule the whole
of race relations legislation on this flimsy basis in what it
called the Scotch porridge case, and with parliamentary
immunity one M.P. therefore calls the whole of the Board
'pompous rather idiotic asses' who had gone off their heads
and should be removed. Parliament could of course have
saddled with costs those who abused the Act in this way by
making vexatious complaints, but it was surely wise to believe
that common sense would ultimately prevail.

In ideal circumstances a better Act could be drafted;
whether more could be expected in the give and take of
politics is another question. Complaints are handled too
slowly, especially in the employment area; presumably trade
union pressures were too strong to permit the quicker procedures of the Board to apply here. The Board has no power
by subpoena to dig out evidence of discrimination by compelling witnesses to attend or to produce documents. The
Home Secretary has failed to give the coloured person adequate remedy against the police. But the citizen in general
has no proper means of complaining about the police. The
same is true in allocation of municipal housing where the
coloured has been given protection which a person unfairly
treated for other reasons does not have. Should the Act have
given the coloured special protection against the police for
discriminatory conduct? Enforcement could be more effective. The employer is not compelled to hire the complainant,
the house-owner cannot be made to sell or let the house to
the aggrieved. Should we wait till citizens have adjusted
themselves to the shock of a Race Relations Act No. 2 before
rounding off the law in Act 3?

THE COMMON LAW

Some rules of the common law still have the effect of protecting against discrimination, though the Race Relations Act diminishes their practical importance. So the West Indian cricketer, Learie Constantine, obtained damages against the Imperial Hotel, London,[15] for wrongfully refusing him accommodation because he was coloured, a law which does not apply to cafés, restaurants or any place other than hotels which refuse accommodation to travellers.

Scala Ballroom (Wolverhampton) Ltd v. *Ratcliffe* [16] is another of the extremely rare cases where an incident concerning colour bar reached the courts. The owners of a ballroom in Wolverhampton would not admit coloured people. Officials of the Musicians' Union told the ballroom owners that they would not allow members of the union to play there while the ban was in force. The owners then sued the officials for damages and for an injunction restraining them from conspiring to cause musicians to break their contracts. The Court of Appeal found that the union contained many coloured members, and that it would have caused bitterness among members had musicians played in the ballroom. They held that, even though the union's material interests were not at stake, it was lawful for the officials to take these steps to protect their legitimate, non-financial interests. The ballroom owners accordingly lost the action.

These random common-law cases matter little. If the law is to be effective in race relations, it will be by the Race Relations Act, which rightly relies on conciliation and enforcement by the Race Relations Board.

CHAPTER 12

CONCLUSION

CIVIL liberties in Britain have been shown to be a patchwork. Some of them rest on the chance that citizens have sued each other and given the courts the opportunity to declare some isolated legal rule. Some rest on sporadic legislation, often passed to meet some specific emergency, real or imaginary. The extent of inroads on certain freedoms rests on the subtleties of ministerial responsibility and the muted insistence of Whitehall to be allowed to govern unhindered.

This is a book about liberties in Britain, and not one about international affairs. Yet a quick glance at the international scene may be useful before a general assessment is attempted. After the Second World War, the United Nations eventually formulated a Declaration of Human Rights which embodied many of the fundamental freedoms which we have been examining. It was hoped to reinforce this by a Convention which would impose on states a binding obligation to respect these rights. Attempts to produce that Convention failed. Europe has had more success in its European Convention of Human Rights of 1950. This Convention is not content to spell out in detail the content of these freedoms : it sets up machinery for investigation and decision. A citizen whose complaint is that a signatory has violated the Convention may ultimately cause that state to be taken before the European Court of Human Rights, which is empowered to award satisfaction to a citizen who establishes the violation. To save the Court from being swamped, all complaints are screened first by a Commission, which decides whether there is a *prima facie* breach and ensures that all other remedies have been tried in vain. It is in line with British official attitudes to constitutional arrangements of this kind that, although it is a party to the Convention and has recognized the Commission, not until January 1966 did the United Kingdom accept the jurisdiction of the Court and allow individual citizens to bring matters before the Commission : it is unfortunate that we lagged behind Austria, Belgium, Denmark, Germany, the Netherlands, and Ireland. Our excuse was the unjustified one that the Englishman would receive no more protection than that furnished by the English common law. An Irish citizen who complained of detention without trial has already had his case against the Government of Ireland adjudicated upon by the Court. It is too early to say what effect on our liberties this acceptance will have. There have been two cases of significance affecting the U.K. In 1967 the Commission treated as admissible a petition by Mohamed Kahn's father alleging that Britain was in breach by not providing a proper hearing of the application to join his father in Bradford :[1] the case was settled in 1968 without being referred to the Court.[2] In 1970 thirty-five East African Asians, denied admission to the U.K. under the Commonwealth Immigrants Act 1968 complained to the Commission. The Commission has treated as admissible twenty-five of the complaints on the ground that they were all subjected to degrading treatment within Article 3 of the Convention, denied the right to security of person and discriminated against.

It must be stressed that only when all remedies in the national court have been exhausted, and all the Commission's efforts to effect a settlement have failed, is the case referred to the Court. The Commission, not the claimant, is empowered to refer the case to the Court. The Court is not a Court of Appeal from the national court; it is concerned only with breach of the Convention. Yet some of the views of the Commission and Court could have application for the United Kingdom; for example, in the context of the *Soblen* case, it is significant that the Commission in one case ruled that the deportation (and even the extradition) of a person to a particular country might in appropriate circumstances constitute 'inhuman treatment' and thereby violate Article

3 of the Convention. It may also be that the protection accorded to privacy in the United Kingdom would fall below the minimum requirements of the Convention.

Membership of the European Communities entails a treaty obligation to ensure that regulations made by the Council of Ministers and the European Commission and decisions of the Court of the Communities are given direct effect in a country's own legal system.

Attempts have been made to construct a general theory of civil liberties in Britain. Best known is the principle of the Rule of Law, expounded by the nineteenth-century Whig, Dicey, who said :

> The general principles of our constitution (as for example the right to personal liberty, or the right of public meeting) are with us the result of judicial decisions determining the rights of private persons in particular cases brought before the Courts; whereas under many foreign constitutions the security (such as it is) given to the rights of individuals results, or appears to result, from the general principles of the constitution. . . . Our constitution, in short, is a judge-made constitution. . . . There is in the English constitution an absence of those declarations or definitions of rights so dear to foreign constitutionalists. . . . Thus the constitution is the result of the ordinary law of the land.[3]

We know that this statement is inexact : for instance, a study, however comprehensive, of decided cases would give the reader a most incomplete picture of the state of British freedom. At the same time it does reveal an important difference of approach between Britain and many other countries. Britain has no one document which can be spoken of as 'the constitution' – Parliament has never attempted to list our freedoms. In sharp contrast is the United States, for example. Here is an extract from its constitution :

> Congress shall make no law respecting an establishment of religion, or prohibiting the free exercise thereof; or abridging the freedom of speech, or of the press; or the right of the people peaceably to assemble and to petition the Government for a redress of grievances.

Dicey, successive British Governments, and many judges

point with pride to this distinguishing characteristic of British liberty and speak disparagingly of written constitutions. They maintain that it is useless to have documents which are merely high-sounding catalogues of freedoms phrased in language so inescapably vague that the little man who finds himself in the hands of the police derives no benefit from them. What counts is whether the judges can give a man a fair trial, whether procedures like *habeas corpus* are readily available to him. These arguments are cogent but not conclusive. The jurisprudential notion of liberty is the same, whether we have the Dicey Rule of Law or a Bill of Rights. For example, freedom of speech can never be a positive power to do something. Every legal system prescribes that you cannot do this and this : you must not defame another, you must not be seditious, you must not be obscene, and so on. The legal concept of liberty is that there are residual areas of great importance where man is free to act as he likes without being regulated by law. In both Britain and the U.S.A. what is not forbidden is permitted. If a country enshrines its freedoms in a constitutional document, its citizens respond emotionally : the American cherishes many of his liberties the more because they are in the Bill of Rights — public opinion is effectively mobilized in their defence. More than that, in a system like the American, the constitution is a special law, one that cannot be changed except by a special procedure different from that for ordinary laws. Was it a good thing that all the restraints on freedom contained in the Official Secrets Act of 1911 were rushed through the House of Commons in one day in time of peace as if they were matters of no moment, the citizen no doubt unaware of that curtailment of his liberty which was thereby being effected? Parliamentary sovereignty in Britain ensures that Parliament can change any law, however fundamental, by the same process as, say, a law which increases the amount which a local authority may charge for dustbins.

Even more important is the power given to courts like the Supreme Court of the United States to intervene if laws inconsistent with the constitution are passed. Judicial review of administrative interference with civil liberties is much more frequent and effective there than in Britain. Here is the explanation why so many of the British administration's interferences with liberty are beyond the courts' control in circumstances where it is inconceivable that the courts in America would stand aside. This has more subtle consequences. Because English lawyers have comparatively few chances to participate in cases affecting civil liberties, there is little interest in the subject professionally – there is no money in it for lawyers – and the dearth of case law makes the universities also inactive in research. This explains, but does not excuse, the fact that this is the first book ever to attempt a detailed survey of the content of British civil liberties, whereas in the United States there are dozens of such books, ranging from the highly specialized monograph to the survey for the general reader.

The British stand on this matter is having unfortunate consequences in the Commonwealth. One of the great unifying strands of the Commonwealth has been the common law. Many members of the Commonwealth are, however, being attracted to constitutions which embody human rights. They maintain that to do so is not inconsistent with the common-law system. They accept the British argument that judicial independence and procedural safeguards are essential for liberty. But they add : why are these inconsistent with a Bill of Rights? Law is not merely a matter of coercion and punishment; is not one of its tasks to set standards of justice acceptable to society? So regarded, a Bill of Rights can provide leadership and set standards. India, Ceylon, and Malaya have guaranteed human rights in the new constitutions which they have formulated since obtaining independence. Most important of all, Canada has recently enacted a new Bill of Rights Act. Linked with this issue is the role of the Judicial Committee of the Privy Council, which used to be a general court of appeal from the Commonwealth and Empire. This is a court composed largely of English senior judges. It could have made a magnificent contribution to Commonwealth relations by aiding the progressive development and unification of the common law. Instead, the measure of its failure is that one member of the Commonwealth after another has dispensed with appeals to it. One of the causes of its failure has been its inability sympathetically to interpret written constitutions, especially the Canadian one. This is a side-effect of our not having a written constitution. American experience shows that judges become much more important where there is a written constitution; they have to immerse themselves in major political questions; they see law as a positive instrument of national policy – the part played by the Supreme Court on racial desegregation over the years is an obvious example. On the contrary the British judge has trained himself as an umpire, avoiding clashes with the Government of the day, cutting himself off from politics whenever possible, and divesting his judgments of social, economic, and political references to the utmost. This outlook has made him unable to provide the kind of interpretation necessary for the written constitutions of other parts of the Commonwealth : hence the by-passing of the Privy Council.

Perhaps in part because 1968 was Human Rights Year there has been increasing discussion recently on whether there should be a British Bill of Rights. The important question to be asked is whether the citizen's freedom would then be better protected. Those who advocate a Bill of Rights have in mind documents like the European Convention of Human Rights. Their characteristic is that they spell out in general terms freedom of expression, freedom of the person, freedom of assembly, freedom of religion, the right of privacy, the right to work and so on, duly qualified by epithets like 'unreasonable', 'arbitrary', or 'necessary in the public interest'. But what legal consequences are you to attach? If it is to be a mere declaration of principles its impact will be insignificant. If you say that this is now the law enforceable in the courts, the courts have to decide these issues of 'unreasonable', 'arbitrary' and the like. For that reason jurists like Lord Gardiner oppose a Bill of Rights; they say that the judges would have an impossible task, so inherently uncertain is the limit of such qualifications. We have seen that, in so far as these rights are now part of English law, they are hedged around with detailed rules; nobody would know how many of these details were still the law until the judges had interpreted the Bill of Rights in the light of them. Or you may say the purpose of the Bill of Rights is to affect future legislation : you would 'entrench' the Bill so that none of it could be automatically repealed by later Act of Parliament. But how far would you 'entrench' it? A mere convention of the constitution would not be enough. The American solution would be to say every statute in conflict with the Bill is to that extent void, and the courts alone would decide the matter. This would be a revolutionary change in the British constitution, giving tremendous powers to the judiciary which it has never been conditioned to exercise. They would be brought into the political arena, and called on to decide the legality of social and economic legislative schemes of the government of the day. The public, the politicians and the judges are not prepared for such radical changes. A lesser 'entrenchment' would be to make it more difficult for Parliament to change the Bill by subsequent Act; at present Parliament can repeal any Act, and in so far as an existing Act is inconsistent with a later one the earlier Act is automatically impliedly repealed. Various possibilities occur : to subject amending Bills to a special procedure or a special majority, and for a special committee to decide whether any Bill introduced does expressly or impliedly amend the Bill of Rights. There is no technical obstacle in the way of passing a Bill of Rights which would be harder to amend than other Acts. Is it desirable? If the purpose is merely to prevent Government from taking our liberties away from us by stealth, it is unnecessary; back-bench M.P.s are not so easily taken in. A large proportion of Bills might impinge on a comprehensive Bill of Rights, so that the legislative process would be clogged, even after any uncertainties about conflict had been resolved by whatever machinery had been laid down.

Another possible reform would be to set up a Civil Rights Commission. This body would be charged with the task of systematically reviewing the law and practice in the various spheres affecting civil liberty. Citizens would bring grievances to its attention, so that it would become a storehouse of information. It would be empowered to go into the departments and learn at first hand what is their practice by examination of the files. The deep-seated British reluctance to learn by direct on-the-spot investigation how administration works must be overcome. Just as the evidence before the Franks Committee showed that senior departmental heads knew little from personal experience of how the administrative tribunals under their control performed their tasks, so also English lawyers seldom reach beyond what the courts have said in their inquiry into legal problems. Such a commission would need full-time expert direction and research staffs to report from first-hand investigation how other countries protect liberty. Its ultimate goal would be to produce codes of civil liberty, which when enacted would reduce the complex, disparate and often unjust existing law into a tidy and reasonable whole. Its methods and aims would be similar to the Law Commission. The Law Commission itself would not be a suitable body, because it takes the view that it should not examine problems such as administrative law which impinge on politics. The main weakness of the Law Commission has been its inability to persuade the Government to find legislative time for its proposals. A Civil Rights Commission would find Governments even more unaccommodating, since many of their proposals would have a politically controversial element.

The reader will now be able to make up his own mind about the adequacy of the protection of an Englishman's liberties in any particular area. One or two other general matters which we have not stressed are always relevant in making such an assessment : especially the independence of the judges and their quality. Our judges may be relied on strenuously to defend some kinds of freedom. Their emotions will be aroused where personal freedom is menaced by some politically unimportant area of the executive : a case of unlawful arrest by a policeman, for example. Their integrity is, of course, beyond criticism. Yet there are obvious limits to what they can be expected to do in moulding the law of civil liberties. Two factors stand in their way : their reluctance to have clashes with senior members of the Government, their desire not to have a repetition of the nineteenth-century strife between Parliament and the courts; and secondly, their unwillingness to immerse themselves in problems of policy, which of course loom large in many of the issues examined here. M.P.s, too, play an important part, especially at question time, in keeping Ministers on their toes with regard to encroachments on the liberty of citizens; but, given the strength of the party system, it would be rash to expect them to safeguard liberty more thoroughly than they are able to do at present. In the U.S.A. private groups like the American Civil Liberties Union and the National Association for the Advancement of Coloured Peoples have played a central role in the civil liberties movement. In Britain the National Council for Civil Liberties has produced many valuable pamphlets and has campaigned vigorously against many forms of oppression. Yet neither they nor other groups like the Society for Individual Freedom have made an impact comparable to their American counterparts. Lack of funds and strict English laws against financing another person's law suit account for their pressing the courts much less. Perhaps it is a further disadvantage when such pressure groups are regarded by Whitehall as being on the far Right or Left. The publications of 'Justice', an all-party group of lawyers under Lord Shawcross's chairmanship, although on a smaller scale than the National Council for Civil Liberties, may produce more legislative reform.

There is much in the history of our freedoms of which we can be proud. They have not been won without much effort. Englishmen should neglect no available means of preserving and increasing their liberties.

NOTES

I. PERSONAL FREEDOM AND POLICE POWERS

1. [1914] 1 King's Bench 595.
2. *Christie* v. *Leachinsky*, [1947] Appeal Cases 573.
3. 5 February 1954, p. 9.
4. *Rice* v. *Connolly*, [1966] 2 Queen's Bench 414.
5. *Donnelly* v. *Jackman*, [1970] 1 Weekly Law Reports 562.
6. (1765) 19 State Trials 1029.
7. (1763) 19 State Trials 1153.
8. [1934] 2 King's Bench 164.
9. *Ghani* v. *Jones*, [1970] 1 Queen's Bench 693.
10. *McArdle* v. *Wallace (No. 2)*, [1964] 108 Solicitors' Journal 483.
11. *Robson* v. *Hallett*, [1967] 2 Queen's Bench 939.
12. Report of Inquiry into the Action of the Metropolitan Police in relation to the Case of Mr Herman Woolf, paras. 112–13.
13. Cmnd 3297.
14. [1918] 1 King's Bench 531.
15. The *New Law Journal*, vol. 120 (1970), p. 665.
16. *R.* v. *Podola*, [1960] 1 Queen's Bench 325.
17. Sheffield Police Appeal Inquiry, Cmnd 2176.
18. Report of Inquiry by W. L. Mars-Jones, Q.C., Cmnd 2526 (1964).
19. Cmnd 2323.
20. Hansard 5th series H.C. vol. 548, cols. 31–4.
21. *Callis* v. *Gunn*, [1964] 1 Queen's Bench 495.
22. *Rochin* v. *California*, 352 United States Reports 165 (1952).
23. *Mapp* v. *Ohio*, 367 United States Reports 643 (1961).
24. *Sommersett's Case* (1772), 20 State Trials 1.
25. *R.* v. *Governor of Wormwood Scrubs Prison ex parte Boydell*, [1948] 2 King's Bench 193.
26. *R.* v. *Governor of Brixton Prison ex parte Kolczynski*, [1955] 1 Queen's Bench 540.
27. *In re Castioni*, [1891] 1 Queen's Bench 149.
28. *R.* v. *Board of Control ex parte Rutty*, [1956] 2 Queen's Bench 109.
29. *Ex parte Daisy Hopkins* (1891), 61 Law Journal Queen's Bench 240.

30. Report of the Committee of Privy Councillors appointed to inquire into the interception of Communications (Cmnd 283).
31. In *R.* v. *Maqsud Ali* [1966], 1 Queen's Bench 688. The police secretly placed in a room in the town hall where two Pakistanis were detained a microphone wired to a tape recorder in an adjoining room. Their conversation recorded on the tape recorder was admitted in evidence on their subsequent trial for murder.

2. MEETINGS AND DEMONSTRATIONS

1. *Hickman* v. *Maisey*, [1900] 1 Queen's Bench 752.
2. *Harrison* v. *Duke of Rutland*, [1893] 1 Queen's Bench 142.
3. *Arrowsmith* v. *Jenkins*, [1963] 2 Queen's Bench 561.
4. (1882) 9 Queen's Bench 308.
5. [1902] 1 King's Bench 167.
6. *Lansbury* v. *Riley*, [1914] 3 King's Bench 229.
7. *R.* v. *Aubrey Fletcher, ex parte Thompson*, [1969] 1 Weekly Law Reports 872.
8. [1936] 1 King's Bench 218.
9. *Jordan* v. *Burgoyne*, [1963] 2 Queen's Bench 744.
10. *Williams* v. *Director of Public Prosecutions*, (1968) 112 Solicitors' Journal 599.
11. Application 3465/68, Collection of Decisions of the Commission No. 29, p. 53.
12. [1935] 2 King's Bench 249.
13. *Papworth* v. *Coventry*, [1967] 1 Weekly Law Reports 663.
14. *Abrahams* v. *Cavey*, [1968] 1 Queen's Bench 479.
15. The conviction was quashed on a technicality: *R.* v. *Clark* (*No. 2*), [1964] 2 Queen's Bench 315.

3. THEATRE, CINEMA, AND BROADCASTING

1. This is the combined effect of *L.C.C.* v. *Bermondsey Bioscope Ltd*, [1911] 1 King's Bench 44, and *Stott* v. *Gamble*, [1916] 2 King's Bench 504.
2. *Ellis* v. *Dubowski*, [1921] 3 King's Bench 621.
3. *Mills* v. *L.C.C.*, [1925] 1 King's Bench 213.
4. Hansard 5th series H.C. vol. 494, col. 170.
5. 24 April 1955. 'Coping with British Movie Censorship'.
6. Cmnd 4095 (1969).

7. Cmnd 8117, Minutes of Evidence of the Committee, Appendix H, Paper 8, para. 2.
8. 62 H.L. Deb. col. 1099–1101.
9. Section 3 (1).
10. *New Statesman and Nation*, 13 August 1955, p. 187.
11. Set out in the Report of the Committee on Broadcasting, Cmnd 1753 (1962), pp. 48–50.
12. Mary Scrutton, *New Statesman and Nation*, 13 October 1956.
13. H.C. 503 (1967), Appendix 2 and 3.
14. Appendix 4.
15. Section 3 (4).

4. THE PRINTED WORD AND ADVERTISING

1. Blackstone's Commentaries, vol. 4, 151–2.
2. Cmnd 7700.
3. Para. 553.
4. Paras. 413–14.
5. Para. 479.
6. Cmnd 1811 (1962), para. 325.
7. *Carlill* v. *Carbolic Smoke Ball Co.*, [1893] 1 Queen's Bench 256.
8. *Hedley Byrne & Co. Ltd* v. *Heller*, [1964] Appeal Cases 465.
9. Set out in full in the memorandum of Evidence before the Pilkington Committee on Broadcasting in Vol. I, Appendix E, Cmnd 1819 (1962).
10. *Ward Labs. Inc.* v. *Federal Trade Commission* (1960), 276 F. 2d 952.
11. Para. 794.

5. OBSCENITY AND DEFAMATION

1. 11 Siderfin 168.
2. (1727) 2 Strange 788.
3. Hansard 3rd series H.C. vol. 146, p. 327.
4. *R.* v. *Hicklin* (1868), Law Reports 3 Queen's Bench 360 at 371.
5. *R.* v. *Secker & Warburg*, [1954] 2 All England Law Reports 683 at p. 686.
6. *Manchester Guardian*, 18 September 1954.
7. See *The Trial of Lady Chatterley*, ed. C. H. Rolph (Penguin Books, 1961).
8. Rolph, 121–2.

9. *Censors* (Rede Lecture 1961), 17.
10. Rolph, 227–30.
11. *Mella* v. *Monahan* (1961), *The Times*, 20 January.
12. *R.* v. *Clayton and Halsey*, [1963] 1 Queen's Bench 163.
13. [1962] Appeal Cases 220.
14. *John Calder (Publications) Ltd* v. *Powell*, [1965] 1 Queen's Bench 509.
15. *R.* v. *Calder & Boyers Ltd*, [1969] 1 Queen's Bench 151.
16. *Director of Public Prosecutions* v. *A. and B.C. Chewing Gum Ltd*, [1968] 1 Queen's Bench 159.
17. It is unfortunate that H.M. Customs is so secretive about its black list, for most of its titles are such as 'Bottoms Up', 'How To Do It', 'Lascivious Abbot', 'There's a Whip in My Valise', and officers are instructed no longer to detain *Lolita*, Genet's *Journal*, *Ulysses*, *The Well of Loneliness*.
18. *Memoirs* v. *Massachusetts*, (1966) 383 United States Law Reports 413.
19. *Youssoupoff* v. *Metro-Goldwyn-Mayer Pictures, Ltd* (1934), 50 Times Law Reports 581.
20. *Byrne* v. *Dene*, [1937] 1 King's Bench 818.
21. *Russell* v. *Notcutt* (1896), 12 Times Law Reports 195.
22. *Cassidy* v. *Daily Mirror Newspapers Ltd*, [1929] 2 King's Bench 331.
23. *Tolley* v. *J. S. Fry & Sons*, [1931] Appeal Cases 333.
24. *Monson* v. *Tussauds Ltd*, [1894] 1 Queen's Bench 671.
25. *Chapman* v. *Ellesmere*, [1932] 2 King's Bench 431.
26. *Kemsley* v. *Foot*, [1952] Appeal Cases 345.
27. *Lyon* v. *Daily Telegraph*, [1943] 1 King's Bench 746.
28. *Hulton* v. *Jones*, [1910] Appeal Cases 20.
29. *Newstead* v. *London Express Newspapers, Ltd*, [1940] 1 King's Bench 377.
30. *McCarey* v. *Associated Newspapers Ltd*, [1965] 2 Queen's Bench 86.
31. *Thomson* v. *Times Newspapers Ltd*, [1969] 3 All England Law Reports 648.

6. CONTEMPT OF COURT AND CONTEMPT OF PARLIAMENT

1. *R.* v. *Almon*, reported in Wilmot's Judgments and Opinions (1802).
2. *R.* v. *Evening Standard* (1924), 40 Times Law Reports 833.

NOTES

3. *In re Labouchère* (1901), 17 Times Law Reports 578.
4. *R. v. Evening Standard Co. Ltd,* [1954] 1 Queen's Bench 578.
5. *R. v. Griffiths,* [1957] 2 Queen's Bench 192.
6. *R. v. Bolam* (1949), 93 Solicitors' Journal 220.
7. *R. v. Odhams Press Ltd,* [1957] 1 Queen's Bench 73. The comments of the Court of Appeal in *Attorney-General* v. *Butterworth,* [1963] 1 Queen's Bench 696, on the case also evince a trend away from the imposition of strict liability for contempt.
8. *Stirling* v. *Associated Newspapers Ltd,* [1960] Scots Law Times 5.
9. *R. v. Beaverbrook Newspapers Ltd,* [1962] Northern Ireland Reports 15.
10. *James* v. *Robinson* (1963), 109 Commonwealth Law Reports 593.
11. *R. v. Savundrayagen & Walker,* [1968] 3 All England Law Reports 439.
12. Collection of Decisions of the Commission, vol. 30, p. 70 (1970).
13. *Manchester Guardian,* 13 February.
14. *R. v. Duffy,* [1960] 2 Queen's Bench 188.
15. Hansard 5th series H.C. vol 640, col. 35, 8 May 1961.
16. *Vine Products Ltd* v. *Green,* [1966] Chancery Division 484.
17. *R. v. Fox ex parte Mosley* (1966), *The Times,* 17 February.
18. *Williams* v. *Settle,* [1960] 2 All England Law Reports 806 at p. 812 (*per* Sellers, L.J.).
19. Hansard 5th series vol. 226, cols. 1238–9, House of Lords.
20. op. cit. col. 191. Of course, after the week-end Press had exposed the error, the Lord Chancellor had to withdraw his advice the following week.
21. See page 97.
22. Cmnd 4078.
23. *R. v. Gray,* [1900] 2 Queen's Bench 36.
24. *R. v. New Statesman (Editor)* (1928), 44 Times Law Reports 301.
25. A Report by Justice, *Contempt of Court* (1959), p. 15.
26. *Ambard* v. *Attorney-General for Trinidad and Tobago,* [1936] Appeal Cases 322.
27. At 335.
28. *R. v. Colsey, The Times,* 9 May 1931.
29. Slesser, *Judgment Reserved,* 256.

30. *R.* v. *Metropolitan Commissioner ex parte Blackburn*, [1968]
  2 Queen's Bench 150 at p. 155.
31. *R.* v. *Chandler Randle and Foley, Guardian*, 9 November 1967.
32. *Sweet* v. *Parsley* [1970] Appeal Cases 132.
33. Hansard 5th series H.C. vol. 443, col. 1100 et seq.
34. 2nd Report from Committee of Privileges 1956–7, 20 December 1956.
35. Report of Press Council, 30 April 1957.
36. 4th Report from the Committee of Privileges, 1956–7, 5 February 1957.
37. May's Parliamentary Practice, 16th ed. 1957, p. 92.
38. See page 204.
39. See page 148.
40. H.C. 112 of 8 April 1948.
41. House of Commons Paper 34 (1967–8).
42. *Stockdale* v. *Hansard* (1839), 9 Adolphus and Ellis 1.
43. *Howard* v. *Gossett* (1845), 10 Queen's Bench 359.

7. FREEDOM OF RELIGION

1. *Attwood's Case*, Cro. Jac. 421.
2. 11 Ventris 293.
3. *R.* v. *Ramsey and Foote* (1883), 15 Cox's Criminal Cases 231 at 238.
4. *Bowman* v. *Secular Society Ltd*, [1917] Appeal Cases 406.
5. At p. 466.
6. (1921) 16 Criminal Appeal Reports 87.
7. Private members' Bills were thrown out in the 1880s. When in 1921 the Home Secretary rejected Gott's petition for remission of sentence he supported the punishment of those venting coarse and scurrilous ridicule on subjects which are sacred to most people in this country.
8. *In re Gathercole* (1838), 2 Lewin 237.
9. At p. 254.
10. *R.* v. *Senior*, [1899] 1 Queen's Bench 283.
11. *Ohuchuku* v. *Ohuchuku*, [1960] 1 All England Law Reports 253.
12. *Sowa* v. *Sowa*, [1961] Probate 70.
13. *Bowman* v. *Secular Society Ltd*, [1917] Appeal Cases 406.
14. *Bourne* v. *Keane*, [1919] Appeal Cases 815.
15. *In re Lysaght*, [1966] Chancery 191.
16. *In re Hummeltenberg*, [1923] 1 Chancery 237.

17. *Schmidt* v. *Secretary of State for Home Affairs*, [1969] 2 Chancery 149.
18. No. 29, p. 70 of Collection of Decisions of the Commission (1968).
19. *R.* v. *Registrar General, ex parte Segerdal*, [1970] 1 Queen's Bench 430.
20. [1955] 1 Queen's Bench 408.
21. *Cummings* v. *Birkenhead Corporation*, [1971] 2 Weekly Law Reports 1207.
22. *Rolloswin Investments Ltd* v. *Chromolit Portugal Cutelarias e Produtos Metalicos S.A.R.L.*, [1970] 1 Weekly Law Reports 912.
23. Cmnd 2528.

8. FREEDOM AND SECURITY

1. (1770) 20 State Trials 870.
2. *R.* v. *Burns* (1886), 16 Cox's Criminal Cases, 355.
3. These were quotations from *Digest of the Criminal Law*, arts. 91 and 93, a book by the leading criminal lawyer of the time, Mr Justice Stephen.
4. *An Editor on Trial*, 1947.
5. *Boucher* v. *R.*, [1951] 2 Dominion Law Reports 369.
6. Evidence of the Director before the Select Committee on Obscene Publications, para. 367.
7. *R.* v. *Leese*, *The Times*, 19 and 22 September 1936.
8. Archbold, p. 1209.
9. *Joshua* v. *R.*, [1955] 1 All England Law Reports 22.
10. [1962] Appeal Cases 220.
11. Wade and Phillips 4th ed., 361.
12. Charles Marvin, *Our Public Officers*, 2nd ed. 1880.
13. Clayton Hutton, *Official Secret*.
14. *Lewis* v. *Cattle*, [1938] 2 King's Bench 454.
15. *Chandler* v. *Director of Public Prosecutions*, [1964] Appeal Cases 763.
16. Cmnd 4089.
17. Para. 134.
18. Cmnd 3309.
19. Cmnd 3312.
20. Cmnd 1681.
21. Cmnd 9715.
22. *Cole* v. *Young* (1956), 351 United States Reports 536.

23. *Greene* v. *McElroy* (1959), 360 United States Reports 474.
24. 197 House of Lords Debates, col. 1275, 21 June 1956.
25. Para. 52.

9. FREEDOM TO WORK

1. *Vine* v. *National Dock Labour Board*, [1957] Appeal Cases 488.
2. *Addis* v. *Gramophone Co. Ltd*, [1909] Appeal Cases 488.
3. *Leng & Co. Ltd* v. *Andrews*, [1909] 1 Chancery 763.
4. *Eastes* v. *Russ*, [1914] 1 Chancery 468.
5. *Spring* v. *National Amalgamated Stevedores and Dockers Society*, [1956] 2 All England Law Reports 221.
6. *Bonsor* v. *Musicians' Union*, [1956] Appeal Cases 104.
7. *Edwards* v. *S.O.G.A.T.*, [1970] 1 All England Law Reports 905.
8. *Huntley* v. *Thornton*, [1957] 1 All England Law Reports 234.
9. *Rookes* v. *Barnard*, [1964] Appeal Cases 1129.
10. *Allen* v. *Flood*, [1898] Appeal Cases.
11. *Lee* v. *Showmen's Guild*, (1952) 2 Queen's Bench 329.
12. *Abbott* v. *Sullivan*, [1952] 1 King's Bench 189.
13. [1964] Chancery 413.
14. *Nagle* v. *Feilden*, [1966] 2 Queen's Bench 333.

10. PROTECTION AGAINST PRIVATE POWER

1. *R.* v. *Tronoh Mines Ltd*, [1952] 1 All England Law Reports 697.
2. *Morgan* v. *Tate & Lyle Ltd.* [1955] Appeal Cases 21.
3. *Dickson* v. *Pharmaceutical Society of Great Britain*, [1967] Chancery 708.

11. FREEDOM OF MOVEMENT AND RACIAL DISCRIMINATION

1. *Schmidt* v. *Secretary of State for Home Affairs*, [1969] 2 Chancery 149.
2. *Re H.K. (An Infant)*,[1967] 2 Queen's Bench 617.
3. Cmnd 4606 (1971).
4. Cmnd 8465 (1952).
5. *Draft Immigration Rules: Control after Entry.* Cmnd 4610 (1971).

6. The United States Supreme Court in fact held that the United States had no power, without a hearing, to deprive Cort of his nationality for remaining outside its borders in order to evade military service.

7. *R.* v. *Governor of Brixton Prison, ex parte Kolczynski,* [1955] 1 Queen's Bench 540.

8. *R.* v. *Governor of Brixton Prison, ex parte Schtraks,* [1964] Appeal Cases 556.

9. *R.* v. *Governor of Brixton Prison, ex parte Enaharo,* [1963] 2 Queen's Bench 455. And see Hansard 5th series H.C. vol. 673, col. 1541–56; vol. 674, col. 581–682; 1271–88.

10. *Zacharia* v. *Republic of Cyprus,* [1963] Appeal Cases 634.

11. *R.* v. *Secretary of State for Home Affairs, ex parte Soblen,* [1963] 1 Queen's Bench 829.

12. *R.* v. *Governor of Brixton Prison, ex parte Soblen,* [1963] 2 Queen's Bench 243.

13. *Kent* v. *Dulles* (1958), 357 United States Reports 116.

14. *Ealing London Borough Council* v. *Race Relations Board,* [1971] 1 Queen's Bench 309.

15. *Constantine* v. *Imperial Hotels Ltd,* [1944] King's Bench 693.

16. [1958] 3 All England Law Reports 220.

12. CONCLUSION

1. 10th Yearbook of the European Convention on Human Rights (1967), 478.

2. Bulletin of Legal Developments (Council of Europe), 1969, No. 1, p. 5.

3. Dicey, *Law of the Constitution* (10th ed.) 203.

TABLE OF STATUTES

TABLE OF CASES

TABLE OF CASES

INDEX

Advertising: aircraft, through medium of, 102–3; anti-smoking posters, 106–7; Association, functions of, 107–8; code of standards, 107; codes of conduct, 106–7

consumer protection: breach of contract, 100

control body required for, 117; controls, U.S.A., in, 117; defects considered, 116; fraud in, 100; guarantees given in, 100; legal controls, 99–105; legislation, new, needed, 117; loudspeakers in street, by, 104; matters to be regarded in, 99–100; misrepresentations in, 100; Molony Committee, 118

newspapers: advertisers' influence on, 93, 255; right to refuse, 99, 255; textual references to, 254

patent medicines, 107; planning controls, 104–5; post, by, 104; regulation of: Joint Censorship Committee, 106; within the industry, 106–9

sites, control over, 104–5; statutory control, 101; 'switchselling', 108

television: advertising committees, 112; advisory committee, 113, 115; B.B.C. precluded from, 116; breach of code for, 114; Code of Standards, 110–16; complaints by viewers, 115; control of, 88; duty of I.T.A., 87; forbidden advertisements, 111; medical advisory panel, 115; political matters, 110–11; religious matters, 110–13; statutory provisions, 107–16; time given to, 112

Altrincham, Lord, 87, 256

Anti-bomb demonstrations, 58

Appeal: contempt of Court, as to, 175; extradition order, from, 276

Architects, register of, 248–9

Argyll case, 177

Arrest, contempt of Parliament, for, 181; police powers, 15–20; private citizens, by, 17; reason to be given for, 19–20; shop detective, by, 16; warrant for, 15–16

Asylum, right of, 274–5

Atheists, removal of disabilities, 187

Australia, telephone tapping, 45

Bail: abuse of system, 30–31; grant of, 36–8; nature of, 37

Bank loans, discretion in, 257

Beveridge Report on Broadcasting, 82–3

Bill of Rights, advocacy for in Britain, 295–6

Binding over by magistrates, 52–3

Blake, George, secrets case, 220

Blasphemy, early prosecutions for, 186; law of, development of, 188

Books: national security, affecting, 220–24; censorship, see Printed matter; obscene, see Obscene publications

Bradlaugh, the atheist, 187

Breach of contract by advertisers, 100

MORE ABOUT PENGUINS
AND PELICANS

Penguinews, which appears every month, contains details of all the new books issued by Penguins as they are published. From time to time it is supplemented by *Penguins in Print*, which is a complete list of all available books published by Penguins. (There are well over four thousand of these.)

A specimen copy of *Penguinews* will be sent to you free on request. For a year's issues (including the complete lists) please send 30p if you live in the United Kingdom, or 60p if you live elsewhere. Just write to Dept EP, Penguin Books Ltd, Harmondsworth, Middlesex, enclosing a cheque or postal order, and your name will be added to the mailing list.

Note: *Penguinews* and *Penguins in Print* are not available in the U.S.A. or Canada

SENTENCING IN A RATIONAL SOCIETY

Nigel Walker

This Pelican is written for a society which still needs and imposes restraints but is affluent enough to devote money and manpower to the handling of offenders. We may rely on superstition rather than science in our use of these resources, but at least we are sufficiently rational to feel the need of more scientific knowledge to replace the superstition.

In the meanwhile, until more scientific knowledge is available, how should we approach the problem of sentencing? What is it rational to do until we know more?

To answer this question Dr Walker discusses here the aims of a penal system, the scope of the criminal law, psychiatric diagnosis and social inquiry, preventive, deterrent and corrective techniques, the young offender, and the reasonable protection of society.

'A stimulating book. It should go at once on the reading lists issued to newly-appointed justices' – *The Times Educational Supplement*.

'So lucid that for anyone thinking in terms of communication it is a *tour de force*' – *Law Society's Gazette*.

CIVIL LIBERTY

THE N.C.C.L. GUIDE

Anna Coote

No constitution or charter protects British rights. At the mercy of any piece of hasty or prejudiced legislation, they must be upheld in every generation.

Do you possess the 'eternal vigilance' required to safeguard liberty? Do you know, for instance, what your rights are if you are arrested; if you want to hold a meeting or a lottery; to demonstrate in public or vote or strike; to eject an unwelcome visitor or evict a tenant; to adopt a baby or get a divorce; to be educated or obtain a council house or a supplementary benefit; to park your car or sue your dentist?

If you are unsure, this Penguin Special will supply the answers. You will find detailed here all those questions of liberty, justice and human rights about which most men in the street are ignorant or, at best, doubtful. In effect this well ordered and useful guide distils the long experience of the National Council of Civil Liberties in standing up (both politically and through case-work) for 'us' against 'them'.

A Penguin Special